MAKING
MEANING OF WHITENESS

SUNY Series, The Social Context of Education
Christine E. Sleeter, Editor

MAKING MEANING OF WHITENESS

Exploring Racial Identity with White Teachers

ALICE MCINTYRE

STATE UNIVERSITY OF NEW YORK PRESS

Published by
State University of New York Press, Albany

© 1997 State University of New York

LB 1775.2 M316 1997

Printed in the United States of America

For information, address State University of New York
Press, State University Plaza, Albany, N.Y. 12246

Production by E. Moore
Marketing by Dana E. Yanulavich

Library of Congress Cataloging-in-Publication Data

McIntyre, Alice, 1956–
    Making meaning of whiteness : exploring racial identity with white
teachers / Alice McIntrye.
        p.   cm. — (SUNY series, social context of education)
    Includes bibliographical references (p.   ) and index.
    ISBN 0-7914-3495-8 (hc : alk. paper). — ISBN 0-7914-3496-6 (pb :
alk. paper)
    1. White teachers—United States—Attitudes. 2. Student teachers-
-United States—Attitudes. 3. Women teachers—United States-
-Attitudes. 4. Race awareness—United States. 5. Discrimination in
education—United States. 6. Multicultural education—United
States. I. Title. II. Series.
LB1775.2.M316 1997
371.1'0089'034—DC21   96-45473
                                                                              CIP

10 9 8 7 6 5 4 3 2 1

To the God of my understanding
and to all the people who "trudge the happy road of destiny with me"—
my deepest gratitude.

CONTENTS

Foreword   ix

Acknowledgments   xiii

Introduction   1

1. Multicultural Antiracist Education and Whiteness   9

2. Participatory Action Research   19

3. Making My Whiteness Public   29

4. White Talk   45

5. Constructions of Whiteness   79

6. Teacher Image   117

7. Implications for Research and Teaching Practice   134

Appendixes   151

Notes   171

References   177

Index   187

FOREWORD

Christine E. Sleeter

Making Meaning of Whiteness by Alice McIntyre is a much needed book at this historical juncture. In this era of the post–Civil Rights movement we are witnessing the turning back of the clock, as white people increasingly believe that not only was racism remedied during the 1960s and 1970s, but also that people of color now have systematic advantages over whites. "When," I hear more and more from students, "are we going to talk about how I am now at a disadvantage because I'm white? When will we do something about reverse discrimination?" On many college campuses efforts to preserve gains of the Civil Rights movement are yielding a growing white backlash, as white students fear that they are now the victims and targets of systematic racism.

Yet abundant data illustrate the persistence of institutional white racism, and persistent gaps between the rhetoric of progress and actual evidence of it. Although people of color have closed the gap in years of educational attainment, large gaps persist between whites and people of color on indices such as poverty rates, average income, average household net worth, access to health insurance, and so forth. One need only peruse U.S. government statistics on the World Wide Web to locate the most current data documenting these patterns (http://venus.census.gov/cdrom/lookup).

At the same time, Americans of all races have experienced massive job loss and downward mobility over the past two decades as industrial jobs have been replaced by service and "high-tech" jobs due to increased automation, and as jobs have been shifted to Third World nations where workers are paid a fraction of what they were paid in the United States. People experience this national shift in the economic structure in a very personal way. In 1979, the average white male income in the United States was $32,030, and the average Black male income was $23,260. By 1991 both had dropped: The average white male income was $30,270 and the average Black male income was $22,080 (U.S. Census Report, 1992). In this context of job loss and income reduction, white people increasingly are turning their frustration toward people of color, attributing white losses to presumed gains among people of color as a result of Civil Rights legislation and policies such as affirmative action. Most white people seem unaware of the racial disparity in incomes mentioned above, and even when presented with such information, remain skeptical. Rather than coming together to address common concerns and to challenge elite power that has manipulated laws and economic policies for its own advantages, racial groups in the 1990s are targeting each other, with white America scapegoating Black and Brown America.

Addressing both institutional racism and the worsening conditions of all Americans will require action directed toward the roots of our problems in the economic and political structure. This action, in turn, requires coalitions that are able to get beyond scapegoating, agree on an analysis of common concerns, share a trust level, and work together. Coalitions depend, in turn, on dialogue that confronts injustice, racist history, and racial divisions, and that builds on our common humanity and shared interests. I am suggesting here that it is in all of our best interests to learn to engage in cross-racial dialogue about racism, for the expressed purpose of dismantling institutional racism, and addressing needs and issues that most people share.

Cross-racial dialogue about racism, which involves white people, however, is rare and difficult to develop and sustain. Dialogue requires that people be able to articulate some analysis of racism and one's own position in a racist structure, one's own feelings and experiences, and the choices one has for acting differently. Most white people do not talk about racism, do not recognize the existence of institutional racism, and feel personally threatened by the mention of racism.

This past week students in one of my courses illustrated this problem. One of my Cultural Diversity courses turned out to be all-white this semester, despite the racial diversity of the student population. The few students of color who initially enrolled dropped the course, explaining to me that it would be too frustrating to spend all semester being one of the only voices of color in a sea of "white talk." I have focused much of the course on examining racial oppression, and exploring our own identities as cultural beings. The course has indeed taken on the character of "white talk," with me pushing students beyond their comfort zones while trying not to lose them in the process. This past week a group of students of color volunteered to join the class to participate in a simulation and follow-up discussion. In the discussion, the students of color tried to engage the white students in talking about race, an experience everyone found frustrating because most of the white students were silent. After class, white students told me that talking about race was new to them, and they were not sure what to say. But most also wanted to continue the process of dialogue because they recognized the importance of building bridges among themselves.

Dialogue requires two-way participation; the students of color wanted the white students to open up, and the white students experienced difficulty finding a voice with which to talk about racism that was different from the tacit acceptance of it they have grown up with. They also feared the frustration they felt in the students of color, and were worried that dialogue might turn into confrontation. There is relatively little writing articulating white perspectives that are critical of white racism and might help to raise consciousness and provide an alternative white discourse: some helpful works do, however, exist (e.g., Frankenburg, 1993; Gaine, 1987; Ignatiev & Garvey, 1996; Kivel, 1996; Schutte, 1995; Stalvey, 1988; van Dyjk, 1993; Wellman, 1993).

In this excellent book, *Making Meaning of Whiteness*, Alice McIntyre has given us a very helpful teaching tool. She presents a fascinating "inside look" at the "white talk" of her own teacher-education students. In all-white environments, white people articulate notions about race that we often sense are adverse to the perspectives of people of color, even as we try to make meaning of race in constructive ways. As McIntyre skillfully shows us, white people fear being thought of as racist or as "bad people," yet at the same time usually do not experience the outrage at racism that would move us to act differently. White people have grown up learning racial stereotypes that inform their thinking whether they consciously like it or not, and usually lack an awareness of the institutional racism in which they participate in everyday. While in an abstract sense white people may not like the idea of reproducing white racism, and in a personal sense, do not see themselves as racist, in their talk and actions, they are.

We, as white people, can talk and act differently from people of color, though, a direction in which McIntyre wants to take us. But to prod us, she lays bare our own taken-for-granted "white talk" and white sense-making about race, so that we can see it, name it, critique it, and move forward. In her book, we can hear our own voices and recognize the dualism that is embedded in white consciousness: believing ourselves to be good, caring people, on the one hand; while on the other hand, believing that the social system is relatively fair, and not wishing to jeopardize our own comfort and advantages by questioning it. This dualism comes through clearly in the words of the students as they are *Making Meaning of Whiteness*.

By holding up to us our own words, McIntyre strives to deepen our own responsibility for race relations. As she notes in this book, some white students can recognize the racism in "white talk" if it is held up to them. By recognizing racism in our own way of making sense of whiteness, white people can begin to examine ourselves critically and listen to alternative perspectives. In so doing, we pave the way for learning to engage in dialogue across racial boundaries, and learning to act differently. McIntyre has produced a volume that will surely help many of us, as whites, to look at ourselves and our sense-making critically.

REFERENCES

Frankenburg, R. (1993). *White women, race matters: The social construction of whiteness*. Minneapolis, MN: University of Minnesota Press.

Gaine, C. (1987). *No problem here: A practical approach to education and "race" in white schools*. London: Hutchinson.

Ignatiev , N. & Garvey, J. (Eds.). (1996). *Race traitor*. New York: Routledge.

Kivel, P. (1996). *Uprooting racism: How white people can work for racial justice*. Philadelphia, PA: New Society Publishers.

Schutte, G. (1995). *What racists believe*. Thousand Oaks, CA: Sage.

Stalvey, L. M. (1988). *The education of a WASP*. Madison, WI: University of Wisconsin Press.

U.S. Bureau of the Census. (1992). *Blacks in America—1992*. Washington, D.C.: U.S. Government Printing Office.

van Dijk, T. A. (1993). *Elite discourse and racism*. Thousand Oaks, CA: Sage.

Wellman, D. (1993). *Portraits of white racism*, 2nd ed. New York: Cambridge University Press.

ACKNOWLEDGMENTS

When I was in my early twenties I had the good fortune to meet a very wise older woman who took the time to teach me a few things about life and relationships, about work and play, about believing in myself and others, and about how to live "the simple life." I continue to learn from her—even though she is with me only in spirit. One of the many things she used to say to me was: "Alice, when someone does something for you, just say 'thank you.' There is no need for melodrama. Say 'thank you.' Mean it. And then go do something for someone else." So, in honor of Vonnie, a simple, but sacred thank you to family, friends, and colleagues who accompanied me in and through the research process described in this book.

A collective thank you to my dissertation director, M. Brinton Lykes, and to committee members, Elizabeth Sparks, and Polly Ulichny—who took a risk with an alternative methodology, a sensitive, unexamined topic, and a strong-willed, high-maintenance doctoral student. And a special thanks to Mary Brabeck and the School of Education at Boston College—your support has been greatly appreciated.

As I was writing my dissertation, I had the good fortune to meet Christine Sleeter, an educator and activist who has contributed enormously to my understanding of whiteness and the role of white educators in dismantling racism. I approached Christine at a conference and asked her if she would talk to me for a few minutes about "whiteness." We are still having that conversation and for that, I am deeply grateful.

Many thanks to the anonymous reviewers of a draft of this manuscript. Your critical feedback and insightful suggestions were very helpful.

To the participants of the research described in this book—your commitment to this difficult dialogue provided us with some very important insights as to how we can continue the task of critiquing whiteness, developing antiracist teaching practices, and exploring strategies for promoting social justice through education. Keep coming.

And last but not least . . . Conducting participatory action research around issues of whiteness and racism for one's doctoral thesis is not an easy task. Neither is writing a book describing that experience. For me, both projects required Brinton. Over the years, Brinton has unselfishly—and with enormous amounts of patience, humor, and tolerance—provided this tough-minded, working-class, white Irish ruffian with a unique opportunity to live out my activism through my research. Brinton challenges me to think reflexively and critically, forces me to question my own assumptions, "expands my repertoire," and provides a safe, stimulating, and rich environment for "intellectual debates."

Boss, I couldn't have done it without you. I would have done something, but I couldn't have done this. Here's to "passionate scholarship," good humor, transformative stoop-sitting, and our mutual commitment to making the road as we go. In palship and solidarity . . .

Through the research experience presented in this book, I have understood, on a deeper level, the responsibility we, as white activist educators, have to rethink, reimagine, and rework our pedagogies, to interrupt racist teaching practices, and to work for social justice. To those who came before me and tirelessly work for the same, I applaud your perseverance and appreciate the work you did—and continue to do. To those of you who I have the privilege of working with now—and for those of you who come after us—on with the action.

Proceeds from this book will benefit the Ignacio Martín-Baró Fund for Mental Health and Human Rights, an organization dedicated to fostering psychological well-being, social consciousness, and active resistance in communities affected by violence, repression, and social injustice. For more information, please write to the Martín-Baró Fund, 1892 Beacon Street, Brookline, MA 02146.

INTRODUCTION

In the 1970s, during the height of the racial tension in Boston around the issues of busing and desegregation, I saw a photo on the cover of the morning paper that I have never forgotten. It was a group of angry white people from South Boston heading down a main street toward a line of yellow school buses. In the foreground was a white male marching down the street, holding a bat, in defiance of Judge Garrity's ruling that called for busing and the desegregation of the city's schools. Beside him was a young, white male, who looked about 5 years old with the same angry face, same stride, and the same type of bat in his white hands. I was shocked. I was angry at the sight of what "these white people" were doing "in the name of their children." "What about the rights of the children?" they demanded. The *white* children is what they meant. The rights of the *white* children. No one seemed to care about the rights of the Black children.[1]

I experienced a moment of racial awakening as I saw that photograph. I realized that I was insulated in, and by, my own skin color. Everyone I knew and had grown up with was white like me. Everyone I played with as a child was white like me. Everyone that I became friends with later in my childhood and into my adolescence was white like me. Every teacher I had in school was white like me. Every babysitter, store owner, relative, neighbor, and family friend who I came into contact with was white like me. And, like others before me, I never thought about it. No one ever asked me about my whiteness. Being white remained an invisible, yet powerful force that was as much a part of my make-up as my gender, my ethnicity, my religion, and my social class. I just never really saw it.

Then I entered the teaching profession where I had numerous occasions to "see" my whiteness and to experience the ways in which race and racism shaped my life, my teaching, my politics, and my understandings of privilege and oppression, especially as they related to the educational system in the United States. Whether I was teaching in an inner-city school in Boston or in a rural school in Vermont, I saw the effects of an educational system that benefits some students at the expense of others and I found ways, both inside and outside of my classroom, to address what I considered to be inequitable practices in the schools in which I taught. Many of those inequities went beyond discriminatory policies and practices based on "race"[2] and had everything to do with socioeconomic class, gender, exceptionalities, sexuality, and religion. But no matter what they had to do with, they were all embedded in the system of whiteness—a system that is largely invisible to those of us who benefit from it.

After 12 years of classroom teaching, I returned to graduate school. During those 12 years, I lived with/under the challenges of conservative Republican policies. I saw the ascendancy of "the right," an increase in racism on college campuses, and in the country as a whole, and watched people in this country grow increasingly intolerant of "difference." In recent years, I saw the beating of Rodney King and the aftermath that followed. I heard the Mark Fuhrman tapes and watched the visible reemergence of white supremacy groups in this country. I saw the wellspring of support for David Duke's run for the Senate in 1990 and the reemergence of anti-Semitism in this country. Recently, I have seen the burning of over 40 Black churches in the South and listened to contested debates about dismantling affirmative action in the United States. Through all of this, I have seen whiteness continue to function as a system that accepts and exacerbates multiple forms of racism within our society.

As a graduate student supervising white female middle- to upper-middle-class student teachers, I "saw" whiteness from a different perspective. During that time, I became very concerned about the assumptions that many of them had about both the students of color and the white students they were teaching in their preservice teaching sites. I found myself increasingly drawn into conversations with them about race, racism, education, and our roles as white teachers. Like my own experience growing up, these students didn't appear to "see" their whiteness. These particular student teachers, like many other college students, are young, bright, idealistic, hard-working, eager, and in a very real sense, want to make a difference in the lives of the children they teach. At the same time, they uncritically embrace a discourse about race, racism, and teaching that serves—many times—to reinforce a white, class-based Euro-American perspective on life. Such a perspective marginalizes and oppresses people of color while it continues to privilege them, as white people, and the white students they teach. I hoped that by examining that discourse with a small group of white student teachers we could begin a process of deconstructing whiteness and racism, thereby gaining a better understanding of how whiteness influences and informs our teaching practices, especially within the area of multicultural education.[3]

This book describes that process. In it, I present a participatory action research project in which we (the participants and myself) explored white racial identity, examined the meaning of whiteness, and confronted the difficulties in thinking critically about race and racism. By whiteness, I refer to a system and ideology of white dominance that marginalizes and oppresses people of color, ensuring existing privileges for white people in this country (see e.g., Frankenburg, 1993; Helms, 1993; Lopez, 1996; Roediger, 1994; and Sleeter, 1995a for further discussions of whiteness). By white racial identity, I am referring "to a sense of group or collective identity based on one's *perceptions* that he or she shares a common racial heritage with a particular racial group" (Helms, 1993, p. 3).

What do those definitions mean for us, as white teachers? What exactly does it mean to be white? How do white people/teachers make meaning of whiteness? What impact does one's white racial identity have on one's notion of what it means to be a teacher? Those are questions I/we sought to explore through this research and ones that launched us on a challenging journey of self- and collective reflection about the intersection of whiteness, racial identity, racism, and teaching. This book invites you to join us on that journey.

THE INTERSECTION OF SOCIAL LOCATIONS

Many scholars in the field of education have positioned "race" as critically important for consideration when we are examining pedagogies and the need to be reflective in our teaching strategies (Cochran-Smith, 1991; Nieto, 1996; Paley, 1979; Sleeter, 1992; Tatum, 1992). In addition, numbers of feminist scholars have succeeded in moving the study of racial identity, particularly in women, "from the margins closer to the center of social science disciplines" (Stewart, 1994, p. 13). Stewart suggests that what has emerged from feminist theorizing over the last two decades is a number of strategies that can serve as guides for better understanding "what has been overlooked, unconceptualized, and not noticed" in the lives of women, men, and children. One of those strategies is to "look for what's been left out" (p. 13).

What has been left out of much feminist theorizing over the years, and what has been missing from much of the educational discourse in U.S. society, is the question of what it means to be white—a white feminist, a white researcher, a white woman, and in this case, a white teacher. This racial meaning-making is co-constructed within the context of one's gender, age, social class, educational experience, and other less visible identities that inform and influence how we understand the world. Furthermore, these contexts are embedded within multiple systems of privilege and oppression that, as Patricia Hill Collins (1990) suggests, form "an interlocking matrix of relationships" (p. 20) all of which function to both conceal and illuminate our understandings of ourselves and others.

In this research project, I highlight one aspect of that matrix. I explore "what's been left out" by those of us who are white educators, feminists, and researchers. I focus on what it means for a group of white middle- and upper middle-class females to be white and how that relates to their/our understandings of whiteness. At the same time, I acknowledge the importance of the participants' multiple positionalities. As the data in this book reveals, making meaning of whiteness for these young women—both individually and collectively—was complicated and paradoxical, highly contradictory, and deeply influenced by their gender, social class background, age, educational experiences, and familial relationships. For the purposes of my research, I "zeroed in" on an analysis that would contribute to my/our understanding of the multiple meanings of whiteness. Notwithstanding the significance of other identifiers and social positions, and their impact on the meaning-making process, choosing to analyze "whiteness" provided us with an opportunity to begin a process of unravelling the complexities of our racial locations as whites. In addition, it gives us a glimpse of the ways in which other identified positions interrelate (i.e., social class, education, gender, age) as we continue to define and redefine ourselves as white women and teachers.

WHY WHITE TEACHERS?

Why study white teachers? The National Education Association (1992) reports that 88 percent of the teachers in the United States are white. In addition, Sleeter (1992) suggests that "the teaching force is becoming increasingly white, and given the lengthened time it is taking to complete teacher certification programs, it may also be becoming increasingly middle class" (p. 208). Concurrently, the student population in our country continues to become more diverse. A "new majority" of students is emerging consisting of African Americans, Latinos, Asian/Pacific Americans, Arab Americans, and Native Americans (Campbell, 1996). Given these changing demographics, it is essential for students in teacher preparation programs, specifically white students, to be well prepared to teach and interact effectively with diverse student populations.[4]

One way for these student teachers to teach more effectively is to develop a range of insights about their own socialization processes and their own locations as white female student teachers. Reflection on their attitudes, beliefs, and life experiences, and an examination of how these forces can oftentimes work to limit their understanding of the multiple forms of discriminatory educational practices that exist in our schools, is an important first step. By examining our racial locations within this society, the participants and I began to recognize the importance of our own racial identities as determinants in how and what we teach, especially within the framework of multicultural antiracist education. In addition, I, as a participant-facilitator, tried to contextualize our locations as white women within the political and ideological field of whiteness. In doing so, I hoped to engage the participants in the task of understanding a system of privilege and oppression that structures many of our institutions, shapes U.S. culture, informs our beliefs, and restricts our understandings of what it means to be white in this society.

In chapter one I link multicultural antiracist education to white racial identity and the system of whiteness. I suggest that one strategy for pulling together multicultural antiracist education, whiteness, and white racial identity is through positioning the white teacher as an active agent of change who is implicated in the teaching/learning process that she/he creates out of the convergence of theory and practice. Cochran-Smith (1991) argues that student teachers can be activists and reformers in the struggle for educational reform. She defines reformers as those who "include alternative ways of documenting and measuring learning, transforming and constructing curriculum, and thinking through issues of race, class, and culture" (p. 306). I add to Cochran-Smith's analysis by suggesting that white student teachers need to be intentional about being self-reformers—in other words, *purposefully thinking through their own racial identities as salient aspects of their thinking through the racial identities of the students they teach*. I also suggest that this kind of self-conscious critique cannot be achieved without also looking at how we, as white individuals, are intimately connected to the pervasive system of whiteness that continues to advantage the dominant group in our society, while oppressing this society's people of color.

This move from acknowledging our white racial identities to locating ourselves within the system of whiteness to teaching multicultural antiracist education was—and continues to be—a profoundly challenging experience. One needs a set of tools that allow white teachers to not only reflect on, but to reinvent, their notions about their racial identities. One needs to also examine the discourse of whiteness that profoundly influences our educational institutions.

In chapter two, I describe a research methodology that provided the participants of this project with a way of reflecting on white racial identity and the meaning of whiteness. I lay the groundwork for how we, as a group of whites, engaged in a dialogue about issues related to race, racism, and whiteness. In addition, I describe how I envisioned this research project as a vehicle for facilitating change. In chapter three, the reader moves *with me* as I elaborate on *my* personal engagement as a white participant-researcher in this PAR project. I use my field notes and personal journals as data for engaging in my own "autocritique" (Ewick, 1994, p. 107) describing how I made meaning of my own whiteness and how it constrained and facilitated the ways in which I engaged the multiplicity of my roles within this experience. In chapters four through six, the reader moves *with the participants* as I present *their* experiences engaging in this project. In these chapters, I examine the principal ways that the participants both illuminated and distorted each other's understandings of the meanings of whiteness. In this section, I invite the reader to "sit in on the group sessions" and listen to us coerce, cajole, collude, and compete with one another for the creation of a collective narrative about the multiple meanings of whiteness. Although the interpretations are mine, I allot considerable space in these chapters to the participants' texts.

This shift from me (chapter three) to them (chapters four through six) requires a change in perspective. The analysis of the participants' group talk becomes the focus in the latter half of the book. Although I illuminate the multiple ways *the participants* made meaning of whiteness in these chapters, *I* remain an intrusive participant throughout the text revealing the ways in which I/we moved in and out of engaging in problematic talk during the group sessions. By illustrating the collective process of meaning-making, I reveal how all of us constructed a dialogue—sometimes critical, sometimes not—about the discourse of whiteness.[5]

In the last chapter, chapter seven, I discuss the significance of what can be learned by conducting a PAR project with white female student teachers aimed at making meaning of whiteness. I advocate for reimagining research methodologies and pedagogical practices, and rethinking what it means to be white, thus, creating a more critical lens through which to investigate—and dismantle—the oppressive ideology of whiteness as it influences educational discourse.

The central thesis of this book is the meaning of whiteness and how we, as white educators and researchers, can develop teaching strategies and research methodologies aimed at disrupting and eliminating the oppressive nature of whiteness in education. It is about how similarity can blind us to our own complicity in the perpetuation of racist talk and the uncritical acceptance of racist actions. It is about the need to learn by doing—to engage and reengage whites in discussions about whiteness and to continue to develop strategies for critiquing the very discussions we generate. It is about publicizing and politicizing our whiteness—being vulnerable and "fessing up" to how we contribute to the routinization of racism in our teaching practices.

As I continue in my own journey of "fessing up" and finding ways to combat racism in my personal and professional life, I have become—and am becoming—better able to "live in accordance with the principles [I am] advocating" (Sleeter, 1992, p. 212). I've made mistakes in that process—some of which you will read about in this book. I've learned from them—which is not to say that I still don't make them, or that I won't again. I do and I will. My hope is that by sharing those mistakes, as well as some of the more successful "aha" moments in this research process, I can assist the reader in her or his own self-reflection and provide some helpful hints about how to engage white students in discussions about whiteness and racism. For, as Maguire (1993) suggests,

> reflection on the flaws and inadequacies, and even the modest successes of *attempting* this [work] will help us, deep in the seriousness of our critiques and criticisms, to come up for air to examine and find ways to encourage small-scale efforts. (p. 158)

CHAPTER 1

MULTICULTURAL ANTIRACIST EDUCATION AND WHITENESS

MULTICULTURAL? ANTIRACIST? EDUCATION

Multicultural education emerged out of the protest movements which occurred in the 1960s and 1970s. According to Gay (1983) three forces converged during this time, giving rise to an approach to education that was aimed at social change and empowerment for minority groups. These included: "new directions in the civil rights movement, the criticism expressed by textbook analysts, and the reassessment of the psychological premises on which compensatory education programs of the late 1950s and early 1960s had been founded" (p. 560).

During this time, many African Americans and other people of color focused on restructuring educational and social policies, revamping school curricula, developing strategies for redistributing power and representation in schools, and inserting their cultural identities in educational institutions. It was evident to most educators of color that white teachers, especially, knew very little about the lived experiences of students of color and that their teaching practices reified the myth that difference meant deficiency. Early advocates of multiethnic education (as it was often called then), saw curriculum reform and inclusionary practices as strategies for educating teachers about diversity and for addressing the heretofore neglected histories and cultures of marginalized peoples.

Multiethnic education was seen as a beacon for those who wanted to cross the educational borders and challenge existing forms of institutional and cultural racism. African Americans and other racial and ethnic groups demanded that educational institutions reform their curricula, hire minority teachers, create ethnic studies programs, and give more control to communities over how their schools were structured. They saw their work as being antiracist in nature and as being situated in a sociopolitical context. Thus, their challenges to the educational system were also seen as challenges to the existing ownership of knowledge and to the larger issues of the distribution of power and wealth in our society.

Initially, this alternative educational approach was met with optimism and a readiness to address the inequities within the educational system. New laws were passed supporting bilingual education. Funding was being provided for multiethnic curriculum development. Students with disabilities were required to be mainstreamed. Feminists were pushing for revisions in the curriculum and, overall, the vision of equality seemed to have captured the educational community.

This apparent success brought with it seeds of discontent and a ubiquitous language that has suffered considerably at the hands of educators and policy makers alike since the mid-1980s. "Multiethnic education" became known as "multicultural education." The focus still centered around issues of ethnicity and racial group representation, but a broader view of culture was added in hopes of providing a more inclusive forum for dealing with the intersection of ethnicity, race, class, culture, gender, and exceptionalities within the educational system.

Watkins (1994) suggests that what is occurring in education *today* is that, "Multicultural education operates under the protective canopy of egalitarianism, inclusion, and social justice" (p. 99). Under this "virtuous" canopy, multiculturalists have had to define, redefine, and defend the meaning of multicultural education. Much like the splintering of feminism into feminisms as a result of women of color critiquing the claims of universality in white feminists' notions of what constitutes "equality" and "power," so too, multicultural education has been subject to challenges and critiques about its content, its character, and its universality. Is it about culture? Is it about ethnicity? Is it about race? Does it include an analysis of class? Is it aimed at individual transformation or is its purpose to dismantle educational policies and practices that are racist and discriminatory? Has multicultural education fallen prey to a type of political correctedness that has removed most of its power to transform the infrastructure of our school systems?

Many antiracist educators in the field today believe that multicultural education needs to be pervasive and provide open access to marginalized groups on multiple educational levels with "a major aim of the field [being] to restructure schools, colleges, and universities so that students from diverse racial, ethnic, and social-class groups will experience an equal opportunity to learn" (Banks, 1992a, p. 273). Those who support multicultural education question its relationship to school reform, to racial politics, to the distribution of wealth, power, and knowledge in this country, and do so *by making racism, and the problematic of race*, its core tenets (see, e.g., Banks, 1996; Grant, 1995; Larkin & Sleeter, 1995; Martin, 1995; Nieto, 1996; Sleeter & McLaren, 1995).

Sonia Nieto (1996) reminds us of the importance of racism as a core construct in multicultural education when she states:

> it is easier for some educators to embrace a very inclusive and comprehensive framework of multicultural education [because] they have a hard time facing racism. Issues of class, exceptionality, or religious diversity may be easier for them to face. . . . Racism is an excruciatingly difficult issue for most of us. Given our history of exclusion and discrimination, this is not surprising. Nevertheless, I believe it is only through a thorough investigation of discrimination based on race and other differences related to it that we can understand the genesis as well as the rationale for multicultural education. (p. 7)

Who Defines? Who Decides?

Today, "multicultural education is entrenched in highly selective debates over content, texts, attitudes, and values" (McCarthy, 1994, p. 82). Simultaneously, we are witnessing an increased emphasis on the importance of teachers developing multicultural skills in order to effectively educate immigrant, non-English-speaking students, and children from diverse racial and ethnic groups (see, for example, Banks & Banks, 1993; Banks, 1995; Mallory & New, 1994; Martin, 1995; Ng, Staton & Scane; 1995; Nieto, 1996; Sleeter, 1995b). This increase in the diversity of students, along with the increased demand for teachers to teach to diversity, coincides with the increasing number of educators, policy makers, and academics who are looking for a multicultural cure.

As one reviews the history of inclusive education within the last 30 years, one observes that the meaning of multicultural education has a great deal to do with *who* is doing the defining and, in a more pragmatic sense, *who* is actually implementing the multicultural perspective. An added question for consideration is *where* is this kind of education being lived out—in what context? under what conditions? Today, when the advocates for multicultural education are African Americans like Banks (1991; 1992b; 1995), Tatum (1992; 1994) and Gay (1993), or Latinas and Latinos like Nieto (1994; 1996) and Diaz (1992), or Asian

Americans like Pang (1992), the discourse[1] is more likely to include a macroanalysis of the structure of social institutions and the need to dismantle hierarchical systems that consolidate power and knowledge construction into the hands of a few—the few usually being middle- to upper-class whites. This is not to say that due to the subordinate status of these racial and ethnic groups that they all speak the same "multicultural language" or that they all place racism as a core variable for analysis. Quite the contrary. They speak from their own individual class, race, ethnic, and gender positions and offer unique perspectives on the role of multicultural education in our schools. They are not to be seen as representatives of their race or gender or class, nor as educators who are automatically opposed to the dominant discourse due to their marginality. As McCarthy (1994) notes, "minority cultural identities are not fixed or monolithic but multivocal, and even contradictory" (p. 82). Nonetheless, their contributions are important as their identities as educators are located outside the dominant educational discourse—a location that is reserved for the white males and females who occupy most of the positions in our educational systems. The authors cited above have developed a critical perspective due, in part, to their positions as educational "outsiders."

    White proponents of multicultural antiracist education like Ahlquist (1991), Cochran-Smith (1991; 1995a; 1995b), Ellsworth (1989), Paley (1979; 1995), Sleeter (1992; 1994; 1995b), and Weiler (1988), though committed to the same goals, don't pretend to see the landscape through the same lens. Both educators of color, and white educators, may work simultaneously to challenge existing educational policies and practices that discriminate against certain racial and ethnic groups under the umbrella of multicultural education, but this challenge is grounded in different life experiences. Being white educators, and having benefited from the present educational structure, we have to be careful not "to reproduce the very practices of domination that we seek to challenge" (Patai, 1991, p. 147). One way to avoid the tendency to reproduce those practices is to commit ourselves to interrogating whiteness within the framework of multicultural antiracist education.

The Teacher as "a" Definer/Mediator of Multicultural Education

Cherry Banks (1992) reminds us that multicultural education is

a process, an idea, and a way of teaching. . . . Multicultural content and insights should permeate the entire social system of the school, because specific norms, values, and goals are implicit throughout the school's environment, including its instructional materials, policies, counseling program, and staff attitudes as well as its hidden and formalized curricula. (p. 204)

Although Cherry Banks addresses important issues in multicultural education, this perspective, like others, ignores the racial identity of the classroom teacher and the system of whiteness that is the bedrock of the education system in the United States. Though there is an underlying assumption that teaching to diversity automatically makes one sensitive to the Other (however the Other is defined), the reality is that the white classroom teacher can "perform the multicultural tricks" while never having to critique her positionality as a beneficiary of the U.S. educational system.

As Nieto (1996) suggests, "many people may believe that a multicultural program *automatically* takes care of racism. Unfortunately this is not always true" (p. 308). Many multicultural education programs may address culture, race, ethnicity, and gender but they "mute attention to racism (and ignore patriarchy and control by wealth), focusing mainly on cultural difference" (Sleeter, 1994, p. 5). The central construct, as Sleeter suggests, becomes cultural difference when it needs to be "white racism and racial oppression [constructs that] disappear from consideration in the minds of white educators" (p. 5) as we/they develop and implement multicultural programs and policies. White educators are implicated in the norms, standards, and educational models set by white academics and institutions. Subsequently, we frame our perspective of multicultural education in such a way that it loses its original critique of the multiple levels of miseducation for children of color, and of white children as well, and the unequal distribution of wealth and power that exists in our nation and is partially lived out within the confines of our educational institutions.

Reeducating Ourselves

Many of us, as white educators, have only responded to the issue of cultural difference, diversity, and multicultural antiracist education because of historical events that have challenged us to rethink the education being provided to the children of this country. Over the years, people of color have forced "us" to reform, restructure, and rethink exclusionary practices that exist on multiple levels in this society. As white educators, we have been advised by many to teach ourselves (hooks, 1990; 1994) but oftentimes, we remain unwilling to do so.

One strategy for becoming more critical about multicultural education *as antiracist education* is for white teachers to be more self-reflective about our own understandings about race and racism and for us to challenge our own constructions about what it means to be white in this country. How do we, as white teachers, become more self-reflective? How do we learn to acknowledge our own sense of ourselves as racial beings actively participating in the education of young people? How are we to take action *against* discriminatory educational practices and take action *for* liberatory educational practices? How do we become multicultural antiracist people?

There is no absolute panacea for the challenges raised by these questions. However, an examination of how white student teachers make meaning of their whiteness and how that meaning informs and influences their beliefs about race, racism, and multicultural antiracist education is needed. What has emerged for me in thinking through these issues is the notion that we, as white educators, need to examine our racial identity in hopes that such an examination will contribute to new ways of teaching and learning that disrupt racist educational practices. Examining our racial identities *and* problematizing the system of whiteness in which those identities are created leads to what Terry (1975) calls "a *new white consciousness*: an awareness of our whiteness and its role in race problems" (p. 17). Terry states that "Too many whites want interpersonal solutions *apart from* societal changes" (p. 2). The consciousness I suggest must go beyond the "interpersonal solutions" and enable white teachers to perceive educational inequities that exist in our schools as being related to larger societal inequities and to mobilize for change.

WHITE RACIAL IDENTITY

The lack of self-reflection about being a white person in this society distances white people from investigating the meaning of whiteness and prohibits a critical examination of the individual, institutional, and cultural forms of racism. As Katz & Ivey (1977) suggest—and it continues to ring true today—being unaware of one's racial identity and being unable to conceptualize the larger system of whiteness "provide[s] a barrier that encases white people so that they are unable to experience themselves and their culture as it really is" (p. 485).

For white educators, in particular, this invisibility to one's own racial being has implications in one's teaching practice—which includes such things as the choice of curriculum materials, student expectations, grading procedures, and assessment techniques—just to name a few. What is necessary for white teachers is an opportunity to problematize race in such a way that it breaks open the dialogue about white privilege, white advantage, and the white ways of thinking and knowing that dominate education in the United States.

Being White

What exactly does it mean to be white? Terry (1981) suggests that,

It is a question . . . that confounded my life and launched me on an exciting and, at times, frightening odyssey. . . . To be white in America is not to have to think about it. Except for hard-core racial supremacists, the meaning of being white is having the choice of attending to or ignoring one's own whiteness. (pp. 119–120)

Katz (1978) posits that,

Because United States culture is centered around White norms, White people rarely have to come to terms with that part of their identity. Ask a White person his or her race, and you may get the response "Italian," "Jewish," "Irish," "English," and so on. *White people do not see themselves as White.* (p. 13)

Helms (1993) notes that,

if one is a White person in the United States, it is still possible to exist without ever having to acknowledge that reality. In fact, it is only when Whites come in contact with the idea of Black (or other visible racial/ethnic groups) that Whiteness becomes a potential issue. (p. 54)

In interviewing a group of white teachers, Sleeter (1993) quotes one of her interviewees as saying:

What's the hangup, I really don't see this color until we start talking about it, you know. I see children as having differences, maybe they can't write their numbers or they can't do this or they can't do that, I don't see color until we start talking multicultural. Then oh yes, that's right, he's this and she's that. (p. 161)

Sleeter goes on to say that "white teachers commonly insist that they are 'color-blind': that they see children as children and do not see race" (p. 161). She then asks a poignant question of these white teachers: "What does it mean to construct an interpretation of race that denies it" (p. 161)?

Another white educator, Peggy McIntosh (1992), "thinks that whites are carefully taught not to recognize white privilege" (p. 71) and that "many, perhaps most, of our students in the United States think that racism doesn't affect them because they are not people of color; they do not see 'whiteness' as a racial identity" (p. 79).

These authors, among others, contend that white people's lack of consciousness about their racial identities limits their ability to critically examine their own positions as racial beings who are implicated in the existence and perpetuation of racism. This invisibility to their own race allows white people to ignore the complexities of race at the same time that it minimizes their way of thinking about racism and about race as being "important because white Americans continue to experience advantages based on their position in the American racial hierarchy" (Wellman, 1993, p. 4).

Thus, white people's lack of consciousness about their racial identities has grave consequences in that it not only denies white people the experience of seeing themselves as benefiting from racism, but in doing so, frees them from taking responsibility for eradicating it (Elder, 1974; Feagin & Vera, 1995; Hacker, 1995; Hardiman, 1982; Katz, 1976; Moore, 1973; Wellman, 1993). Being unable to conceptualize "whiteness," white people are unable to see the advantages afforded to the white population within this country. Furthermore, they fail to see how these advantages come at the expense of the disadvantaged.[2]

The Emergence of a White Racial Identity

Over the years, many sociologists, psychologists, and educators have argued that racism is a white problem and a problem that needs to be addressed by the white community (see, e.g., Corvin & Wiggins, 1989; Feagin & Vera, 1995; hooks, 1994; Katz & Ivey, 1977; McIntosh, 1992; Ryan, 1976; Sleeter, 1993; Wellman, 1993; West, 1994). These authors assert that if white people would become aware of their own racial beings, accept the reality of white privilege that exists in the United States, and act to alleviate the forms of racism that emerge from this imbalance of color-power, then they would be more effective in dealing with the racism in this country. The focus, they argue, has to move from "blaming the victim" (Ryan, 1976) and looking at a "view of race . . . that still see[s] black people as a 'problem people'" (West, 1994, p. 5) to a view of white people as profoundly implicated in the maintaining of racial oppression and deeply affected by white racism.

During the 1970s and 1980s, perspectives on racial identity centered on the consequences of racism on the victims. Rarely were the implications of racist attitudes for the dominant group considered. Though there were some scholars studying how white people view themselves as racial beings (Elder, 1974; Katz, 1976; Moore, 1973), it has only been within the last two decades that theorists have begun to investigate white racial identity and propose stage models of white racial identity development (Hardiman, 1982; Helms, 1993; Ponterotto, 1988). These models attempt to conceptualize the process by which white people come to understand their racial identity. Though the stages and phases may differ in name, the processes are similar in each model. The white person progresses through a developmental continuum of "statuses" where she or he is confronted on multiple levels with the issues of whiteness and its meaning in contemporary society (Helms, 1994).

This confrontation may take multiple forms, but is most clearly viewed in terms of its impact on one's racial identity. As Wellman (1993) so cogently notes, "What is crucial to American identity, . . . is not that Americans hate black people. Rather the fundamental feature of their identity is that they do not know who they are without black people. Without the black Other, the American [white] Self has no identity" (p. 244). Though Wellman situates the white identity in terms of its relationship to the Black identity, the formation of white racial identity, and the need for transformative strategies for thinking about whiteness, is not limited to the white-Black relationship.

As Wellman (1993) notes regarding his research for the book, *Portraits of White Racism,*

> Although this book focuses on the issues dividing black and white Americans, the analysis is applicable to relationships between white Americans and other peoples of color. The differences and relations between European Americans and Asian, Latino, or Native Americans are also rooted in the organization of racial advantage. (p. 4)

Similarly, the developmental stage models are investigations into what constitutes whiteness and are conducted, not in isolation, but in relation to white people's attitudes, feelings, beliefs, and behaviors toward people of color. Helms developed the White Racial Identity Attitude Scale to assess attitudes related to her stages of racial identity. Recently, the WRAIS has been used to study the relationship between racial identity attitudes and counseling interactions (Carter, 1993; Helms & Carter, 1991; Sabnani, Ponterotto, & Borodovsky, 1991). Researchers have also begun to investigate the relationship between racist attitudes and racial identity among whites (Block, Roberson & Neuger, 1995; Carter, 1990; Carter, Gushue & Weitzman, 1994; Claney & Parker, 1989; Pope-Davis & Ottavi, 1994; Yang, 1992).

IN SEARCH OF THE MEANING OF WHITENESS

Though educational literature is inundated with new and improved suggestions for training teachers about multicultural education, what the literature lacks is innovative research into the relationship between white racial attitudes, beliefs, and how white teachers make meaning of whiteness and its relationship to multicultural education. Using the stage models of racial identity theories would be one strategy for examining white racial identity in white student teachers. Another method would be to investigate white student teachers' notions of their whiteness in relation to typologies that have been developed by Jones (1972) or Terry (1975). These typologists have presented various "white-types," attempting to examine how white people construct notions of themselves as "white."

In this participatory action research project (which from now on will be referred to as PAR), I examined white racial identity, and the meaning of whiteness, through a different lens. Rather than a developmental model consisting of statuses and various transitions to the formation of a healthy racial identity, or a model that relies on assessing the types of white people the participants might be, I looked at white racial identity as a social activity that is constantly being created and recreated in situations of "rupture and tension" (Minh-Ha, 1996). Like Cochran-Smith (1991), I believe that teachers are both critics and creators of the knowledge that circulates in their classrooms and that they are forever creating (and re-creating) their identities.

One way for white student teachers to become creators of their *racial* identities, is through a commitment to (1) investigating whiteness, (2) educating themselves about the relationship between their racial identities and the existence of racism within U.S. society, and (3) taking constructive action in the naming of racism and the renaming of what they can do about it within the context of multicultural antiracist education.

CHAPTER 2

PARTICIPATORY ACTION RESEARCH

Paulo Freire has had a considerable impact on educational thought and practice over the last two decades. Freire (1970) outlined his methodology and his educational philosophy in *Pedagogy of the Oppressed*, a work that has been the foundation for popular education projects, in not only Third World countries, but in industrial countries as well. Though Freire's work was aimed at the dispossessed in Latin America, the struggle for social identity, for a participatory role in the creating of society, and for the opportunity to "name the world" in Latin America is similar to the struggle that marginalized groups experience in the United States.

Freire's (1970) discourse on power, dialogue, and the idea of *conscientizacao*—"learning to perceive social, political, and economic contradictions, and to take action against the oppressive elements of reality" (p. 19)—has been the cornerstone of Freirean theory and practice. For Freire, this learning process is aimed at transforming the individual/collective consciousness by providing a context for people to become active participants in creating their own knowledge and critically examining their realities.

This participatory action research (PAR) experience is an attempt to incorporate Freire's educational philosophy into a social science research project. One of the contradictions in this effort was working with the oppressors, rather than the oppressed (an issue I address in chapter seven). Notwithstanding the contradictions, I believe that Freire's work offered me a framework for engaging in a PAR project that put the focus on the oppressor and broke the silence about what it means to be a white in our society. By breaking that silence, we, as a group of whites, were able to engage in dialogue about our racial identities, the meaning of whiteness, and our positionalities as teachers, thereby fostering the development of critical consciousness. This dialogue is not a mere technique in the education/research process, but a dialogue that Freire (Shor & Freire, 1987) believes "must be understood as something taking part in the very historical nature of human beings" (p. 13). This dialogical setting that Freire creates is not a manipulative strategy, but a setting that allows for open exchanges, as well as for silence and reflection. It is contingent on human beings engaging in a process of transformation, a transformation that can only be achieved with a commitment to humanistic education and, in this case, to humanistic research.

For this transformation to occur, within individuals and groups, Freire (1970; 1973) proposes a methodology for learning, which is participatory and egalitarian in nature, and which I incorporated into this study.[1] Freire's authentic dialogic idea of education, with its emphasis on inquiry, shared knowledge creation, and critically stimulating communication between teacher and student, was integral to the PAR design and to the context in which the researcher-participant relationship was created.

PARTICIPATORY ACTION RESEARCH: A RESOURCE FOR EXPLORING WHITENESS

Participatory action research emerged during the 1960s and 1970s as a social, educational, and political movement aimed at transforming the daily realities of oppressed people in developing countries (Fals-Borda & Rahman, 1991). Since the 1970s, educators and researchers in North America have appropriated the participatory action research methodology as evidenced in and through multiple projects designed to address a number of social and community issues (see, e. g., Forrester, Pitt, Welsh, 1993; Maguire, 1987; Park, Brydon-Miller, Hall, & Jackson, 1993). Although there are varying understandings of what constitutes a PAR project, and multiple ways in which they are carried out, most participatory action research projects include a collective commitment to (1) investigate a problem, (2) rely on indigenous knowledge to better understand that problem, and (3) individual action, collective action, or both to deal with the issue under examination. These aims are achieved through collective investigation, education, and action at different moments throughout the research process. Although not widespread in university settings, I felt that PAR was an appropriate methodology for engaging the participants in a process of illuminating white racial identity and whiteness with the hopes of facilitating change. PAR provided an opportunity for us to (1) examine what it means to have a white identity, (2) discover ways of making meaning about whiteness and thinking critically about race and racism, and (3) recognize how our white racial identity and the system of whiteness are implicated in the formulation of educational practices, thereby fostering the development of individual transformation, collective transformation, or both. Through this process, we were provided with opportunities to view ourselves as "white"—an experience that was relatively new to all the participants. It also provided us with a challenging and highly provocative way to envision change and to view our positionalities as white teachers who are important actors in how antiracist education is played out—or not—within our respective sites of teaching and learning.

A recurring question in the PAR literature is whether the researcher needs to be requested as a resource by a community or group, or whether the researcher can determine that a problem exists and then decide to engage with a group in a participatory approach to solving it. I chose the latter approach and entered this study recognizing that there were many predetermined aspects of this research that seem antithetical to the overall methodological stance of a PAR project. Whereas some PAR projects involve joint research designs between the participants and the researcher, the very fact that this was a dissertation proposal initiated by me and that it was contingent on institutional approval—prior to investigation and action—made that specific step problematic. Notwithstanding, I pursued the project because of my belief in the underlying tenets of PAR: (1) an emphasis on the lived experiences of human beings, (2) the subjectivity and activist stance of the researcher, and (3) an emphasis on social change.

The first characteristic included the development of critical consciousness and the importance of the participants' lived experiences within this project. This consciousness-raising experience was created when the participants were given opportunities to share their experiences, beliefs, assumptions, and confusions during the group sessions. Thus, these particular participants were expected to be researchers about their daily lives, to pose questions that arose from the complexities around their own racial identities, and to strategize ways for making meaning out of their individual and collective experiences as white female student teachers. Feminist research and the Freirean philosophy emphasize that this raising of consciousness occurs when spaces are created wherein "inquiry is pried open" (Fine, 1992, p. 220). Within a context of dialogue and shared risk-taking, we could "critique what seems natural, spin images of what's possible, and engage in questions of how to move from here to there" (p. 220).

This is not to imply that dialogue and risk-taking, in and of themselves, resulted in transformation and the disruption of racist attitudes and actions among the participants. Quite the contrary. "Coming to consciousness about one's racial identity and/or race privilege as white is not . . . by any means the same as transforming it" (Frankenburg, 1996, p. 4). In this research experience, opening the Pandora's box labeled "whiteness" oftentimes resulted in the participants *maintaining* their racist attitudes when it "should have" (according to me) led to critical self- and collective transformation. That was not always the case. But we had to begin somewhere. And the somewhere for these participants was the conversations they had about race, racism, and the meaning of whiteness that emerged out of their own lived experiences—experiences shaped by their race, social class, educational background, gender, and other less visible identities. By documenting the lived experiences of these white female student teachers, and by analyzing their group talk, new possibilities emerged for me, as the researcher, and for us, as participants, in constructing knowledge about white racial identity and its relationship to racism, the ideology of whiteness, and our images of what it means to be a white teacher.

The methodology I employed "stresses the importance of human subjectivity and consciousness in knowledge creation" (Maguire, 1987, p. 19). Within this paradigm, the researcher acknowledges his or her own social position—a second characteristic addressed within this study and one that I explore in the next chapter.

The third characteristic that informed this research was an emphasis on social change, a characteristic in the writings of Paulo Freire. To study white racial identity in white student teachers was to break the silence about who white teachers are and how they position themselves in relation to their pedagogy. It was to challenge deeply embedded assumptions about the Self and Other, while "seek[ing] to unearth, interrupt, and open new frames for intellectual and political theory and change" (Fine, 1992, p. 220). As Maguire (1987) suggests, "We are forced to abandon the myth and safety of neutral, value-free work, be it education, activism, or research" (p. 27). Embarking on a PAR project with the clear understanding that this was a continuing process ensured a perspective of creating knowledge and meaning that was intimately tied to a deeper need to make individual and social change. Yet, just as uncritical dialogue does not result in the development of critical consciousness an *emphasis* on social change does not necessarily *result* in social change.

I attended a PAR conference with a group of academics, graduate students, community activists, educators, and social workers while I was in the initial stages of my dissertation. During our 2-day meeting, we engaged in many heated and informative debates about what constitutes "participation" in a PAR project, what is the meaning of "research" in PAR, and how does one define "action" in a PAR project? There were a range of responses to the questions we articulated and we found ourselves reconfiguring combinations of the three aspects of PAR—participation, research, and action—in ways that challenged our assumptions about the "right" way to do PAR. We discovered that there are multiple ways of designing a PAR project just as there are multiple ways of addressing the distinctive challenges that emerge out of and through actual PAR experiences.

For me, in particular, I encountered a set of issues that challenged me to think about the cooptation of PAR within a university setting. I grappled with questions of ownership, coanalysis, power relations with both my dissertation committee and the research participants, and the larger issue of who, exactly, was going to benefit from this project? I wanted to see this work as "part of a larger discourse on emancipatory, liberatory, or transformative practice" (Hall, 1993, p. xiv), yet, oftentimes felt constrained by the complexities of conducting PAR with a privileged group of white females in a university setting, *and* by my occasional feelings of self-doubt concerning the "purity" of this project.

Yet, I was also excited about the idea of engaging in an alternative research methodology for examining whiteness, and was enthusiastic about the prospect of "breaking new ground" in an educational setting that oftentimes gets comfortable with complacency. The PAR methodology attracted me. And the attraction *to* was greater than the fear *of*. In addition, Brinton Lykes, my advisor and dissertation director, had years of experience working with a PAR model in Central America and worked closely with me in developing a framework for the research that was at the intersection of research and action.

Thus, what started out as a written proposal loosely outlining the path this project might take, turned out to be a much more complicated, complex, and highly charged experience for me/us. In this research, unlike many other PAR projects that are aimed at breaking the silence for the oppressed, the silence that needed to be broken was the silence of the oppressor. This was not about liberating the marginalized but about prying open self-criticism among those who occupy the center in ways that would challenge us to think about what life is like on the margins and how we, as the center, can alter existing inequitable structures.

The Participants

The thirteen, white, undergraduate female student teachers who voluntarily participated in this project were all enrolled in a teacher preparation program at a private northeastern university and were all engaged in a prepracticum field experience (practice teaching) during the course of this research.[2] All thirteen self-identified as middle- to upper-middle-class females. Of the six participants who provided parental incomes on an initial questionnaire the average was $100,000 per year. Seven of the participants had two siblings, three of them had one sibling, and three of the participants had no siblings. The average age of the participants was 20 years old. One of the participants lives on the West Coast, another lives in the Midwest. The rest of the participants live on the East Coast, eight of those living in New England. Twelve of the participants were juniors in the university during this research project; one, Julie, was a senior.[3] Four of the participants were majoring in early childhood education. Six were majoring in elementary education and three were majoring in secondary education.

Methods of Data Collection

Semistructured Interviews

I conducted semistructured interviews (see Appendix A) with each of the thirteen participants within the first 2 weeks of the semester, prior to the initial group session. These interviews lasted for an average of 1 hour. These interviews were an initial tool for my understanding of how the participants made meaning of whiteness. They were also opportunities to investigate some of the participants' ideas about how "being white" functions within the field of education. Conducting the interviews also provided both the participant and me with an opportunity to meet one another, thus beginning the process of being with one another in a PAR process/project.

Group Sessions

In order to explore white racial identity and the meaning of whiteness, the fourteen of us participated in eight group sessions lasting approximately 2 hours each during the fall semester of 1994. During these sessions, we discussed readings, shared personal stories and teaching experiences related to the subject of race, and engaged in a consciousness-raising process that involved critical dialogue and the naming and analyzing of the participants' realities around the issues of whiteness, white racial identity, race, racism, and teaching. These discussions were audiotaped and transcribed. Like the interviews, these transcriptions were presented to the participants for their feedback and critique prior to—and during—the formal analysis.

An important aspect of participatory action research is the attention to the daily lives and the subjective realities of the participants. Though our respective realities are only partial representations of the whole, it was essential that these realities had a place to be defined, examined, and challenged. Creating predetermined exercises and imposing a preset recipe for studying our realities, ran the risk of constraining the emergence of the participants' experiences. Nonetheless, there was a necessity to define certain goals for the group sessions and to develop a framework from which to proceed in our investigation.

The goals of the research sessions were varied. They were also subject to change, since one of the facets of participatory action research is sharing the construction and the creation of knowledge with all participants. The overall goals for the sessions were to (1) engage the participants in dialectical consciousness-raising experiences around the issues of white racial identity and whiteness, (2) provide an opportunity for the participants to locate themselves within the larger educational arena as white female student teachers, thinking critically about educational practice in relation to their own identities as white teachers, and (3) make explicit the need for examining whiteness and how we, as white teachers, can be committed to a process of teaching and learning that is antiracist and transformative in nature.

The data were created through a dialectical process of demystifying the expert, while simultaneously, "living a participatory process" (Scheepers, personal communication, June 17, 1994). Scheepers suggests that when the expert is seen as the vehicle for imparting knowledge to the inexperienced, the "spirit" of participatory research is lost and the participants are no longer the emancipators of their own transformation. The participants in this study would not grow and become self-reflective and praxis-oriented teachers through being *told* about their white racial identities. They did, however, engage in a consciousness-raising experience through being creators of their own research story—a story that evolved as a result of using the multiple resources that we, as participant researchers, brought to the overall project.

The specific resources that I brought to this project emerged out of my continued engagement with the various aspects of participatory action research. They were jumping-off points for participants who were "just beginning to feel their own [racial] stories" (Greene, 1992, p.

252). They ranged from readings that stimulated critical thinking about white privilege (e.g., McIntosh, 1992), to co-constructuring group discussions about the students' field practicum experiences and their daily encounters with "race," to discussing the problematic terms that arise in the field of multicultural antiracist education. The participants also had opportunities to individually and collectively discuss their interviews, share their own interpretations of that experience, and make meaning of what emerged from their personal and group encounter with an experience of having their own words "read back to them." Symbolic art (for example, collages and visual designs[4]) was also used as a tool for living out the participatory process. Combining visual as well as oral representations about the issues raised in the discussions provided different entry points into the research experience. The participants created visual images that were reflected back at them, both individually and as a group, thereby eliciting a number of ideas and realizations that would not have occurred in the verbal exchanges.

I was a participant, a coordinator, and a researcher in these sessions. I also facilitated many of the conversations, cognizant of the fact that the need to discuss the lived experiences of the participants is a central tenet of PAR. I began each session with a brief overview of the previous session inviting comments, clarifications, or both from the participants. Following this introduction, I either suggested that we take up a question or an issue raised from previous conversations, or, I requested that the participants join in an activity related to the research topic. For example, after 3 weeks of discussing various definitions of racism and sharing a myriad of personal stories about race, racism, and being white, I asked the participants during session four to create collages that represented whiteness. They formed small groups and using magazines, glue, and scissors, created collages that they then shared with the larger group. This session was structured around an activity and it required active participation by the group members.

In preparation for session six, a much different session than the one just described, I suggested that the participants revisit their interviews. In particular, I was interested in whether the participants made new meaning of themselves as white people since the project began. We were going to use some of the interview questions as points of entry into that discussion. Yet, due to a group discussion that took up most of the session time, we never reviewed the interviews, neither did we investigate the possibilities of individual change, collective change, or both. Instead, the session turned into a discussion about group dynamics that then led into a rather lengthy conversation about the racism in the schools where the participants were student teaching.

Thus, even though all the group sessions were organized around a theme, a question, an activity, an experience the students had at their field sites, a problem posed by the researcher or the participants, or an idea that emerged from the project itself, the very nature of PAR is one of surprise. Therefore, the "aha" experiences that emerged in the research project oftentimes worked to redirect the sessions. The topics of whiteness, race, and racism, and the issues they raised for all of us, caused a reformulation of even the best thought out exercise or activity. The participants were thereby integral agents in the direction of the discourse and were instrumental in creating the data.

Field Notes and Personal Journal

As a participant-researcher, I kept detailed field notes, as well as a personal journal, to record my observations of the group sessions and my personal reactions to the resulting dialogue. These documents also helped me to reflect on my own consciousness-raising experiences that occurred during this project. The field notes and the personal journal guided me in the process of remembering events and experiences, describing and interpreting situations, developing (and redeveloping) ideas, questions, and goals, and reminding me that my own subjectivity—and positions within this research—were important factors in the research process and product. They also served as data for my own self-analysis and self-critique, which I discuss in chapter three.

DATA ANALYSIS

Within the context of participatory research, dialogue encourages people to look at the "whys" of their lives. Why do problems exist? What causes these problems? Participatory research assumes that reality and history are human-created, thus knowable. In participatory research, the researcher might not "put ideas" in someone's head, but the researcher certainly encourages people to reflect on parts of their lives that they might not ordinarily question or pay attention to. People are encouraged to begin to look at "reality" differently, that is, more critically. (Maguire, 1987, p. 134)

One of the underlying assumptions about participatory action research, and one of the tenets of a Freirean methodology, is that problem-posing provides opportunities for knowledge creation and self- and collective reflection, which, in turn, generates themes and patterns for analysis. The knowledge is created through dialogue and is constructed in the context of the overall PAR process. Although I had initial questions that informed the analysis, these questions existed in the abstract and were only concretized as the project developed. How did the participants make meaning of their whiteness? What did it mean for them to be white? How did their white racial identity relate to how the participants thought about race and racism? What has changed, or is changing, in how the participants think about themselves as white female student teachers? were initial questions that provided the initial framework for the overall analysis.

Charmaz's (1990) social constructionist grounded theory method for analysis, which she reconceptualized from the work of Glaser & Strauss (1967), fosters the development of analytic and conceptual constructions of data. It also stresses the active stance and positionality of the researcher as crucial to the interpretation of the data. For those reasons, I used a modified version of Charmaz's social constructionist grounded theory method to analyze and interpret the group session talk.[5] I made conscious choices about how to include myself—or not—in the data analysis. Although the discourse that was produced in the sessions was cocreated by the participants and me, the research question focused on how the *participants'* made meaning of whiteness. My contributions to the group discussions informed and influenced the direction of the talk, yet, I chose to situate the data analysis in the participants' meaning-making. Notwithstanding that decision, I highlight the participatory dimension of my role in various sections of the book by including my own questions, comments, and challenges within the group dialogue. I do so in hopes that it will assist the reader in gaining a better understanding of how all of us constructed a dialogue—sometimes critical, sometimes not—about our meanings of whiteness.

I present the participants' group talk with very little editing to illustrate how they, as young white students, not only engage in informal conversation, but also how they struggle to articulate their feelings, beliefs, and attitudes about issues related to race and racism. I chose not to analyze the individual interviews but to use them as supplemental resources providing me with necessary information that contributed to the overall analysis. The techniques I used to analyze and interpret the group's talk can be found in Appendix B.

CHAPTER 3

MAKING MY WHITENESS PUBLIC

I entered into this research experience as a student, an educator, a white, North American, working-class feminist, who has been afforded multiple opportunities in this society. My story intersected with the participants in a variety of ways, yet there remained differences within our similarities. I lived with my own contradictions as I, too, engaged in understanding my own white racial identity. These contradictions, and the complexities of being a participant-researcher, were not resolved within this research project. However, I acknowledged and attended to them throughout the experience, and as revealed in the remainder of the book, they surely influenced the direction of this work.

My own assumptions about whiteness informed my thinking and had a profound influence on how I conducted and participated in this research. Griscom (1992) suggests that whiteness becomes the norm, creating a situation where we fail to see that whiteness is indeed a significant aspect of our social location. A recurring question for me then, was: "And how does *my* race, gender, class, status, and self-interest position me within this process?" This self-examination was not without a great deal of struggle. Refocusing the lens with which I view my own reality was an exercise fraught with contradiction and questions. Like Facundo (1984), "I believe that the most important questions are those that resist a simple, factual, individual answer" (p.v). There are/were no simple answers to racism, neither are/were there simple strategies for being a white participant-researcher investigating the meaning of whiteness with a group of white student teachers.

Michelle Fine (1994) argues that participatory qualitative researchers who are interested in self-consciously "working the hyphen" between Self and Other must do so by "unpacking the notions of scientific neutrality, universal truths, and researcher dispassion." She invites qualitative researchers "to imagine how we can braid critical and contextual struggle back into our texts" (p. 71).

This chapter is an attempt to braid *my own* critical and contextual struggles into this text, thus, illustrating the intricate network of experiences that challenged me in this project. To render these experiences meaningful, I expand on Fine's thickly dichotomous metaphor of "working the hyphen." Engaging in a PAR project as a doctoral student, researcher, participant, teacher, feminist, and white female required that I "work the intersection" of my varied positionalities, negotiating the boundaries that frame this project with both eagerness and caution. I found it extremely challenging to conduct white-on-white participatory action research and experienced what a colleague and I refer to as the "seduction of similarity" (Hurd & McIntyre, 1996). I also found myself struggling with what I refer to as the politics of engagement and the politics of critique—a complicated and contentious experience that exemplifies what it was like to be a white participant-researcher invoking Freirean principles of consciousness-raising and self-reflection with a group of white participants.

In this chapter I describe my own fumbling path as a participant-researcher and document my own "gradual process of misunderstanding and misrecognition, occasionally illuminated by small beacons of recognition and clarification" (Scheper-Hughes, 1992, p. 24). I offer my reflections to assist educators and researchers in our practical efforts to understand the importance of conducting white-on-white research as a tool for disrupting the dominant ideologies that permeate white institutions and U.S. societal structures. Yet, the experiences I outline here are not outside of or divorced from the participants' experiences. We struggled with similar questions and challenges. We were all seduced by similarity. We were all in a constant process of negotiating engagement and critique and we were all drawn to and ran from opportunities to learn by doing—to make our whiteness public. The themes I describe in this chapter are threaded throughout the remainder of the book and link the participants and I—and the participants to each other—in complicated and confusing ways. They invite critique and certainly alert us to the need for rigorous self- and collective reflection about how—and why—we, as white educators, talk about whiteness and the role of education in that discourse.

WHITE-ON-WHITE PARTICIPATORY ACTION RESEARCH

I share similar points of entry into the study of whiteness with the participants of my/our research. We both share characteristics that profoundly shape our life experiences: sex, race, and choice of profession. We differ most dramatically in age and level of education. Due to these shared similarities, I experienced moments of unspoken connection with my participants. Although this type of connection felt "comfortable" at times, it also worked to divert my attention away from challenging very problematic race talk—what I refer to as white talk: talk that serves to insulate white people from examining their/our individual and collective role(s) in the perpetuation of racism. My own unexplored experiences of sameness, especially at the beginning stages of this project, were ever-present reminders to me, throughout the remainder of the research experience, about how seductive sameness can be and how easily white talk is constructed.

During the third group session, the participants discussed how they experience being white student teachers interacting with Black children. Following is a brief exchange that occurred between two of the participants (please refer to Appendix C for transcription code):

FAITH: *I think little Black kids love white girls. Like I don't like to make that little stereotype but like . . . they play with your hair. . . . They just love you.*

MICHELLE: *I had so many kids, so many Black children, like if I wore it down at camp this summer, if I wore it down, it was inevitable that they would come and touch my hair. It was inevitable. I I never, if I wore it down, there was never a day where they didn't come and touch my hair.*

This exchange was accompanied by a number of the other participants nodding in agreement, sharing similar stories of Black children playing with their earrings, sitting on their laps, and braiding their blonde hair. My own memories of being a white elementary school teacher placed me in familiar territory with the speakers. This cogent feeling of similarity distanced me from countering the participants' racist assumptions and distorted realities. The participants' stories resonated so closely to mine that I maintained a "racially privileged naïveté" (Roman, 1993, p. 189) and failed to challenge the participants' constructions of whiteness. Although I was clearly frustrated and angered by their interpretation of the relationship between Black children and white teachers, I closed the session with a story about my early days of teaching and the experience of having my hair corn-rolled by a fourth-grade Black girl who was one of my students and who lived next door to me. I was totally unaware at that moment of how I colluded in white talk.

A few days later, Brinton, having listened to the taped session, questioned my reasoning for sharing that story. She not only named the racist talk of the participants, but confronted me about my collusion in a discourse situated in white stereotypes about Black children. After a highly contentious discussion, I returned to my office, sufficiently demoralized. The following is a brief excerpt from my journal entry for that day:

> What a mess! Is it a process that I let go of or is it a process I interrupt? . . . [I]s this about me informing them that they are racist and better get their acts together or is it about how they make meaning of it all? Well, one week I think it is the former and the next week I think it is the latter and by the time I figure the thing out, it will be over. I am so thrown by Brinton's reaction to the conversation of 20 year olds who AT LEAST are talking about it [racism and whiteness]. Maybe I put more stock in that than she does and maybe that is why I am more willing to accept their contradictions. . . . (Oct. 3, 1994)

In retrospect, I understand my hesitancy about and resistance to challenging the participants' racist mythmaking about how "little Black kids love white girls." On one level, I was very concerned about my position as a participant-researcher. As noted in my journal, I was preoccupied with the tension between "letting go" and inserting critique. I was also struggling to gain control over my personal anxieties around doing and completing a dissertation. My journal entry illustrates how I assumed a defensive posture toward Brinton, yet developed a more protective stance toward "my" participants. These conflicting postures emerged out of the multiple anxieties of conducting an alternative methodological dissertation around a topic that, by its very nature, is an "excruciatingly difficult issue for most of us" (Nieto, 1996, p. 7). Would the participants stay with the project? Would they keep coming back? Would they be "transformed"? were questions that were omnipresent during my initial encounters with them.

On another level, I experienced a powerful moment of identification with the participants. This reconstructed memory pulled me into the conversation in such an effortless and seductive way. The group collegiality—formed through shared *unchallenged* story telling—muted my desire to disrupt misinformed, racist group talk. I opted for the comfort of shared similarity. I aligned myself with the participants' lived, *but critically unexamined*, experiences.

This encounter—both with the participants and with Brinton— was transformative for me, profoundly influencing and changing my sense of self. I remember feeling paralyzed with inadequacy after this experience. I was convinced that I was now going to ask the wrong questions, give the wrong answers, do more harm than good. I questioned the epistemological and methodological contributions of my work and wondered about what the effects of being anchored in white privilege would be on my research.

The numbing effect of group homogeneity and similar life experiences, and the complexities of the participant-researcher role, which are discussed throughout this chapter, converged at times to silence my activism and center my complicity. Yet, as the days passed, I was better able to critique my own speech, to hone in on white talk as it was being formulated, and to be vigilant about my own story telling. My experience suggests that conducting white-on-white research requires that we, as whites, work diligently to critique the cultural and racial encapsulation that blinds us to our own biases. What is taken-for-granted by many whites—both researchers and participants—as normal, self-evident, and typical is precisely what needs to be identified, challenged, and reimagined.

MULTIPLE POSITIONALITIES IN PAR: LEARNING BY DOING

The methodological commitment to a PAR design challenged some of my predetermined assumptions about what it meant to conduct a research project. For example, two methods of data collection that I had decided to use—prior to the beginning of the PAR project—were participant journals and visits by me to the participants' field sites. The journals were going to be a tool for the participants to reflect on their feelings, thoughts, and reactions to the readings, discussions, and group activities as well as for helping the participants relate the group sessions to their prepracticum experiences. The visits to the participants' field sites were planned so that I could familiarize myself with the students' prepracticum experiences and contextualize the stories and questions that were being raised in the sessions with their actual teaching experiences. I had discussed these strategies for data collection with my dissertation committee who supported my methods and approved of their addition into the rest of the project. Due to the nature of PAR, and to the inherent complications that were created out of my own multiple positionalities, neither tool for gathering resources materialized within the research process.

During the first group session, I explained my goals for the project, reviewed my dissertation proposal, and explained the requirements for this dissertation. In the midst of explaining all of this, and trying to assuage my own anxiety about the fact that I was actually beginning my dissertation, I panicked and began to distance myself from the predetermined participant expectations that I had documented in my proposal. One of those expectations was the weekly journal entries I had previously thought so important. What became more important *at that particular moment* was keeping the participants engaged in this project. After listening to them talk about how heavy their schedules were that semester, I muted the journal requirement, merely mentioning it as a possibility, as something we could discuss as a group once the sessions got under way.

Although the journals were discussed from time to time throughout the research project, and although a few of the participants intermittently wrote their reflections in their journals, I, as the researcher, was never able to restore the significance of journaling into the overall project. In the months that have followed the research project, I have continued to learn about the multiple aspects of PAR. In addition, I have revisited my role in this research experience many times, reflecting on the choices I made regarding, among other things, the use of the journals. In retrospect, I consider *not* being more intentional about journal writing a failure on *my* part rather than a group decision. I was more concerned with the "doctoral dissertation, a central gatekeeping document of an academic's career" (Lenzo, 1995, p. 20) than I was with the process. The product became the foreground in an experience that is much more about process and consciousness-raising than it is about product and fulfilling requirements.

The fear that I would be conducting a PAR project with no participants subsided as the project evolved. I mention it here to remind myself—and other students who may be thinking of conducting a PAR project for a dissertation—that completing a PAR dissertation in an institution of higher learning is highly contradictory and inherently problematic. Decisions have to be (re)negotiated as the process develops. Sometimes, those decisions "feel" inauthentic and seem contradictory to the assumptions that underlie PAR. But it is to be hoped that those types of experiences will move us "toward a more self-critical and self-acknowledging appreciation of the actual messiness, political complexity, ethics and ambiguities of effective PAR processes" (Forester & Pitt, 1993, p. vii).

As previously mentioned, I had planned to visit the participants' field sites hoping I could establish an explicit relationship between the participants' actual teaching experiences and the discussions we were having in the group sessions. I originally scheduled the group sessions on alternate weeks throughout the semester which would have given me ample time to visit all the sites and record my observations. The participants voted against that idea during the very first session. They agreed to meeting eight times during the semester, but declined to meet during the weeks immediately prior to their exams. Subsequently, we rearranged the meeting times of the sessions and met every week with 1 week off during midsemester exams.

This scheduling change resulted in reformulating my plan to visit the classroom sites. With an entire semester to visit sites and familiarize myself with the classroom contexts, I felt that the discussions in the sessions could be more experientially based and that there might be immediate opportunity for connecting the participants' theorizing about whiteness and race with their actual teaching practice. Once the participants decided to change the meeting schedule, the opportunity to include the classroom visits as points of entry into the group's discussions became problematic. With the new schedule, there was little time to visit the participants at their classroom sites and then relate those visits to our discussions in a meaningful and productive way. As a result, the original dissertation proposal had to be modified and the already loosely structured sessions reorganized.[1]

Reorganizing schedules and shifting agendas coexisted inside the framework of this PAR project. This coexistence of sometimes competing forces is as "normal" in PAR projects as it was disquieting for me. Yet, there was significant benefit for me—and for the participants—from the experience of instability and unpredictability. Research for social change, research for transformative praxis, does not occur in a bubble. It is lived out within the research process itself. As a participatory action researcher, I was committed to including the participants in all aspects of the research agenda, recognizing that there were certain constraints to that ideal when PAR is conducted as part of a dissertation. The participants did not stand outside of their own discourse, neither did they become objects for data collecting. Unlike the claim of positivism that knowledge can be apprehended "out there," I believe that the participants were active agents "in here"—*in* the PAR process. I also recognize that such an engagement is complicated. It required that I grapple with uncertainty and be willing to adjust the process as we went along.

THE DIALECTIC OF ENGAGEMENT AND CRITIQUE: BEING A PARTICIPANT-RESEARCHER

As noted in chapter two, the aim of Freirean methodology is to transform the individual/collective consciousness by providing a context for people to become active participants in creating their own knowledge and critically examining their realities. In order to be both reflective and critical about their life experiences, I provided the participants with a context for critically examining those realities. According to the "ideal" PAR design, there is full participation in all phases of the research, and the engagement in critical dialogue leads definitively to the development of critical consciousness and transformative praxis. In reality, I experienced great difficulty enacting—and seeing the results of—Freire's authentic, dialogic idea of reflection and action leading to consciousness-raising and transformation.

Tensions were created for me as a white participant-researcher working with white participants. I tried to simultaneously engage *and* critique a group of white participants around issues that threatened our/their white self-concepts and racial identities. Moments of contestation emerged for me as I tried to determine the "right amount of engagement" and the "right amount of critique" within this PAR project. I found it extremely challenging to find a balance between "allowing" the participants' to engage in individual and collective meaning-making, *and* inserting my own critique of their uncritical "sense-making" that resonated with a "Dysconsciousness . . . that justifies inequity, and exploitation by accepting the existing order of things as given" (King, 1991, p. 135).

I had a complicated agenda as a participant-researcher. I wanted to provide a space for the sharing of the participants' own lived experiences (politics of engagement). It was also my goal, as a white feminist activist researcher, to be explicit about my own antiracist stance and to penetrate our white consciousness so as to transform it (politics of critique). The dilemma, and ensuing risk, was being a white researcher negotiating the boundaries of "engagement and critique." If the research was to be dialogical, I needed to participate in creating a forum for sharing knowledge and life experiences. Concurrently, that shared knowledge and those life experiences needed to be challenged and problematized so as to provoke an in-depth critique of the participants' white worlds. This false dichotomy between engagement and critique (for, in reality, they were *braided* into the group sessions) manifested itself in ways that blurred the boundaries of being a participant-researcher.

Politics of Engagement

Many times during the group sessions, the participants made meaning of their white worlds without direct input from me. The use of intercommunicative strategies among the participants—laughing, talking, free-associating, participant-led conversations—were emphasized as tools for extending the discussions about whiteness and race. My hope was that by shifting the control of the discussions to the participants, they would be better able to "name their worlds" (Freire, 1970) and in doing so, find those worlds problematic—an extraordinarily difficult thing for members of a privileged group to accomplish. Deconstructing our privilege and critiquing our roles as oppressors in a racist society are not what most whites choose to do when considering the problem of racism. The next step (in the ideal world of PAR) would be that the participants would then engage in a more reflective discourse critiquing themselves and their "white worlds." The risk, in this particular project, was that as I distanced myself from directly participating in the formation of dialogue, I simultaneously contributed to "engagement without critique."

For example, during session three the participants were discussing the role of white people in the racist history of the United States. (I present a detailed analysis of that discussion in Appendix D. For the purposes of illuminating the complexities of "engaging and critiquing" I focus on my own positionality within that discussion here.) At one point in this discussion one of the participants said, "Well, now they [African Americans] . . . they want to go back? Go. You know what I mean?"

I vividly remember my reaction to that comment, as well as to the overall discussion. I wanted to disrupt the racist white talk by directly challenging a host of comments that I had been listening to. At the same time, I was trying to encourage continued participant engagement with the topic—an engagement that would hopefully lead to a consciousness-raising experience for the participants rather than an experience that reified their racist assumptions. I was hoping that *one of them* would take up the challenge of critiquing racist talk. If *I* directed the critique, would that ultimately silence the group? If *I* became the sole gatekeeper for what needed critique and what didn't, would that relieve *them* of having to take responsibility for their own talk? How was I going to keep the participants "at the table" in ways that would lead to self- and collective transformation? Those questions haunted me throughout the project. I never discovered "a right" answer. Rather, I tried to stay close to my choice of methodology and to the research question: How do *the participants* make meaning of whiteness, while simultaneously, working the intersection of my varied, and complicated, positions?

Prior to the above discussion, I made a firm decision to be more of a silent, observant researcher. My decision to be a quiet bystander stemmed from my engagement with the tapes from session two. After listening to the session tapes, I felt that I had taken over the latter half of session two by "teaching" the participants about racism. As a PAR project, that is clearly acceptable and an important aspect of knowledge construction. Nonetheless, I felt that I was a bit overbearing and therefore, I decided to try a new strategy for session three—I was not going to teach and I was not going to direct the discussion. In my journal that evening, after session three, I was quite proud of myself when I wrote: *"I actually did it. I kept my mouth shut!"* I also noted that

> It is one thing to write about [the research] process but it is another thing to experience it and to stay with it when it isn't going the way I think it should. . . . There is the language they use. Language of white people. Stuff I have heard and read for years. Justifications. Denials. Lies. Insinuations. It's unbelievable to me . . . how uncritically whites/we/they talk about racism. So many times during the session I wanted to say, "Wait a second. Listen to what you just said." But I didn't. And other times I wanted to say, "Exactly. Yes. That's what we need to look at." But I didn't. Sometimes I just feel assaulted by all the language . . . I am still unsure of how much they should direct the flow and how much I should. (Sept. 30, 1994)

I insert that notation, not to excuse my silence during extraordinarily problematic talk, but to emphasize the complexities of being a white participant-researcher conducting a PAR project within this particular context. One of the paradoxes about my involvement in this research, is that I operated in extremes, dichotomies, highly polarized states that are antithetical to the "gray and messy areas" that characterize PAR. I found myself repeatedly deciding between *this* or *that*, thereby leaving little room for thinking about the multiple options afforded to participatory action researchers. My journal is replete with references to needing to control, direct, and teach the participants about race, racism, and multicultural education. Decisions of "when to engage" and "when to critique" were ever-present, significantly polarized, and highly negotiable aspects of this project for me. My tendency to think in the extreme left me with little room to discover alternative strategies with which to frame our discussions. I very much wanted to know how these young women made meaning of whiteness. I was looking for "purity"—for the absence of the researcher as being perceived as teacher, knower, and director. Competing with that aim was the desire to be a white activist researcher working for social change.

These clashes of instincts—to act or not to act—resulted in a number of frustrating experiences. Along the way, I realized that critique would never be the byproduct of guarded, dispassionate engagement. Creating a stimulating environment that provoked possibilities for conscious-ness-raising among the group of participants was essential if we were to free ourselves from the tenacious grip of "safe engagement."

Politics of Critique

As noted in this chapter, I experienced a rather long wrestling match with myself concerning discourse control and the extent to which I should be inserting myself, not just as a researcher and/or partici-pant, but as an antiracist white educator. Like Roman (1993), "I found it difficult to pierce the *veneer of polite interchange and consensus* that appeared to characterize [the participants'] interactions" (p. 189). Brinton suggested that I reread Paulo Freire. On doing so, I reflected in my journal:

> [My perspective about PAR] is definitely formed and shaped by the constraints of a dissertation which forces me to make some decisions that I might not make had we had more time. It has also been shaped and formed by my own resistance to thinking differ-ently about how to maneuver myself. Reading Freire was a really good idea—not so much for the techniques but for the spirit of it all. I needed to feel that it was OK to have an active, dialogical, critical and criticism-stimulating dialogue. And we can't have that unless there is some intentional intervention in the "talk." I have been vacillating between allowing the participants to construct the content and the flow of the sessions (something that is an aspect of PAR) and drawing attention to the points that are raised that are unclear or naive or problematic (another aspect of PAR). I have a hard time managing this. (Oct. 10, 1994)

"Managing critique" continued to be negotiable, debatable, highly contextualized and very subjective. By "managing critique," I mean the capacity I had to rupture the entrenched modes of the participants' racist speech that subverted the interrogation of whiteness. For instance, during session four, I forcibly interrupted the participants when they tried to avoid the question, "What does it mean for you to be white?" Although I validated the time they had spent in creating dialogue around issues that had been heretofore unexamined in their lives, and valued those experiences as important aspects of PAR, I reminded them that they had also spent too much time staring at "them" and that it was now time to fix the gaze on "us." I asked them: "What about *your* whiteness? What about *your* position as a teacher, *your* position as a white female in this society?" My comments about the direction of the discussion were met with silence, a smattering of nervous laughter, and a tenuous commitment by the participants to gather in small groups and create collages depicting their representations of whiteness.

Similarly, I began session six by summing up some of the participants' concerns about the "culture of niceness" that pervaded the discussions we were struggling with, and in. This addiction to polite discourse was suffocating critique. I explained to the group that unless they addressed the group dynamics, we would have difficulty moving the discussions beyond agreeable banter. Again, my intrusion into the group dynamics was met with an uncomfortable silence, followed by a group decision to develop a set of strategies for disrupting polite conversations that only served to insulate us from taking our own racial inventories.

The following week, during session seven, I pounded my fist on the table—not once, but twice—in response to some of the participants whose resistance to focusing on the "white us" constrained our understandings of how race relations are re-created and maintained through the individual and collective actions of white people. Some of the participants fell silent. Others reformulated "what they meant." Still others chose to focus on their pizza and avoid eye contact all together. In this instance, I didn't facilitate critique. Rather, I forcibly inserted the need for it.

There continued to be times throughout the group sessions when I directly addressed problematic statements and exchanges. I also chose to interrogate whiteness in less direct ways. Oftentimes, I questioned the participants about their contributions to the discussions. I also attempted to engage in critique by asking a participant—or the group—for clarification of a problematic comment or story. There were also times when I listened more than I intervened as another participant interrupted problematic dialogue (a detailed example of this is found in Appendix D). I reviewed prior sessions at the beginning of each meeting, recalling earlier statements made by the group and compared them to the present discussions in order to illuminate possibilities and contradictions. We also had some hopeful exchanges during our group sessions whereupon one or more of the participants unearthed the underlying assumptions that seemed to keep the participants in a state of resistance and confusion.

The competition between grasping the "purity" of the participants' experiences—even if those experiences were blatantly racist and were grounded in the ideology of whiteness—and my own need for the research to be grounded in some kind of consciousness-raising did

result in some "aha" experiences that triggered a few of the participants to hold onto their whiteness long enough to attend to it in a critical and self-conscious manner. At the same time, the tension between
engagement and critique left me questioning my own ability to create a
rhythm within the group that both attracted and secured the participants' critical involvement in the group sessions.

Could my critique have been more liberatory? Could it have been
more transformative? Could I have been more deliberate in naming
my/our racism(s) *during* the sessions? Those are difficult questions to
answer given the nature of PAR, my own subjectivity, the constraints of
time, and the intensity that marked the project. Nonetheless, I did manage to construct a dialogical experience that has resulted in the compi-
lation of a disturbing, compelling, and challenging story about how
these young white females make meaning of whiteness. This story has
implications, not just for white researchers, but for white educators as
we work to develop pedagogies for teaching white students about
whiteness and its relationship to education and teaching.

Freire (1973) suggests that "Time spent on dialogue should not
be considered wasted time. It presents problems and criticizes, and in
criticizing, gives human beings their place within their own reality as
the true transforming Subjects of reality" (p. 122–123). My participation in this project has led me to transform my own reality as a white
person and reminds me not only of the importance of engaging other
whites in the unveiling of our racial positionalities, but of the significance of critiquing those positionalities as well.

MAKING WHITENESS PUBLIC

My experience as a white participant-researcher and educator suggests the importance of "going public" with the types of racism that
we, as white educators and researchers, encounter in our work, as well
as the racism that some of us perpetuate. By "going public," I refer to
the necessity of/for white people to speak openly and honestly about
our own collusion in maintaining and sustaining the fabric of racism
that weaves in and out of the social systems in our society. It has been
my experience that "critical friends" (Tripp, 1993) are essential for white
people who are committed to engaging in a process of individual, institutional, and social change around issues of racism and whiteness. By
"critical friends" I refer to the people—both white people and people of
color—who accompany whites in our journeys of becoming more self-
reflective about our understandings of racism, and who join us in our

individual and collective determination to challenge racial injustice.

Unfortunately, my introduction to dialoguing about issues of race and racism with "critical friends" emerged out of friction (an experience I describe below). This experience suggests to me that it is more beneficial for whites to initiate dialogue out of a desire to better understand our racial positionalities, to interrogate the parameters of experiences for both whites and people of color, and to be committed to developing ways to make meaning of race and racism—together. *Volunteering* to make our whiteness public suggests a willingness on the part of white people to expose our whiteness to critique.

During this research project, I was invited by two African American women-colleagues to join two other white women-colleagues in a discussion about the explicit and implicit racism that students of color were experiencing in the doctoral student group of which I was the representative. Brinton, whom we all trusted and who, herself, has engaged in antiracist work for many years, facilitated this first meeting (along with a second follow-up meeting). Her presence, and her ability to facilitate a difficult conversation, was essential for creating a context where we could begin the process of making meaning of whiteness, race, racism, and our individual and collective experiences as white students and students of color in the university.

I was unprepared for the examples these African American women shared with me about my own racism within our doctoral student group. These African American women are acutely aware of multiple forms of white racism. My own white antennae is not so fine-tuned. Thus, even though I *thought* I was acting one way, in some instances, I was sanctioning and legitimating "the white experience." Like some of the participants in this study, I responded to aspects of these women's critique with defensiveness, anger, and a desire to reject their claims. Yet, I also responded with a willingness to continue the dialogue. I am committed to engaging in antiracist pedagogy and consciousness-raising research. Thus, I feel it is necessary that I not only *listen* to the contributions that people of color can make to my understanding of racism and my positionality within that system, but also join them in cocreating opportunities for critical reflection and dialogue.

This first meeting was a painful one for me and severely tested my limits and knowledge about my own power as a white woman in the university. This dialogue also challenged me to redouble my efforts at paying attention to my daily interactions with people of color. We have continued to meet and after a year of sharing many life experiences with one another, invited two other African American women-colleagues and two other white women-colleagues to join us in the dialogue. There are eight of us now working together to better understand ourselves in a racist society. We are also committed to finding ways to address racial injustices in our personal lives and in the workplace. We have not reached total agreement on some of the issues that get raised in the group and we tentatively approach others. Yet, our willingness to engage in candid discourse and speak with one another about what many whites think is "the unspeakable," represents an important framework for how white people can better understand whiteness and racism.

During one of our conversations about how uncomfortable it is for whites to talk about racism, one of the African American woman asked, "Well, what can we do about that?" I found her to be referring to the dilemma of "engagement and critique" which I addressed in this chapter. How do we engage white people in the conversation about racism long enough so that they/we can honestly critique it? My response to that dilemma is that there is no comfortable way. There is no comfort zone for white people when it comes to discussing white racism. There may be safety zones and we may be able to create nonthreatening environments to discuss white racism, but my own experience suggests that there will always be moments of discomfort that accompany the process. "Being uncomfortable" is the price I, and other whites, must pay (and a small price it is) if we are serious about the business of honestly confronting— and "doing something about"—white racism. As Naidoo (1992) suggests,

> A [white] teacher who perceives racism as only at the obvious personal or behaviourial level will not be able to take students very far. A teacher who has not begun to examine how living in a society culturally seeped in racism for centuries has infiltrated their own substratum of beliefs, assumptions, perceptions and values, will not be in a position to help her students engage in that difficult and often uncomfortable task. (p. 147)

My own experience suggests that white people coming "to the table" with people of color can be a difficult and uncomfortable task, moreso, if the dialogue's genesis is conflict. Embracing dialogue, rather than avoiding it, invites us to learn by doing, rather than learn by "being told." As Golden (1995) suggests when she describes Black and white women writing together about race and racism:

> The aching honesty, the willingness to critique and unveil . . . is testimony to the bounty we all share if we tried as hard to see each other as we try not to, or to "fess up" rather than be nice. Show me yours, I'll show you mine. (p. 3)

SUMMATION

Patai (1991) writes that "the world will not get better because we have sensitively apologized for privilege" (p. 150). By making my struggles with whiteness public, I do not intend to apologize for privilege as much as to "puncture any illusions" (p. 150) about how powerful the lenses of whiteness can be within our personal and professional lives.

This participatory action research project recognized the multiplicity of the lenses of whiteness. PAR assumes an interdependency between participant and researcher, and advocates for the creation of social spaces where both parties can "name their worlds." As participants name their worlds and shift their lenses, they begin to challenge the multiple levels of power and authority that inform, shape, and determine those worlds. Theoretically, that paradigm "feels good" to an activist educator-researcher. It's the kind of research that "punctures illusions." Yet, enacting PAR with members of the dominant group *and* being a member of that dominant group myself, raised a set of complex issues, some of which I addressed in this chapter. These same issues informed how the participants experienced this project. In the following three chapters, you will see that, like me, the participants were seduced by similarity, struggled with the dialectic of engagement and critique, and grappled with how far they would go in making their whiteness public. For myself, grappling with those issues forced me to (re)imagine and (re)construct what transformative praxis looks like from the vantage point of the "elite."

I am still "working the intersection," still questioning my positionalities and still making meaning of whiteness. I hope that by sharing my own experience within this PAR project it helps "others find the courage to learn by doing rather than being immobilized by ideal standards" (Maguire, 1993, p. 158).

CHAPTER 4

WHITE TALK

What is so striking about whites talking to whites is the infinite number of ways we manage to "talk ourselves out of" being responsible for racism. As you will see in the next three chapters, whether the topic is defining racism, or what it means to be a white teacher, or the lived experiences of people of color, or how whites "feel" about being white, many of the participants' conversations continued to rigidify the discourse of whiteness. In the remainder of this book, I reveal how that rigidification occurred in our group sessions. I present some of the participants' struggles and illustrate how they, like myself, fell victim to the seduction of similarity, how they "worked the hyphen" of engagement and critique, how they grappled with learning about whiteness by doing something about it (or not), and lastly, how they struggled with "how far they would go" in making their whiteness public.

WHITE TALK

One of the most compelling and disturbing aspects of the group talk was the way in which the participants controlled the discourse of whiteness so that they didn't have to shoulder responsibility for the racism that exists in our society *today*. Just as I slipped into uncritical talk that reified myths about children of color, so it was with the participants who, many times, found themselves embroiled in what I refer to as "white talk"—talk that serves to insulate white people from examining their/our individual and collective role(s) in the perpetuation of racism. It is a result of whites talking uncritically with/to other whites, all the while, resisting critique and massaging each other's racist attitudes, beliefs, and actions.

The discourse of white talk in this research experience was created, shaped, reproduced, and contested by a multiplicity of voices. It was an ongoing speech event, conjointly constructed and grounded in the assumptions that meaning-making—particularly as it pertains to racial issues—is inherently contextual, highly subjective, and deeply paradoxical. White talk is a discourse that, in many respects, happens "naturally" among white people in our every day conversations with each other, and with people of color. It's just that most of the time, we are unaware of how we contribute to its formation. In this case, white talk was generated when a group of young white women began to problematize their racial identities and critique the system of whiteness. I don't think it is a discourse that can be avoided.

During the group sessions, the participants used a number of speech-tactics to distance themselves from the difficult and almost paralyzing task of engaging in a critique of their own whiteness, some of which served to push the participants to be more self-reflective about being white and some that resulted in the perpetuation of white talk. These tactics are characteristic of white talk and consisted of: derailing the conversation, evading questions, dismissing counterarguments, withdrawing from the discussion, remaining silent, interrupting speakers and topics, and colluding with each other in creating a "culture of niceness" that made it very difficult to "read the white world." How the participants accomplished group commonality, for instance, profoundly shaped the discourse they created around the issues of race, racism, and their own white identities. "Caring" for each other, not wanting to disrupt the niceness in which they embed interpersonal relations, and not wanting to deal with the discomfort of personal racism, prevented them from naming injustice, holding each other accountable for injustice, or from enacting principles of equity and justice as these creep into consciousness (see Eaker-Rich & Van Galen, 1996, for a discussion of the complexity of care within interpersonal relationship and institutions of learning). The participants' repeated attempts to gain control over the discourse and to keep the discourse safe, revealed the deep complexities and dilemmatic nature of white talk. As noted in my own experiences, the dilemma—engaging white people in conversations about whiteness while simultaneously being cognizant of the strategies we use to derail those discussions—resists a simple explanation.

White talk among the participants flourished due to a host of reasons, many of which appear to be related to their educational histories. The participants of this PAR project were unfamiliar with how to question preexisting knowledge about whiteness. They have been successful students in the traditional "banking" sense (see Freire, 1970, for fuller discussion), yet are unaccustomed to a dialectical process of critique. Much like me, the participants of this study had to be open to uncertainty and take responsibility for the direction of the discussions if they were to engage in a consciousness-raising process. They needed to relinquish their need to be *spoken to* about their own racial identities. Instead, they were being asked to *speak about* their racial identities and to challenge long-standing beliefs and ideas about their whiteness and their social locations as white female student teachers in this country.

The language of white talk actively subverts the language white people need to decenter whiteness as a dominant ideology. The language of the participants' white talk, whether it was intentional or not, consciously articulated or unconsciously spoken, resisted interrogation. Interruptions, silences, switching topics, tacitly accepting racist assumptions, talking over one another, joining in collective laughter that served to ease the tension, hiding under the canopy of camaraderie—these maneuverings repelled critical conversations.[1]

The themes created from the participants' group discussions that are most salient for the discussion of white talk are (1) how the participants constructed difference from "the Other," (2) how they reconstructed myths about whites and people of color, and (3) how they privileged their own feelings and affect over the lived experiences of people of color in our society. These themes worked to distance the participants from the difficult and almost paralyzing task of examining whiteness.

CONSTRUCTING DIFFERENCE:
WE'RE AFFECTED BY RACISM, BUT WE'RE NOT RACIST

I knew from the initial interviews, and from the first group session, that the participants had a myopic view of what it meant to be white and/or a person of color in this country. I also knew that they had differing ideas about what constituted racism. As a way to initiate a discussion about racism during our second session together, I gave the participants packages of magic markers and pieces of poster paper and asked them to form small groups and create collective representations of racism that they then presented to the larger group.

After the groups had completed their presentations, and after we had discussed the myriad ways the participants made meaning of racism, I took the opportunity to "play teacher." I headed for the chart paper ready to provide a more comprehensive definition of racism. Although I hadn't planned on "teaching a lesson," the participants' confusion over the multiple dimensions of white racism—which they interwove with discrimination, prejudice, and individual attitudes— required clarification. For some of the participants, the expressions of these varied dimensions of racism added up to a contradictory notion of racism that rationalized and justified the privileged location of white people. Their understandings of racism were more about prejudice and discrimination than they were about the institutionalization of racism. Thus, to help the participants gain a better understanding of the varied dimensions of racism, I followed up on the posters they had created by describing white racism as a system of power and advantage that manifests itself on individual, institutional, and cultural levels. We talked extensively about power relations and how power is a core variable when we examine the roots and causes of racism. We discussed how power and privilege metastasize within a system of white racism. Our conversation about the dimensions of white racism was a starting point for thinking more critically about our positionalities as white people in our society but was not necessarily accepted by the participants as the way to think about racism overall. There was an uncomfortable tension in our conversations about racism that brought with it a resistance to decentering whiteness and our racial locations in the midst of that system. The resistance played itself out in a number of different ways— one of which was to continually redefine racism in the group sessions so as to justify certain racist practices. The disparate views on what constituted racism worked to derail critical conversations that we attempted to have regarding white racism and frustrated me because hadn't I "taught" them what it was in session two? Didn't they hear me? I saw them nod in agreement. I knew that they intellectually grasped what I was saying. So why the resistance?

The participants told numbers of stories during our project that illustrated the difficulty they had understanding the nature of racism as a system that privileges and maintains the social practices, belief systems, and cultural norms of the dominant group, and believes in the superiority of that group over the inherent inferiority of others. Three of the stories that reflected the participants' understanding of racism are presented below.

Elizabeth shared her story during session five.

ELIZABETH: *I have to share this story 'cause I think it's just guilt inside of me and (laughs) it makes me, having to share this but I waitress at [a restaurant] right here at [the Square]. And um, there's a lot I mean there's plenty of white people around here but there there tends to be a lot - just I've noticed from being there since all summer, a lot of Black and a lot of different people I guess I should say. But I've noticed there are a lot of Black people that come in and um, you know, when I first started working there I noticed this without anyone saying to me, you know, telling me this what I noticed. But every time I had someone that was, it was basically just Black people, like the Black customer or family. They were horrible tippers (laughter) and I was kind of like, "Listen," (laughs) you know, but um, and I noticed it was really like a trend. It wasn't like OK, the occasional family that just doesn't tip good. It was every time I got a Black party whether it was a single person or a family of six, whatever. Bad tips. So I just kind of kept to myself well you know said, "Well, whatever" you know? But just thinking that I was like, "Well, am I just being racist or" you know? And I'm like "but isn't that kind of odd" (laughs) you know? And I I just didn't know what to think. And so one day, I was um, I don't know how it came out but another co-worker said this to me. They said, "Oh, I had a bad day of tips. Well, I had a lot of Black parties." And I said, "Well, why do you say that?" you know? And they said, "Well, every time I get a Black party" and so then now every time you know, you get a Black party, you think or just everyone there is like, "Alright, how good is the tip gonna be?" You just kind of expect a lower tip and every time I get a Black party I'm like, "What am I thinking? Did I think this" and I just, it's horrible 'cause I say to myself, "I am being racist in expecting a lower tip" or maybe trying to go out of my way to be extra nice and hope for a good tip or whatever. But it kills me 'cause I know that just thinking it is being racist, but I also know that I try my hardest not to be. I mean we're all sitting here talking about this and it's like I don't know. I don't know how to change those little thoughts when . . . it's like perpetual, you know what I mean?*

LYNN: *Quick comment. Is that when I fight . . . with the definition of racism. Is that being racist or is that being stereotypical?*

ELIZABETH: *Well, see that's what I don't know[*

. . . .

ELLEN: *I I had another question was do you think that they would tip a Black waitress better?*

ELIZABETH: *Well, that's another thing. At you know, I go up to you know like say we get a party of 12 and if they're white people, I will think, "OK. Cool," you know? I'll have to work a lot harder but it's probably a real good tip. And if they don't tip well, I'm surprised. Whereas a party of 12 of Black people come in, I think, "I'm gonna work my butt off and not get a very good tip." And, I never thought anything like this before I started*

working there and it's, you know, it's just the trend I've noticed. It's not
that I before I waitressed I (unint.) Black people tip horrible. I never even
considered it you know? But it's I don't know. I just don't know if it's
racist or I'm just noticing it and[(S5)

This story exemplifies how deeply ingrained racism is in "the
souls of white folk" (Feagin & Vera, 1995). Elizabeth seems to "pick up
racism" by osmosis. She notices that Blacks don't tip as well as whites
"without anyone ever telling me." She describes it as a "trend" and
that "you just kind of expect a lower tip" from Blacks. In addition, "it
kills" her to be racist—to accept the stereotypes that have been created
about Blacks by the white people in her restaurant. The "guilt inside of
me" motivates Elizabeth to question her assumptions about Blacks. Her
desire to "know if it's racist" to perpetuate the idea that "Blacks are
horrible tippers," appears to stem from her need to be free of guilt.

As the discussion continued, Christine asked Elizabeth if she
noticed whether men or women tip more or less and if so, does she cat-
egorize one group as bad tippers and is it sexist to stereotype like that?
This led to a larger discussion where Gerry told a story about hostessing
at a restaurant and being "really bothered . . . when older people would
come in [because] if they didn't like a table or if there was a wait or
something like that. . . . It was too much of a hassle." The group questioned the stereotyping of "old people" and wondered if all forms of
stereotyping had similar effects. In an attempt to bring some clarity to
the discussion I reminded the group about Peggy McIntosh's (1992)
suggestion that there are interlocking systems of oppression and they
are hierarchical in many instances but not experienced by all oppressed
groups in similar ways. I asked them: "What is different about racism?
What is different about Elizabeth's story?"

Rather than address those questions some of the participants
immediately returned to Elizabeth's "plight," alleviating their own feelings of discomfort by refocusing on Blacks and failing to attend to how
whites perpetuate racist behavior. They remained *engaged* in the conversation, but without any sense of how to *critique* their own speech.

FAITH: *I mean I understand totally what you were saying because I was a host-*
ess for like three years and I would hear the waitresses come up and say,
"No Black people tonight. I'm not in the mood." (laughter) And before I
started waitin' tables I was like, me and my girlfriend, I was talking
about this in my interview. We were like, "We are never gonna say that.
We're gonna work so hard and every single Black people they're gonna
give us the best tips. We're gonna be great. We're gonna be great."

ELIZABETH: *It doesn't matter how good you are.*

? *It doesn't.*

ELIZABETH: *It doesn't. And that's what*[

FAITH: *It's so frustrating because you see them and then they go outside and they pull away in their Mercedes and then you're like, "I was giving you the benefit of the doubt that maybe you were like spending this all your money on the really nice dinner but then it's like I see you. I know you have money. I know you just I know I gave you excellent service."*

ELIZABETH: *Right.*

FAITH: *And I and maybe it I do do that. I know I do this. But I see a Black person in my station, I'm like, "Alright. I'm not gonna," I'm like, "I'm gonna give them exemplary service. Exemplary. There's nothing to complain about. I'm gonna make sure everything's great" and I mean that's what I should be doing with every table but, you know, I just do it and then there are times when I will get a great tip and then the one the time that stinks is, "You were the best waitress. You were such a great waitress.*[

OTHER PARTICIPANTS: *"Yeah." "Ohh."*

FAITH: *"Thank you so much. Here. Keep the change." It's like a thirty cents on like a fifty dollar bill, you know? And the it stinks because it's the money that you're taking home, you know what I mean? And it's hard. It's really it's such a struggle in your head but you know, I don't know. When you've been waiting tables for three years and it's like statistics. You can look at statistics. You can look at the numbers you know and lay it out and that stinks.*

ELIZABETH: *But the thing is like you wonder, "OK. Do these people just always tip bad like I'm sure there's plenty of white people that tip bad. Sometimes I wonder well, are they using their race as an excuse to not tip?" Do you know what I mean? Like I have noticed that the majority, I'd say out of every ten Black parties I get, nine tip horrible. I mean like we're talking not even 10 percent, you know? And out of like ten white tables, I'd say one might tip bad, you know? And it's just like like why is that? Do you know what I mean? (S5)*

I was disturbed by the direction of this conversation. It was one of those "engagement or critique" moments for me. I had already tried to generate a more critical discussion by questioning the substance of Elizabeth's story and my attempt had failed. As the conversation wore on,

I found myself waiting expectantly for one of the participants to intervene in the discussion and highlight the myriad racist comments being made. Using those remarks, I hoped that she would raise the consciousness of the others regarding the terminology they used in our discussions. Instead, the participants revert to a "white-as-victim" stance (something I discuss in chapter five) and rigidify the boundaries that get established when white people talk to white people without self- and collective criticism. Elizabeth states: "It doesn't matter how hard you work." No one disagrees with Elizabeth's comment or, if they did, failed to make it known. Faith expresses her own frustration over not being rewarded by a Black patron for her "exemplary service" and by suggesting there are statistics to prove her point that Blacks are bad tippers. Her indignation that "they" would "pull away in their Mercedes" leaving her "thirty cents on a fifty dollar bill" seemed justified. It appeared to me that the other participants accepted her reporting of such an incident as a common occurrence, thereby, facilitating the growth of white talk.

The participants' strong resistance to keeping the focus on themselves and on "us"—the white people—was difficult to interrupt. In an effort to refocus the above discussion and divert the participants' attention away from "them," I interrupted the above exchange again and asked the participants if we, as white people, use *our* race to *our* advantage? This *did* begin a lengthy, more critical discussion about white privilege that did not totally undermine the power of the participants' racist speech but momentarily managed to disrupt the "fixed gaze" (Fine, 1995) on people of color that seemed to prevail in many of our discussions.

Notwithstanding the disruption, Elizabeth and Faith shared stories and comments that were all too common in this project—stories that served to minimize the marginalized history of Blacks in this country, that perpetuated the white-as-victim syndrome, and that clearly showed how whites absorb the presumptions of racism. Once absorbed, many whites accept these presumptions as "truth," reproducing and cultivating an ideology that supports white racism. These stories—and the lack of critical intervention by the participants' themselves to *challenge* such stories—increased the ease with which the participants created a discourse embedded in racist thoughts, beliefs, and attitudes. As Essed (1991) suggests, "When dominant group members implicitly or explicitly rely on group consensus in support of anti-Black actions, they make use of an important power resource" (p. 41).

Gerry shared a story with the group shortly after "the waitress stories" that took a different view of "what and who is racist?" and generated a discussion that again, found the participants grappling with the definition of racism.

GERRY: *A few nights ago I was walking into [a store] down at [the Square] and I mean, I just had on like shorts and a T-shirt whatever. And um, as I was opening the door, they have a cop on guard there. I don't know if he's on there all the time or what. I've never noticed him before. Um, and there were three Black - they looked about high school age guys standing outside [the store] and they had just come out from buying something. And I overheard their conversation and they were like, "What's he lookin' at? He's lookin' at me 'cause I'm a nigger and he thought I stole stuff from that store." Goin' on and on about it. And they had another friend who was still paying for something and they were just like watching their friend to make sure no hassles went on or anything. And I would never even think number one, that the cop was even looking at me. If he was looking at me, that he was looking at me because he thought I stole something or my race or anything like that. And like it was so weird 'cause you never even think about it but the cop watched him the whole time and I just . . . I was standing in line just watching the cop do it and there was like 40 other people in the store and then he's focusing on the three outside the store. But it was just so blatant and it was like I would never even think that if a cop was looking at me like that, it would just kind of be like the thing that was going through my mind is, "Oh, he's watching me to make sure that like I'm OK or something."*

ALICE: *Now, would you consider that racist?*

GERRY: *Mhm.*

CHRISTINE: *No.*

ALICE: *. . . Can all people be racist?*

OTHER PARTICIPANTS: *"Yeah." "Mhm." "Mhm."*

. . . .

GERRY: *I was gonna say that I think that probably like when you get down to reality, white kids have probably stolen as much as the Black kids but the Black kids are caught because they're the ones being focused in on.*

ALICE: *And why are they being focused in on?*

GERRY: *And that right there is racism.*

ELIZABETH: *'Cause they're Black.*

GERRY: *Because of their color.*

CHRISTINE: *I think you can think anything you want whether it's stereotypical or whether it's racist. But what you do with it. It's blatant [action] about your thinking that shows that [it is] labeled as racism. You're being racist.*

ALICE: *What about what you don't do as blatant which is what she's talking about?*

FAITH: *So everything, every encounter that you have with someone of an opposite someone of a minority is racist? Every interaction? Whether it's blatant or intentional or whether it's blatant or not? I'm confused. (S5)*

Gerry clearly sees that what happened at [the store] was racist. For the participants, her story raises even more questions about the definitive characteristics of racism. Intentionality is equated with "blatant racism," thereby, exonerating the participants from racist thoughts and actions *if* those cognitions and behaviors are not premeditated and intentional. Such an analysis of racism excuses whites who "have little acquaintance with the parts of their psyches that are congruent with the spirit of the acknowledged racists" (Ezekiel, 1995, p. xviii).

Michelle attempted to clarify the positions of white people regarding racism at the end of session five when she shared a perspective on racism that she learned in one of her classes. Basically, she told the group that there was no such thing as an inactive antiracist; that in order to be antiracist, one had to take some kind of action. The following exchange occurred during session six and was in response to an ongoing discussion about racism that invoked a reference to the white racist typology presented by Michelle.

FAITH: *I guess I just see a person who is racist is a person who practices racism. That's how I perceive a racist to be. And I don't think that by coming here and by thinking about it all the time and things that I do, I think about it all the time. I think about things that I might do in my practicum. I make connections. I recognize things. I'm out there writing to my Congressmen. I'm not out there, I'm not in the streets. I'm not going to you know, all these movements and demonstrations. But I have my own goals that I have and that is my movement. That's my activity towards against racism. Do you know what I mean?*

ELLEN: *We're sitting here. We're 20 years old. We have so much time ahead of us to do and right at this point our life, we're still forming our thoughts and ideas and planning on what we're gonna do and thinking about what we want to do and what's really important to us - and it could be that we find out that racism isn't the most important issue to us and it could be that it is and that in the next 60 years of our lives, we could you know, we could do something to change that - or we could find something else that is really important to us and go for the gold on that, but[*

? And that's OK.

CHRISTINE: *But that's when we'll be the racist or antiracist. I think right now and what you're saying is that in planning towards what we're going to be acting or not acting I think um, that we can still be antiracist at this level. I mean without acting, without physically acting or teaching or conveying attitudes. You don't have to you're not racist if you don't, I don't know. I just don't agree with those.*

ALICE: *You don't agree with [what Michelle presented]?*

CHRISTINE: *No. . . . I just like I see racism as actively conveying racist thoughts. I don't know.*

. . . .

CHRISTINE: *You can be actively against racism in yourself and not have to be projecting to others your beliefs[*

MARIE: *Can I say something? I just wanna be play devil's advocate and I just think it's funny that we're sitting here as a white people and like controlling like what happens to racism. Like that's --- we're sitting here trying to like you know, when's it a good time for me to like when's it convenient for me to do this. (laughter)*

JULIE: *That's so true. (S6)*

Marie's comment about how we, as whites, control the discourse about what constitutes racism was insightful. Still, the convoluted discussions concerning racism left me wondering to what extent these participants, as white student teachers, will enact antiracist pedagogy when they are so tranquilized by the power of white racism in U.S. society. Repeatedly, the participants shadowboxed the idea of being racist. Rather than admit that we, as whites, have all internalized various dimensions of racism, the participants persistently rejected that notion. They opted to exercise "privileged choice." As Ellen suggests, "And it could be that we find out that racism isn't the most important issue to us." Only white people can exercise such an option when it comes to dealing—or not—with white racism. That is a disturbing thought for me, both as a white person and a white educator. It's distressing to think that we are educating young white teachers and failing to "teach" them that racism is a form of injustice and that we, as white educators, must redress that injustice—whether it's *convenient* for us to do so or not.

The group sessions ended with some of the participants—not all—experiencing more clarity around the multiple dimensions of racism in our society. Many of them continued to shift locations between seeing racism as attitudinal and grounded in one's personality, and viewing racism as a collective white problem grounded in power differentials and maintained by multiple forms of individual, institutional, and societal structures. Their resistance to conceptualizing racism in terms of power and privilege reinforced the construction of difference between whites and people of color—a difference that proved to be difficult, but not impossible, to address. For many of the participants, the seeds of doubt were planted. They began to doubt the constructions of racism that had informed and influenced their lives. They began to think about racism differently. For instance, Mary arrived at the last session with a different outlook on racism than the one she brought to the project—an outlook partially created by her commitment to engage in the group dialogue.

> I came into this I was like, "I am not racist. I just am not and that's how I'm going to be when I'm a teacher and that's that." But I kind of realized that's not the case and I sort of see it that that like in my mind I see that there's a problem and I see that somewhere there's probably a solution. Don't know what it is. Know what the problem is but . . . (S8)

Likewise, during session five, Julie struggled with understanding her classed and raced positionalities and how they intersected with her notion of racism.

> It's so hard for us to acknowledge that we are as a class, privileged and um, it's like it's hard to admit that you're a racist 'cause you don't wanna be. I don't wanna think that you know, I hold these stereotypes against people of other races but I think there are also times when you know, things run through my head that are racist and I'm like, "What am I thinking? Why is this going through my head?" You know? So, I mean it's like I don't wanna say that I am a racist but in essence, I think as a product of society maybe there's a little of that in all of us. (S5)

Kathleen shared with the group her own doubts about what it means to admit one's privilege and acknowledge one's racism.

> I thought when I came in here that admitting that I had a lot of privilege and that I was like was better off than other people was very racist, 'cause I didn't want to [be racist], but I've learned that you have to not, I mean I have to admit that, to come up with a solution and I think because of that I feel like I'm now walking around with a magnifying glass and everything I look at or everything I hear, it just gets magnified and like,

"Oh, no. What does that mean? What does that mean?" And I don't know. I haven't decided if that's good or bad because maybe that's what we need to do. (S8)

These examples illustrate how the participants began to get tangled up in the very white talk that they were creating. They also provide us with glimpses of how critical dialogue *can* provoke possibilities for (re)thinking how we, as whites, conceptualize racism, thus, moving toward developing strategies for addressing it.

IF THEY GAIN, WE LOSE

I remember listening to the tapes of the sessions one night and being (re)struck by how concerned the participants were about "having" and "not having" and about "sharing their privilege" but not wanting to "give it up." Even though they didn't want to admit that they have unearned skin color privilege (McIntosh, 1992) they were definitely concerned about losing what goes along with it. Another paradox—they couldn't admit to having "it" but they didn't want to lose "it." That paradox added to the formation of white talk and informed how the participants constructed difference between themselves and people of color. The participants felt that if they were going to make things equitable for people of color, they, as whites, would have to "lose something" (Mary). This idea of "losing something" is especially significant at this moment in time as white middle- and upper-middle-class workers experience levels of economic insecurity that have contributed to rigidifying further racism. The participants see the effects of "downsizing" on their parents' generation and worry that they may not achieve the same level of comfort their parents have achieved. They fear "not having," which contributes to a kind of zero-sum thinking that positions "we"—the whites—as "having" and "them"—the nonwhites as "not having." We create a "we" versus "them" situation that polarizes any substantial discussion about the incredible amount of time and energy that we, as whites, spend on maintaining racial stratification in this country.

Many whites see nothing positive in demystifying this "we/them," zero-sum system of thinking. As Feagin and Vera (1995) suggest, "This kind of zero-sum thinking leads many white Americans to take imaginary threats very seriously. Unexamined myths of this sort help to keep America balkanized along racial lines" (p. 3).

This zero-sum mentality was evident in a discussion the participants had during session four while discussing white privilege and how that manifested itself in their lives.

MARIE: *If we're not gonna maintain a white status and we want people of minority to be equal to us, we have to, as white people, as individuals, and as a race as a whole, give up something. Like something has to give and that's what you're saying. Like you're willing to give individually, you're willing to give your white privilege to someone else and to someone who doesn't have it.*

. . . .

MICHELLE: *I I'm not willing to give up my privilege. I just want someone to have equal privilege. I don't want to sacrifice mine own. I mean[*

? But then we won't get anywhere[

MICHELLE: *I know it's self-centered but realistically I mean, I like being privileged. I would hate to be not privileged and I wouldn't want to give up my privilege. I just want somebody else to be able to have privilege too[*

MARIE: *But that's what all white people think and that's why we maintain status. I I feel exactly the same way you do to be completely honest[*

MICHELLE: *I mean if we could give up I mean if that was possible then you know, we might solve a lot of problems but it's not possible like[*

(ct)

ELIZABETH: *(unint.) the whole "we-they" thing though. It's like why are we giving up something like why can't they just have it? Like why do we have to be giving up something?*

. . . .

FAITH: *I don't know how my life would change, my own personal life by helping someone of a minority. Do you know what I mean?*

ELLEN: *Yeah, what if what if they had a job you wanted? . . . Wouldn't you rather not help them out and get the job or would you rather help them out, that's the whole thing of giving up something for someone else for helping[(S4)*

Challenged by the thought of racial equality, the participants encase themselves in their own white privilege and embed themselves in a white-on-white discourse that was sustained by shared similarity. Decentering their white privilege resulted in feelings of vulnerability that fuels zero-sum thinking. Michelle's contradictory comments: "I'm not willing to give up my privilege. I just want someone to have equal privilege. I don't want to sacrifice my own," illustrate the tension around *speaking* equality and actually be willing to *live* equality.

It was also during this session that the participants examined
white privilege itself—a topic that resulted in complicated and frustrating discussions for both me and the participants. Along with their
conversations concerning white privilege—what it is and what they
should "do with it"—came this idea that white privilege was a fixed
commodity—something that could be measured and dispensed. During
session five, Marie suggested that privilege could be conceptualized
like water in a drinking glass.

MARIE: . . . *The other thing is that I wanna say, I, the analogy I thought of was
like I feel like there's like two glasses of water and like this glass is three-
quarters full and this glass is a quarter full and this is the white [3/4s]
and that's the Black [1/4] and you can't add any more water like you
can't put any more privileges into the glass. Like you have to mix the
stuff that's already there to make it even. You can't add more*

MICHELLE: . . . *I understand your analogy to the cup where you have only
that much to work with in the water and you have to like level 'em out
and if you're leveling them out, you're thinking that you're lowering
your privilege but I'm thinking there's gotta be something we can do
where we can reconstruct the entire social system. (S5)*

The participants were not ready to think about reconstructing the
entire social system. Their concerns centered around negotiating a space
where they could live comfortably with their advantaged positions,
while at the same time, allow people of color to share some of the
advantages they, as whites, experience. They framed this shared advantage around the notion of leveling the playing field, which created an
uncertainty about what would happen to them—and their privilege—if
that logic became a reality. Would they lose something on an individual
level? Would the entire white race lose something? What would happen
to privilege as a construct? "I just think privileges wouldn't be if everyone came up to a higher level. It just wouldn't be considered a privilege
anymore" (Kerry).
       The impact of the participants' socioeconomic backgrounds on
their understandings of "who has" and "who doesn't," and the lack of
critique about how whiteness and social class function to polarize discussions about racism and what it means to be white, cannot be overem-
phasized. The participants focused their conversations around a way of
thinking that resisted a critical analysis of the consequences of racism
for both people of color and for whites. White society's continued fetish
about controlling the racial discourse around a "we/them-win/lose"

mentality, resulted in these young white females accepting an ideology embedded in fear and distortion.

Gerry asked to listen to the tape of session four prior to returning to session five. She was overwhelmed by the discussion in session four and needed some time to relisten and think through the conversations. During session five, she summed up her reaction to the "we/them" dualism to the group.

> *If you listen to the tapes, it's really shocking how it is such a "we-they" thing. Every comment is either "we" or "they," "we" or "they," "we" or "they." And you don't notice it until you really sit down and listen to it and you're not talking or contributing anything to it and you just listen and it's like, "Well, 'they' this" and "we," "they" and "we" and you're like, it's just so divisive and that's just the prime example. There's just a big division and it's "us" and "them" and I don't know how you can change that. (S5)*

Lack of clarity in defining racism and zero-sum thinking contributed to the group's construction of white talk for they are both strategies for insulating the speakers from tackling the underpinnings of whiteness. The group construction of white talk reified the distance that was created between the participants and people of color. Distancing themselves from Blacks, in particular, was not a difficult thing for these participants to do. As was noted earlier, they have had limited interaction with Blacks, little education about the realities of Black life in this country, and false teachings about what it means to be Black in the United States. As Elizabeth mentioned to the group when I asked them to think about their own whiteness, "It's hard though. It's hard to think about yourselves without comparing it to something other. Do you know what I mean?" Her comment resonates with one by Wellman (1993) which was mentioned in chapter one, "The fundamental feature of [white people's] identity is that they do not know who they are without black people. Without the black Other, the American [white] Self has no identity" (p. 244).

BUT I KNOW A PERSON OF COLOR WHO "MADE IT"

Feagin and Vera (1995) argue that "Among the most important of the myths to which whites cling is that the United States is a land of equal opportunity for all racial and ethnic groups" (p. 142). Reinforcing this myth was a characteristic of white talk. The participants shifted locations repeatedly when it came to supporting the white American ideals of hard work and individual effort. They vacillated between acknowledging their advantaged positions as white females and suggesting that people of color have similar advantages if only "they" would both work hard and develop more inclusive strategies for assimilating themselves into American culture. What is missing in this model is the fact that America keeps Blacks—and many others—"so far behind the starting line [that] most of the outcomes will be racially foreordained" (Hacker, 1995, p. 34).

The participants admitted that, as whites, they benefited in and from a society founded on the principles of egalitarianism and individual freedom. Nonetheless, some of the participants felt that people of color needed to take some responsibility for the fact that they oftentimes excluded themselves from the mainstream, thus, marginalizing themselves from a host of opportunities open to all Americans. Rather than seriously considering the reconstruction of a system that favors whites, the participants privilege the foundations of that system. Some of the participants supported the notion that people of color should not only work hard to achieve the American Dream—just like their white counterparts—but also that people of color need to work hard to *include* themselves in the culture of the mainstream. The participants reinforced these notions by questioning the individual and collective actions of people of color and by sharing "exception to the rule" stories (Christine). These were stories about individual people of color who have "made it." They were stories that defended a myth that operates in our society that if only Blacks would do what we, as whites do, they, too, would achieve the American Dream. These "exception" stories served to soften the blow of white racism. The stories that were produced reverberated with the notion that racism was rooted in the psychological dispositions and actions of both whites and Blacks—a notion that made it extremely difficult to connect the multiple levels of racism operating in our society. Instead, racism became lodged within specific contexts and specific kinds of people. Although the participants are young white females who are "acknowledging or trying to get a better understanding of our race, of how we can acknowledge the other race" (Elizabeth), they oftentimes got entangled in talk that constructed barriers to fully grasping the racial hierarchy that exists in the United States. This white talk unproblematically re-created and reconstructed myths about Blacks and whites that exist within our society.

My analysis suggests that the participants value the ideals of individualism, equal opportunity, and hard work. Although the participants recognized that those ideals can be lived out more easily if one is white, they also believed that similar principles should apply to people of color. The participants had competing priorities: on the one hand, they were concerned about what people of color lack in terms of societal resources. On the other hand, they refused to make a radical break from a system that protects the resources available to them, as white people, due to their skin color. They attempted to consolidate their self-interest *and* their concern for people of color under the canopy of inclusion, failing to recognize the fallacy of such a system when that system is grounded in racial hierarchy.

I use the term inclusion rather than assimilation to emphasize the power and hierarchy that still exists within the construction of a myth that invites *all* people to participate in the American Dream. Assimilation denotes a sense of absorption, of acclimatization. Whites "invite" Blacks to acclimate themselves into white culture. Once acclimated, Blacks will realize the significance of white values, attitudes, and beliefs, there will be equal opportunities for all, and we can all live happily ever after. On the other hand, inclusion denotes a sense of power. "We" will include "them" in our culture, our ways of life but only on our terms. "We" demand that "they" work hard at including themselves in white society, and yet, we are the gatekeepers, the ones who decide the boundaries of that inclusion. Whites talk assimilation, when what we really mean is dominance and control. Inclusion says that Black Americans can be part of white society—in some measure— but they will remain subordinate and living on the margins. Inclusion is about circumscription, about whites determining the limits to which Blacks will be incorporated into the white culture.

Like many colleges and universities, the university that the participants attend has an organization for African American, Asian American, Hispanic, and Native American students. This organization is supported by the administration and has a visible presence on campus. The aim of the organization (which from now on will be referred to by the pseudonym UNITY) is to provide a variety of academic, financial, and social resources to the students of color at this campus. An example of how some of the participants had difficulty understanding the need for such an organization is illustrated in the following exchange which took place during session seven when the participants were discussing the different experiences students of color and white students have at this predominantly white institution. This exchange further illustrates the power of myth. Here, some of the participants reconstructed the myth that it is the people of color who are distancing themselves from white society. They portrayed students of color as being the ones who were separating themselves from the very university that was trying to support them.

ELLEN: *But I don't have the same experience at [this university] as any of the other people in this room do.*

ALICE: *But not because of your color, Ellen. For other reasons.*

ELLEN: *But do they, but do they have a different experience because of their color?*

ALICE: *Do you think that Black people on this campus have a different experience . . . than the white people on this campus?[*

OTHER PARTICIPANTS: *"Incredibly." "Yes." "Uh huh." "Mhm."*

ALICE: *Due to skin color? Do you think that you both experience it the same way?*

ELLEN: *(sigh) No. . . . Is that because of the organizations of the school?*

ALICE: *Meaning?*

ELLEN: *People, meaning every day in the mail, my roommate gets something from UNITY. And is invited to something new that UNITY has put on. And it's something that they are involved in purely because of their race. Purely because of their skin color. So that they feel connected to these other people in UNITY purely based on skin color.*

ALICE: *Why do you think they need to do that?*

ELLEN: *I don't know ---*

FAITH: *I walk into The Club, which is usually mostly, and I'm not, I'm stating a fact, and most times I go in there is mostly Black people or you know, people of color, whatever, go in there. And I feel like, I think it kind of increases the separation between people of color and white people. How can it not if you have your own group and I know it's important for them to feel united and for people of color to feel united and to feel you know like there's support and everything else - but I think it might also increase, I mean I I just hear white people talking on campus who are like you know, "Oh, why do they you have to have a group?" You know people who don't know why they have it think that they have it so that they don't have to hang out with white people. That's just a general thing that I've picked up that whites think.*

. . . .

ELLEN: *Why does [this university] as an organization feel that the minorities on this campus need an official organization in order to feel united but they don't feel that the majority, the whites, don't need their own official organization to feel united?*

(ct)

JULIE: *Because we don't need it. I mean everyone around us is white. Everywhere we go we have people to I mean we have people of our own race to relate to - whereas maybe there's one Black person in a class you know of all white people so why should, I mean I I think we have a hard time understanding why they have to have it because we don't, because we're the majority, you know? But when you don't have people around you that are you know common to you, it's completely different. I don't know.*

MICHELLE: *But I don't even think it's on that level. I don't think it's a relational level. It's a form of empowerment and I mean they have their, like, we have been granted so much power and we all in this room have been granted so much power being white - like in every facet of our life on a personal level, institutional level, cultural level anywhere you want to look at it we have all been granted some kind of privilege or power. I don't know if everyone's ready to admit that . . . all five or six sessions that we've been here no one has been, like it seems like everyone is like avoidant like scared to admit that they have privilege and scared to see it. (S7)*

This exchange resonates with some of the ways I interacted with fellow doctoral students—both white and of color—around issues of how whites and students of color experience life at this university. As I described in chapter three, I was taken to task by my colleagues of color for not being sensitive to the very thing that the participants are being insensitive to: the power of whites to include—or not—people of color in the daily exchanges that occur on a college campus. At the time it was pointed out to me, I was unaware of how I was using my privilege to exclude people of color from fully participating in the doctoral student meetings. I mistakenly thought that the group was a space for all students to feel/be "empowered." Yet, my actions were saying, "You can be empowered in this group but only if you do it the 'white' way."

My questioning Ellen about the differential experiences of Blacks and whites on campus opened the door to understanding how myths of inclusion are operative in discussions among white people and how what we might *think* is empowerment is really just white people controlling the extent to which people of color are allowed "in." Julie and Michelle interrupted the white talk and the mythmaking that was produced and tried to develop a different perspective about the presence of UNITY on campus. They attempted to refocus the discussion onto the responsibility of white people, not the actions—or inactions—of the students of color. Rather than debate the concept of inclusion, they tried to situate the discussion around white privilege and how that was related to the ways the participants reconstructed myths about people of color. (To see the continuation of the above dialogue concerning white privilege, see Appendix D.)

The taken-for-granted myth of inclusion was difficult to contest. The participants have been advantaged by a system that "feels" very normal to them and therefore, "should feel" normal to every other American. The discourse they created though, managed to disrupt their sense of normalcy and raised questions for them about what it means to be "included" in white society. What was "normal" to them became problematic. They were "suddenly made to feel 'white' which [was] a new experience for most of them" (Wellman, 1993, p. 246).

Exceptions to the Rule

If you are a white person who is actively seeking to work against racism, then you are bound to run into another white person who will be all too willing to tell you an "exception to the rule" story. That's another strategy for reconstructing the myth of "equal opportunity for all" and one that was prevalent in many of our group discussions. These "exception to the rule" stories helped the participants—who continue to benefit from racial privilege—to feel secure in their social and racial locations. The stories are testimonies to the "pull up your bootstraps" mentality that permeates white American culture. This skewed framework for thinking about American success continues to ignore and deny the multiple barriers that are consciously or unconsciously built to advantage white people in this country. These exceptions function to alleviate the multiple consequences of white racism.

> The assumption, moreover, is that American society actually operates according to principles of fairness and merit, that the "deserving" are rewarded for their efforts, and that the "undeserving" are left out. Thus, these formulations allow students to see themselves as the rightful recipients of rewards based on individual achievement, *and* to defend a process that advantages them as a group, *without* ever having to justify their location in the organization of racial advantage. (Wellman, 1993, p. 233)

Like Wellman's students, the participants of this project constructed inconsistent formulations about individuality and merit, the work ethic, and equal opportunity. Rather than question the underpinnings of entrenched white American ideals, some of the participants defended the existence of the universality of these ideals across racial groups, and questioned the commitment that people of color have to equality and hard work. In order to solidify the necessity and value of these ideals, the participants shared "exception to the rule stories," protecting their own images of self, and illuminating a positive representation of the Other. Representing a "positive Other" was used by the participants to demonstrate their proactive stance against racist stereotyping. The participants' stories also generated some moments of critical dialogue providing us with opportunities to more deeply engage in—and challenge—the prevailing discourse.

During session four, Gerry shared her confusion about "white status." She questioned the idea that the Other—in this case, her Chinese roommate—does not have the same opportunities for success that she, as a white person has living in this country.

GERRY: *I'm really confused. Are we talking about just white-Black relations or are we talking about all minority? Because I have a roommate who's Chinese and she has everything that any of I mean the rest of us have. She's been taught the same way that all of us have that she can do anything. Like I don't know.*

ELLEN: *There's Black girls that are in my high school that are taught the same the same thing I was.*

GERRY: *So is it socioeconomic? She doesn't feel like the world like my roommate doesn't feel like the world's against her or that like me, as a white person, has a that I have a higher status than she does. Like we talk about it too. And that's why I I mean I don't know if it's a white-Black thing or if it's a white-all minority thing or what. (S4)*

The conversation continued with some of the participants agreeing with Gerry and commenting on this roommate, who a few of them knew personally.

GERRY: *She's never had it be like oh, she's Chinese. Like it's never been that. Her boyfriend for three years was white. Um, and like she's seen white guys at this school. It's like that's never been an issue as far as like her relationships with males go and like we've never seen it. She's obviously felt blatant things towards her um, but honestly like we have never blatantly seen it done to her and she'll tell us if it is 'cause she comes home and rants and raves about it if it [racist behavior] does happens. (S4)*

Michelle commented that the roommate was probably "immune to it" by now "because she's just she's lived with them for so long."

Gerry responded with a comment that was challenged by Kerry who questioned the validity of using one example to represent an entire race or particular experiences that happen to members of a racial group.

GERRY: *Yeah. No. I totally understand what you're saying. I just I have such a hard time like grasping that because I don't know. Maybe it's just me. When I look at her, she's just she's had everything that the white people like that the white people have had. I mean her parents are both professionals. They came from China. They're not they were not born in America. Her parents both came from China. They're both professionals. Like she's been given everything, every opportunity. She's at [a university]. So, that's why I don't understand the status thing, I guess. I don't know. I'm just very confused.*

ASHLEY: *Maybe she's a lucky[*

KERRY: *Because you also, you're looking at her as an example of all Chinese people. You're taking her out and saying, "Well, she's not really being, you know, she's not really seeing prejudice because she's made it. She had everything I did. But is that true of all Chinese people? (S4)*

Being a Chinese student at the university appeared to evoke a different set of assumptions for the participants than the ones they seemed to have if the student (or students) they were discussing was Black. It was assumed by the group that this Chinese girl and her family would arrive in this country well-equipped with exemplary educational backgrounds, good values, and respected traditions that exemplify a "model minority." Nonetheless, this story—which illustrates one of the few times that a member of a racial group, ethnic group, or both other than Black was used to demonstrate a participant's point of view—reveals, once again, the propensity for the participants to elevate "a" story so as to solidify "equal opportunity for all."

Faith shared her own story in session six. We were discussing institutional racism as it is maintained and sustained within the educational system and how they, as white teachers, could and would deal with it. Ellen commented that "We're all optimistic teachers who plan on not having racism in our classroom." The rest of the participants agreed and so I asked them, "How . . . as a white teacher in this society can you not have racism in your classroom?"

FAITH: *Like I work with this girl at my work up here [in the city] and she went to school in um, Hartford. And or New Haven? And she's Black. And she is completely urban, 50 kids in her class went to college. Her Mom's on like welfare whatever. I'm like, "Are you kidding? Like was it ever a thought that you weren't going to college?" I'm like, "This is perfect." She totally loves talking about this [race, racism] and she's like, "I never experienced racism in my classrooms." I'm like, "How could you not?" She had all white teachers. And I'm like, "Do you think that you can identify to a white teacher the way that you can identify to a Black teacher?" She's like, "It's my teacher." She's like, "Fine. They're white. They're Black." She's like, "What matters to me is how they treat me. I always felt encouraged by like to do things and sometimes I would feel discouraged but" she's like, "I knew what I wanted. I have my goals and there was no way I wasn't going to college." And here she is at a really good school, you know what I mean? And doing it and doing really well. . . . You know what I mean? I don't know. I lost my train of thought." (S6)*

The participants never did answer my question directly. Rather, embedded in Faith's story were multiple strategies for how she felt racism could be addressed as a white teacher. They were difficult strategies to argue against. How can one oppose high expectations of students? How can one not be in favor of the principle of merit? Thus, her "exception story" fits nicely with the humanistic and American-sounding philosophy of education. She presents an example of a "completely urban" Black girl who has "made it." Not only is this girl Black, but she was on welfare and had to go to school with 50 kids in her class. The more roadblocks to success, the more powerful the story becomes as a way to glorify white American ideals, and show the world that yes, Blacks can make it too if they work hard, "have [their] goals" and know what they want.

The temptation to accept "exception stories" unproblematically and therefore, privilege the myth of equal opportunity is characteristic of many white people in our society. In conversations that Bellah and his colleagues (1985) had with 200 mostly middle-class white Americans in the early 1980s, they "have found an emphasis on hard work and self-support can go hand in hand with an isolating preoccupation with the self" (p. 56). This preoccupation with the (white) self distances white people from understanding the exact nature of a meritocratic system that privileges the individual who is a member of the dominant group in very particular ways. Individualizing racism and looking for "needles in the haystack" as ways to disprove the effects of racism, lead to misrepresentations of people of color and the systemic nature of racism. As Roman (1993) suggests, if these misrepresentations are "left unchallenged, they may silence, or worse yet, eclipse any memory of the historical, economic, and cultural conditions under which they were produced" (p. 214).

IT'S OVERWHELMING—YOU FEEL REALLY HELPLESS

The participants met the complexities of racism with a variety of affective responses as well. Expressions of powerlessness, defensiveness, and fear were the most prominent feelings displayed during our project. I refer to these expressions as "privileged affect"—affective expressions experienced by white people that are related to positions of privilege. When met with many of the realities of racism, the participants appropriated a set of affective strategies that minimized the consequences of racism for people of color and maximized the "feeling realm" of the participants. Privileging their own feelings increased the likelihood that the participants would continue to construct white talk and fail to consider plans of action for changing the face of racism.

The question of who was going to "do something" about the problem of racism was a recurring theme throughout the sessions and is evident in many of the examples provided in the text. It was much easier for the participants to describe personal experiences related to issues of racism and their constructions of whiteness than it was for them to think about realistic and effective strategies for taking individual action, collective action, or both against racist practices, behaviors, and institutions. Feeling powerless over such overwhelming experiences resulted in subtle and not so subtle forms of abdicating responsibility for determining strategies to work against racism.

Since the participants felt most at ease and "most powerful" in their future classrooms, I decided to ask them how far they would take their commitment to "doing something" in the institutions in which they worked. We had talked a few times during the project about standardized tests and the continuing debates in education about their validity and reliability in representing both white students and students of color. The conversation below addresses that issue.

ALICE: *Well, let me give you a teacher scenario since you all relate very well to teaching as a place where you think you can have some influence. And this goes back to last week's collage about the standardized tests and someone's remark that they are biased. So, if those tests are biased and if they favor white children and you're in your classroom and you've decided that you are going to influence these 20 kids and not be racist[*

? You have to give the test.

ALICE: *. . . Your school district . . . says, "We're doing these tests." What are you going to do?*

LYNN: *Well, it's funny because I had to teach a class today, give an exam. . . . And next to [the students' names], they had their standardized tests scores and most of them were like 58, 59, just 60. Um, none of them really got over 70 except for one child who got 98 and he was a white kid who had transferred from another school. Um, the teacher didn't understand why they were so low because she knew these kids were so smart and what I've always learned about standardized tests and when I give these to my students, is I have to understand that these tests are not absolute. I have to use them and judge them and see them for what they really are. Like I can't use those as a basis for anything and in other words when I get my test scores back, with all these Black kids doing poor and these white kids doing um, fine, I can't say those Black kids are stupid or are not as smart and I cannot pay much attention to those. I would pay more attention to what they're doin' in my class rather than their standardized tests scores. Unfortunately, as a teacher, you're gonna have to give the test. There's not much you can do right now except make known that they are biased so that when people read the scores, they realize what may be a contributing factor to the low scores. I mean I I can't not give it. I'd probably be fired as a teacher if I did not give them.*

MICHELLE: *But what if the whole school system didn't give the test?*

? *They can't fire everyone.*

LYNN: *Right. So if I was a teacher I would pose a complaint and then, I'd have to give the test but in the aftermath, I would uh, go to my principal, go to the people making the test 'cause there are steps now to make these tests supposedly more unbiased but until that's done, all I can do with my kids, is not really put much weight in those standardized tests.*

ALICE: *I asked you the question because again, that's very laudable that teachers do that and say, "Well, I don't pay a lot of attention to the scores." But the scores follow these children until they get to where you were a couple of years ago, which is graduating from high school and you're trying to get into a college and now you have complied this group of test scores and every teacher that's had these kids has said, "I don't pay attention to those because I think differently." Now you point to, until those are changed, this is what I'm going do as a white person who is in a position of responsibility, who has avenues from which to do things. Well, who, what I'm asking is who's going to do that? While teachers are educating the children in their room, who is going to make those changes?*

ELLEN: *How can you make changes?*

LYNN: *Get involved in I guess, pose complaints, go to wherever the committees are that deal with standardized tests and say, "Look. You gotta be making these changes."*

KATHLEEN: *You know, when we talk about trying to change the standardized tests or whatever. That's gonna take a lot of time. And are we willing to, is it more important to try to do that and give up the time we could be preparing to teach in the classroom? Or we could be making a difference in the classroom.*

As was evident in the discussion, few of the participants were willing to jump on the bandwagon of critiquing and taking action against institutions that oppress students and create failure (Sleeter, 1992). Many times, it felt as if we were sitting around talking about what we are going to do *when*, which is very different than applying what we talk about *now* in our everyday lives. The sense of powerlessness over what to do about what many of the participants referred to as the "awesome" nature of the problem prevented them from being able to feel a sense of agency in their personal and professional lives. It was a tension that I wrote about often in my journal.

Is "hearing" enough? So these girls "hear" something different and they experience themselves differently as white females. Maybe. One of them was telling us the other night that all she does now is think about race and [asks herself] "is *that* racially motivated?" and "is *this* racially motivated?" and it is driving her crazy - this preoccupation with racism. But that's a mind game. And I don't think we can *think* ourselves out of this problem. I don't think raising consciousness is enough, though I believe it to be crucial to the dialectical relationship between reflection and action. But the reflection pieces of it can be seductive. It can very easily turn into "intellectual" talk. And that lets us off the hook too easily. . . . I know that I can discuss, argue, and study all I want [but] it's also in the action. It's in the doing. It's in the actions I choose to engage in that will make or break my response to racism. And here I sit thinking that this experience could end in lots of discussions and study and arguing (I *wish* they would argue) and still, we could talk ourselves deeper into denial. (Oct. 15, 1994)

At the end of the penultimate group session, Michelle asked the group if they would be interested in "doing something" on campus about the issues that had been discussed throughout the project. Again, the feeling of powerlessness was palatable in the conversation and appeared to immobilize the participants from engaging in any kind of group action.

MICHELLE: *Do you think that we could like focus in on some certain aspect and as a group address some sort of aspect of racism? Or[*

FAITH: *As a group here?*

MICHELLE: *Yeah. Don't you think we could focus our energies on something and make a difference somewhere? I mean not in the whole entire level but focus in[*

FAITH: *But by focusing in, do you mean discussing or do you mean doing[*

MICHELLE: *Doing something[*

(ct)

LYNN: *Then mention something.*

(lots of ct)

ELLEN: *None of us know where to focus.*

(lots of ct)

? *That's why we came here.*

(ct)

MICHELLE: *. . . Obviously we all know we can't tackle this entire thing. I mean it's overwhelming. We learned that. But there's got to be somewhere that we can focus in on. Something that we can focus in on that we would be able to do as 13 white individuals working together as a group to do some to fight racism, to actively fight it and not just talk about it.*

FAITH: *Like what?*

The end result of these types of conversations is that the participants shift responsibility and free themselves from the complexities of a global and societal situation they feel powerless about changing. "[T]he situation . . . like I mean I I think obviously by the way none of us know what to do or know what to say we feel helpless too. Like it's an overwhelming thing and you feel really helpless in it" (Michelle).

I'M AFRAID I'LL SAY THE WRONG THING

Many of my white colleagues in the school of education have invited me to come to their classes and talk to their undergraduate and

graduate students about "whiteness" this past year. They specifically
want me to use the group collage activity mentioned in chapter three,
and described in more detail in chapter five, as a way to generate small
and large group discussions about whiteness, race, and racism with
their students. Having been an elementary and junior high school
teacher for many years, I am familiar with, and have benefited from, a
wide variety of teaching experiences: team teaching, coteaching, teaching with colleagues across age groups, and participating in shared mentoring of student teachers. Therefore, I am all too willing to engage in
more collaborative teaching experiences in the university—an educational setting that is usually resistant to methods of teaching that go
beyond the traditional professor-student paradigm. Yet, I am not convinced that the invitation to teach in these classrooms is about collaboration as much as it is about assuaging an underlying fear that my white
colleagues have about their own whiteness *and* about "saying the wrong
thing" to their students. Whiteness is not a topic that is usually cov-
ered in college classrooms. One of the concerns then becomes not knowing enough about whiteness to conduct an effective and educative class.
In addition, talking about whiteness with white students is not easy. It
generates uncomfortable silences, forms of resistance, degrees of hos-
tility, and a host of other responses that many of us would prefer to
avoid. From my own experiences teaching about whiteness in a university with predominantly white students, I can attest to the fact that
there are many "How do I deal with what was just said?" kind of
moments and many times when the question arises: "Did I handle that
student's remark appropriately? Did I say the 'right' thing?" My colleagues might disagree with the above hypothesis, but it has been my
experience, especially since conducting this research, that as white people and teachers, no matter how intelligent, well-read, progressive, liberal, or outspoken we might be, we do not feel comfortable talking
about whiteness—our own or anyone else's.

My colleagues' hesitancy to "teach" about whiteness is similar to
what the participants experience as they enter unfamiliar school settings where they are faced with what many consider insurmountable
problems, only one of which they see as racism. Not only do they fear
their own performance as teachers, they fear students of color in a very
real sense. What if they say the wrong thing? What if they don't understand "them?" What if the students of color sense their fear?

In addition, the participants feel that they might "say the wrong
thing" in a class, in conversations with people of color, in papers they
write, and in everyday situations that occur in which race is a factor.
They have a generalized fear of people of color—*and* about what to say

about people of color—that is fed by white America's representation of the Other—especially African Americans as Other. This fear resulted in a variety of responses that were expressed during our project: anger, frustration, confusion, defensiveness, guilt, and feelings of victimization.

At our third session, Faith asked if she could share her "whiteness experience" that had occurred during the previous week.

FAITH: *I was walking and it was raining and I was like walking through the rain back to my house and I saw this guy come towards me and he had a hood on and he was Black and I'm like, "Oh my God" and like I think immediately I was like, he's a man. I'm alone. It's raining. It's night. Rape on campus. You know what I mean?*

? Right.

FAITH: *But I was like if he were a white guy would I be, "Oh my God" or would I be like, "Yeah, what's up?" you know what I mean? (laughter). I don't know. I don't know how I was reacting. When I reacted that way I was like, "I just came back from two and half hours of discussing my total open-mindedness and my (laughter) liberal role and now here I am jumping on the other side of the street" and I couldn't believe it and I think, I don't [know] if that's ever gonna go away, you know what I mean? . . . And if I was talking to like say someone like my father, and I was trying to talk to him about it, he would be like, "Well, you know, Faith, statistics say that of all the rapes on campus, 98 percent of them are done by Black men" so you're just thinking, "Of course I'm gonna be scared because most of the people who do it are you know, Black." And you know, not that he's a racist but some people might think he is. (laughs) I don't know. But you know what I mean? So, I don't know. I'm just very confused. (S3)*

Faith's story was immediately followed by Marie's—a story that resonated with the same kind of fear we heard in Faith's narrative. Marie's fear was accompanied by a feeling of embarrassment about "looking racist." Marie picked up where Faith left off.

MARIE: *I I don't mean to interrupt[*

FAITH: *No.*

MARIE: *I had a similar experience today. (laughter) One of my friends was telling me a story about how she was held up last night at McDonald's and she was telling me this blah, blah, blah and they like, they came in and she noticed they were wearing like bandannas and they had hoods on and she's like, "Oh, they're from a gang" and then they pulled out guns and she was like, "No they're not." (laughter) . . . They put them all in the freezer and nothing happened. They took the money and they left and I had to ask her. I said and I don't know why I said, "Were they Black?" and she said, "Yes." and I said, "Why did I immediately think that?" and I was like and I and I try so hard. I really do. (laughter) I do. (laughter) It was like this burning question and it made me feel like really embarrassed and I even said it to her and I'm like, "I'm really embarrassed that I just asked you that question because now you are gonna think that I'm like" and I did and I assumed and I was right but I assumed. (S3)*

Immediately following Marie's story, Michelle told a story about how uncomfortable it was for the white students in one of her classes to claim their racial and ethnic backgrounds. This led to a discussion about how to describe people of color and was it "OK" to use color as a descriptive term. Lynn joined in that conversation and stated, "I should not have to feel uncomfortable saying, 'That *Black* guy over there.'"

As noted in chapter three, I had made a firm decision to remain a "silent bystander" during session three. As I sat and listened to Faith's story—and the rapid succession of others that followed—I began to question that decision. In my journal entry the following day, I wrote: "I have to admit that there were some tempting moments there when I wanted to ask a question, make a comment, refocus the group, interrupt a talkative participant, but I kept thinking, 'Al, you promised yourself that you wouldn't say anything so be quiet'" (Sept. 30, 1994). So, instead of challenging Faith's father's assertion that 98 percent of the rapes on campus are committed by Black men, or commenting on the small number of Blacks on this campus, or expounding on the realities of rape in America, or discussing *why* some Blacks commit violent acts in the United States (i.e., poverty, unemployment, lack of opportunity), or explaining how justice is meted out among this country's racial groups (see, e.g., Wellman, 1993 and Hacker, 1995), I remained silent, and the participants continued to privilege their feelings. In doing so, *I* failed to correct misinformation and *they* resisted any attempt to undercut their negative and racist images of Black men. Their feelings became justified, their disparaging conceptions of Black men were reified, and I took solace in the fact that I had kept my promise to myself! It was only after listening to the tapes and being challenged by Brinton about my silence that I realized how badly I had handled those discussions. After a meeting with Brinton about the above stories, I wrote in my journal:

I don't know whether I should cry or kick the door in here. . . . One minute I am flying high over the immense accomplishment of not talking - even though I wanted to - and then, in a flash, I am devastated because I SHOULD HAVE said something. Well which one is it? Is it a process that I let go of or is it a process I interrupt? Didn't I already write about this? (Oct. 3, 1994)

In order to clarify my position, and provide a critical response to the above stories, I explained to the group the following week what I should have explained during the discussion itself. The participants listened to my interpretations (briefly summarized in the following paragraph) and although they didn't openly disagree with them, they didn't necessarily accept them as fact either.

What resonated in their stories from session three was a feeling of shared acceptance of a particular stereotype and a feeling that all the participants would have assumed the same things Faith and Marie had. Instead of looking at how whites construct images of the Other, how Blacks are prohibited from entering the "white world" on a variety of levels, how racism is implicated in the amount of crime in this country, the talk continued to center around how uncomfortable the participants *felt* dealing with racism.

Privileging their own feelings over the conditions and feelings of people of color was a strategy for the participants to ignore their own whiteness. As has been shown, locating the discussion around the powerlessness, fear, and defensive posture of the participants stalled the conversations and led to highlighting the discomfort of the white self and dismissing the daily life experiences of people of color. Roman (1993) raises the important question of what educators should do "when white students recognize not only that racism exists at levels deeper than the expression of individual prejudices [and here I would add, individual feelings as well] but also feel ashamed to be implicated in its structural practice—ashamed to face those who have suffered racism" (p. 214). Her response to that question is an important one:

> Ashamed contradictory whites subjects are not absolved of their responsibility to build effective social alternatives to structural racism. If white students are to become empowered critical analysts of their own claims to know the privileged world in which their racial interests function, it strikes me now that such privileges and the injustices they reap for others must become the *objects* of analyses of structural racism, to the effect that subjects move from paralyzing shame and guilt to stances in which we/they take effective responsibility and action for disinvesting in racial privilege. (p. 207)

SUMMATION

The examples of white talk presented in this chapter demonstrate how the participants' uncritical talk resulted in the domestication of the multiple issues we raised concerning the meaning of whiteness, white racial identity, and white racism. Constructing difference from people of color was a continuous thread heard in the group's discourse. In addition, many of the participants reconstructed myths and stereotypes about people of color. Finally, the participants' instinctive emotional reactions to a variety of issues raised in our group sessions proved formidable barriers to interrupting the flow of white talk. Oftentimes, their affective responses resisted individual and collective critique. Feelings of powerlessness, fear, and defensiveness shielded many of the participants from challenging the polemic nature of race talk.

However, the participants' strong, affective responses were not only tools for resisting critique. Becoming aware of their feelings about racism and their own racial identities was an integral and very important aspect of how the participants made meaning of whiteness. Their willingness to share their feelings about themselves and people of color was crucial to being able to move the discussion beyond the feeling realm—even if the move was slight. In reflecting on the intensity of their feelings, some of the participants gained a much deeper sense of themselves as white women and were able to construct new forms of knowledge about racism, whiteness, and the lived experiences of people of color. For example, during our last session, I asked the participants what they were going to take with them as we ended our experience together. Below are a few of their responses:

JULIE: *Mine is um recognition of white unearned privilege because I think just recognizing it is a first step to having solved the problem.*

KATHLEEN: *This is a very wide problem on many different levels and that I no longer need to have, I shouldn't have, tunnel vision and I should have a wider perspective of everything in order to understand it.*

MARY: *I'm um taking three things. Well, I'm taking a lot but three things came to mind. A new understanding about myself. Um, a new perspective about everyone like the whole problem and um, a little bit of optimism.*

ASHLEY: *I wrote introspection. I think this group helped me to really stop and think and not just say things without backing it up. I have such empty statements sometimes and like this group has made me like really think about if I really believe that or not and stick to when I do. Stay with it.*

King (1991) suggests that whites need to identify, understand, and bring to conscious awareness our "uncritical and limited ways of thinking" (p. 140) about racism if we are to move toward a more critical consciousness-raising dialogue. In this PAR project we identified the problem of racism and whiteness. We brought to consciousness our "uncritical and limited ways of thinking." Subsequently, through critical self- and collective dialogue, many of us experienced a new awareness about the myriad issues that were raised in our group sessions. Such an engagement was excruciatingly painful at times. At the beginning of session five, we were discussing how disturbed and confused everyone felt following session four. Elizabeth summed up the group's feelings quite well when she said:

> *I remember like Mary, Marie, and I were leaving and we were just like, my whole body was like AHHH! There was so much going on and it was like I wish we could've just sat, I don't know. I almost felt like we were all in like this huge fight (unint.) and it wasn't. It was just a discussion but it was like (unint.) being almost like angry and I don't even know why. (S5)*

Discovering why, making meaning, and engaging in dialogue and critique are a continuing process. As Freire (1994) argues, "Changing language is part of the process of changing the world" (p. 67–68).

My analyses of the participants' discourse both documents the participants' paradoxical language and illustrates the enormous complexities involved when white people begin to examine racial issues. The conversations presented thus far make clear the need to examine the multiple dimensions of camaraderie, group homogeneity, social locations (including gender and social class), and the lived experiences of white people when we problematize whiteness. When we are creating spaces for groups of white people to attend to race relations, and to our own white racial identities, we need to be aware of how easily we can fabricate white talk—a kind of talk that doesn't just obliterate the lives of people of color. It also anesthetizes the white psyche, and serves to minimize white culpability for the existence of individual, institutional, and societal racism.

CHAPTER 5

CONSTRUCTIONS OF WHITENESS

As was illustrated in the previous chapter, there was a strong tendency on the part of the participants to focus on people of color as a way to make sense of their own racial identities. In addition, the participants carried a variety of conflicting beliefs, attitudes, and ideas about white people and the meaning of whiteness. Participants reported that until they were interviewed, they had never been asked, "What does it mean for you to be white?" Although a heretofore unexamined phenomenon, the participants did recognize "their own whiteness." How this recognition related—or not—to their own lives, and to their relationship with membership in the white race, was something they were less sure about. Subsequently, the participants' encounter with their racial identities contained elements of surprise, concern, frustration, and resistance.

As a way to work through and think through this "white dilemma," the participants framed their notions of whiteness around three interlocking themes: (1) whites as living a fairy tale, (2) whites as keepers of the American Dream,[1] and (3) whites as dualistic. These mutually interacting descriptors of whiteness share certain features that illustrate the conflict that existed in/for the participants as they tried to make sense of their racial identities. Whites were represented on a continuum from those who were the ideal, the perfect, the norm, to whites as bad, racist, and ignorant. The participants described whites as those who "have" and those who "have not." Whites were portrayed as powerful, dominating, and afraid of losing their privileges and advantages. In addition, whites were presented as wanting/needing to "rescue" people of color who the participants see as less fortunate than many whites.

The tendency to dichotomize whites into this or that category was prevalent throughout our discussions and seemed like an almost effortless exercise. It was the attempts by all of us to refrain from creating polarized notions of whites, and find a more realistic sense of ourselves as white women, that proved to be the most difficult, the most complicated, and at the same time, the most illuminative experience.

WHITES AS LIVING A FAIRY TALE

ASHLEY: *Basically we being white is about being a fairy tale. Like our life is we can reach the moon. We can have serenity in a household. We can we can be political leader if we want to be. We can be beautiful. We can be classical like if you look at the old movies and like everyone wants that loving life, elegance and and we can be heroes in our society and it it's just like we can have a view and as a white person that's what it means to us. I mean it sounds it's horrible but it's not the same way for a Black person or any other minority. It's just it's not that available to them. This is everything that is for us. (S4)*

"Whites as living a fairy tale existence" illuminates the lived experiences of these participants in a particular way. As was suggested during the sessions, if this research project were being conducted with students at a state college, where the experiences of the white students intersect with class discrimination in differing ways from its intersection among white women of privilege, a different conversation would have been constructed. The life histories of these middle- and upper middle-class participants played a crucial role in how they viewed white people as "the ideal" and "the norm." The participants' limited interactions with people of color, their geographical locations growing up, their education, and class backgrounds, and the range of opportunities they have been afforded interact in a powerful way to create this idealized notion of what it means to be white. Although it was mentioned in the sessions that not all white people experience life as a fairy tale, there was a shared acceptance that white people "can do anything in society" (Mary).

In session four, the participants were asked to form small groups and create group collages to represent whiteness. The groups then presented their representations to the larger group who was asked to reflect on what they saw and then individually and collectively interpret the creations. This is an exchange that took place in response to the collage created by group number two (see Photo 1).

PHOTO 1
REPRESENTING WHITENESS

FAITH: *Well, it's like all the words you have are kinda like you can achieve anything like you're free and you're having a ball. It can happen to you. You're beautiful. (unint.) Like you can do anything. Like it's kinda like a freedom. . . .*

GERRY: *(unint.) perfect daughter . . . and then you have your perfect (unint.) family. (laughter) But then like in this corner, you have your perfect little family like all gathered around the coffee table, having snacks and like bonding. And they're white.*

MARY: *Yeah, you have leaders up there like leaders whatever so[*

ELLEN: *White white men going to the moon.*

MARIE: *They were the first to achieve something[(S4)*

Observations continued to be made supporting the idea that whiteness symbolized the "All-American" image of the at-home mother with the white nuclear family and everyone looking like the actors on the once popular television program "Happy Days." In response to the collage created by group number three (see Photo 2), Gerry remarked: "When I see some of these things, I think like, 'Oh my God. That's so all-American. Like so typical.' The first thing I think is, 'All-American. White.'"

MICHELLE: *There's no like expectation for us or anything. Like it's just assumed [that we are perfect].*

GERRY: *We're allowed to screw up and they aren't.*

MICHELLE: *Yeah, basically.*

? *There's more of us.*

GERRY: *We get the second[*

? *There's power in numbers[*

GERRY: *and third chances too like[*

? *Yeah[*

GERRY: *people are always there to pick us up. Like you could screw up all I know like I could do anything and my parents would still be there like*

PHOTO 2
REPRESENTING WHITENESS

encouraging me and trying to get me back on my feet, whereas I think that that's because society's still saying, "Well, you know, she had this type of a life so far, you know[

MARY: *You could do anything in society[(S4)*

This idea that whites are born with the proverbial spoon in their mouths is at once similar to the participants' own life histories but also in many ways, contradicts aspects of their own personal experiences as well as the experiences of many white people. As students, these participants have very high expectations for themselves and work extremely hard at achieving good grades and learning how to be "good teachers." They are also aware of the tremendous number of white people who do not have equal access to the kinds of opportunities that are afforded to more advantaged white Americans. As Faith noted during a discussion of white advantage,

FAITH: *Um, I know people I mean, my friend, for example, doesn't have any money and he goes to a very expensive private school because he's on scholarship and because he works and his parents don't give him any money and he's not Black. He's white and he went to a good high school because he got a scholarship. Do you know what I mean? And I feel like we're forgetting about those white people who also have to work really hard. Do you know what I mean? Like just because he was white doesn't mean that he was given this great education, you know because he doesn't have any money so - and I feel that a lot of people you know, maybe people start to take for granted things you know that, I don't know. (S5)*

Although there were attempts to represent white people in a more realistic way, the overall portrait of white America created by the participants was one where white people were the ruling class in the hierarchy of racial order. In the group talk, the participants speak about the racial hierarchy that exists in this country. What was problematic in this talk was their failure to explore and/or question how whites continue to dominate people of color and keep this racial hierarchy in place.

When asked to interpret a poster that a group had created representing racism during session two (see Photo 3) the participants remarked:

ELLEN: *I feel like it's like there's like one big person and that's the white person kinda not ruling over the all the other colors but[*

JULIE: *Dominating*

PHOTO 3
REPRESENTING RACISM

ELLEN: *Domin dominating. That's a good word[*

KATHLEEN: *Someone who's dominating some other group or two groups. (S2)*

The participants were able to acknowledge white power and they were able to recognize how "normal" it is for whites to dominate the Other. Yet, acknowledging and recognizing white "supremacy" (my term—not theirs) is not the same as critically examining how and why it continues to exist. They did not interrupt the notion that whites are the ideal with a more substantial discussion of the origins of white domination and oppression. Rather, the participants moved the discussion to "white as normative."

WE SET THE STANDARDS

Along with idealizing the white race, the participants also felt that white people were the "norm reference group" in this country—the group that "sets the standard" for everyone else. Throughout the sessions, I heard the participants make reference to the extent to which white people dominate aspects of our society—the media, government, law, and education. The preponderance of white people in all areas of society, some of whom are positive role models, some of whom are not, serves a dual purpose: it sends a message to white people that "We can do anything" (Michelle) and "We have it all" (Gerry). At the same time, it sends a message to people of color that they are excluded, marginalized, and do not represent the norm.

FAITH: *And I think also like a white person, like a girl, like think of a little like white girl when she's little. She goes to the ballet and she sees the Nutcracker and she wants to be a ballerina and you know, that's her new role model and then it's Mary Lou Retton (laughter) and like, you know? You go on and do all these things, like you always have all these dreams and your parents keep saying, "You're gonna be the next whatever" you know? And then you have these little Black kids who - society doesn't tell them that they can be great. You know what I mean? Like society just tells them, "You're lucky if you make it out of high school" . . . and you know, white kids, there's a lot of you know, "You can be what you wanna be" and everything else. So of course we are gonna have role models, like my role model is whoever, Hillary Clinton (laughter) and where's Black people? Their role model can't be Hillary Clinton because she's married to the President and unless I'm gonna marry a white guy and he won't even be elected President if he's married to a Black girl anyway (laughter) so you know, that totally wipes that out, you know what I mean? (S3)*

This idea that opportunities for Blacks are "totally wiped out" is striking and resonates with Michelle's interpretation of her group's collage depicting whiteness—an activity conducted during session four (see Photo 4 that depicts people of various racial and ethnic groups on the right, white people on the left).

MICHELLE: *This is America's standardized test. Everything in society is compared to the norm reference group of whites. . . . So this is our norm reference group and this is the test takers, the Blacks, and the people of color are the test takers and they're not measuring up to our standards because we set the standards and our standards might not be theirs. But the way our test is set up is that we represent the norm.*

? *We are the standard[*

MICHELLE: *(unint.) Yeah, exactly[*

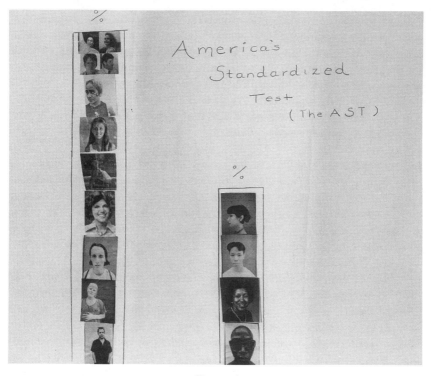

PHOTO 4
REPRESENTING WHITENESS

MARY: *We don't have anything to prove[*

MICHELLE: *We don't have to work up to anything. . . . You are the norm so you don't have to work at it.*

ELLEN: *So it's just sort of assumed that you that you're as good as the norm just because you're white?*

MICHELLE: *Mhm.*

MARY: *I don't think you ever even think about it.*

MICHELLE: *Yeah. You don't have to to think about it.*

MARY: *I think you just you just know it. (S4)*

Clearly, this recognition of differential standards for whites and people of color is an important step for white people in unpacking the systemic and systematic structures that advantage one group over the other. For some of these young women, it was a point of entry into the more complicated discourse of institutional and cultural racism. This entry point resulted in a heightened awareness for some of the participants about the extent to which the United States is a divided nation, at the same time that it evoked a powerful resistance in the participants to thinking about the racial divide in our country. Sleeter (1995) suggests that it is crucial for white people to "think institutionally" about racism. I would add that it is as important for white people to "think culturally" about racism as well. Throughout the sessions, the participants displayed a powerful resistance to thinking institutionally, culturally, or both about racism. They preferred to think of racism as individual discriminatory behavior against another, not as a system of policies and practices that metastasize as they permeate the multiple dimensions of our society. At the same time, the participants juxtapose this limited perspective of racism with the various characteristics associated with white group membership as that membership relates to "the norm." This tendency to locate racism within the individual, and the struggles of locating oneself within the larger white group, will be explored later in this chapter. For now, it is important to note that the above exchanges move beyond the description of racism as a one-to-one confrontation to an expanded perspective about racism as a system that maintains and sustains racist practices, denigrating people of color through exclusion and marginalization. The participants began to recognize this stratification between whites and people of color, a stratification that has enabled white people to experience life as "normal." If whites are the norm, if whites set the standards, if "we don't have anything to prove" (Mary), then one can understand why Michelle could ask the following question as she pondered the collage that was created to represent "whiteness" and which was presented earlier (see Photo 1):

MICHELLE: *Well see I can look up there and point like the little picture of the kids down there and say, "Oh, that's my childhood and that's my best friend." But what if I was Black. I'd be looking up there going, "Mmm." You know? What what symbolizes me up there? (S4)*

Michelle—and some of the other participants—pushed the discussion beyond the surface descriptive white talk and disrupted the "fixed gaze" (Fine, 1995) that white people have on, not just the-Other-as-deficient, but also on whites-as-normative. They began to question their own meanings of whiteness and how those meanings intersect with their lived experiences, their place in history, their social class, and gender. Examining what it means to say that "white is normative" and that "white is the ideal" challenged the participants to break through the "white noise" (Fine, 1995) that oftentimes masks the multiple realities of what it means to be white in this country.

We are the Keepers of the American Dream: White Power and Privilege

Griscom (1992) suggests that "power permeates every aspect of our life." She goes on to quote Nancy Henley who argues that power is "the oxygen of our social life" (p. 400). If, indeed, power is an energy that fuels every facet of our lives, then white power is an energy that fuels the implicit and explicit realties of racism in this country.

I listened often as the participants tried to make sense of this kind power and how it related—or not—to their understandings of white privilege. The participants were never able to *clearly* define power and privilege in an agreed on, collective manner. Many times, the conversations became entangled in feelings of frustration for not having a shared understanding of what constitutes power and privilege.

MARIE: *Yeah. I was gonna say something. . . . It's you know, I don't like, I don't know. I don't do any, I don't, I know I do but I don't mean to do anything that gives me a white privilege. But it's given to me by society so I accept it and I take it and it's OK. And I expect it now and it's like, so I am maintaining the status just by accepting it and saying, "Yeah. If that's OK for you to give that to me and now I expect it because you've given it to me for as long as I can remember."*

GERRY: *I'm really confused. Um, . . . I don't understand how, as an individual, you maintain white status. (S4)*

Marie and Gerry summed up what many of the participants felt when they talked about status, power, and privilege—constructs that were problematic for the group and resulted in many convoluted exchanges. Assumptions about the privileged positions of white people in this country continued to be discussed:

ELLEN: *What [does] the white race still need to achieve?*

MARY: *I think the white race is like I don't think, like I can't think of anything that would be a goal for a white person[*

MARIE: *Maintain maintain our status.*

ELLEN: . . . *I feel like there's nothing left for the white race, as a race, to achieve.*

MARY: *Like we've achieved freedom. We've achieved equality.*

ELLEN: *Yeah[*

MARIE: *Yeah but now we just have to maintain it[*

ELLEN: *Yeah[*

MARIE: *Now we've got it so let's just keep it[(S4)*

. . . .

ELIZABETH: *But I think, as teachers, or as future teachers . . . I mean the group of what 13 of us, we can't go and just change the world you know what I mean? But if we show our students, no matter what race they are that they can at least try to do whatever whatever they want to do, you know what I mean?*

ALICE: *Can they do whatever they want to do though[*

ASHLEY: *Yeah. What happens when they do it and it doesn't work?[*

ELIZABETH: *Well, that's the thing[(S4)*

These exchanges exemplify how many of the participants conceptualized white power. We have it. It has worked for us. With power, we have "achieved freedom . . . equality." This recognition of power is related to, but different from, the participants' tendency to engage in zero-sum thinking—a characteristic of white talk presented in chapter four. Unlike zero-sum thinking, which is more about lodging the discussion about whiteness and racism within a limited, uncritical "we/them" paradigm that keeps whites from decentering power and privilege, conceptualizing white power is about recognition of what whites have acquired, what whites "have," and what it means to be situated in the dominant positions in our society. Unfortunately, how white people achieved this power was not attended to in the participants' discussions. Their lack of understanding about the history of white dominance in this country, and in the world, resulted in a skewed understanding of what constitutes white power and privilege. This uncritical acceptance of white power and privilege fosters the belief that white people are the keepers of/for democracy and, therefore, our power is legitimate. It's a painful realization for white people to admit that our history is fraught with the destruction of other peoples in the name of democracy, freedom, and equal rights. This admission is a point of entry into the history of colonization and slavery that many white Americans choose not to examine. These participants were no exception. They recognized their own race's power but failed to see its origins and its impact on the lives of marginalized groups or on themselves.

Instead, they saw power as situated in multiple contexts. For them the safest way to construct power was in their roles as teachers. In their classrooms they felt that they could use their power and the influence that comes with it in positive ways, thus, giving their students power so they could "do whatever, whatever they want to do"—a fallacy in many educational contexts where success is mediated by classroom materials, teacher expectations, access to resources, ability to take advantage of opportunities and a "society . . . racked by the problems of poverty, homelessness, unemployment, community dislocations, and racial division" (Campbell, 1996, p. xxx). The participants' connection to the larger phenomenon of white power was seen as a good thing in the classroom. They were not misusing their power, only tapping into it to improve the lives of others. As Lynn mentioned in one of the sessions, "It's not about us losing it. We're trying to bring them [people of color] up too. . . . I don't have a problem with trying to help them to get to the point where I am."

The paternalism inherent in Lynn's remarks is striking and is uncritically constructed by the participants out of "where the participants are"—which is a privileged position in this society. They are young, healthy, intelligent, responsible, idealistic white women who are attending an expensive, private university where they are, as Elizabeth suggested, "getting the best education of my life." She then went on to wonder why she couldn't share it with others. Since the participants felt that the whole idea of racism and what to do about it was too overwhelming to deal with on a societal scale, they chose to use the classroom as a site for "sharing" their power and privilege. It was within the four walls of a classroom where they felt in control and able to manage at least a piece of the problem.

ASHLEY: *As a white teacher, I would tell my students it's my minority students if they needed anything like any like backing not not I wouldn't blatantly say, "Ask a white person," but I would be like, "Ask me and I will help you" 'cause I know as a white person I would have more influence than these teenagers that were minorities would have. Like I would not I'd try to 'cause I don't think they realize that when they're younger that they don't have well, I don't know. Um, what I'm trying to say is basically that I think as a white person I have more influence than a Black person does and that I would help a Black person but[*

ELLEN: *Use your influence?*

ASHLEY: *Yeah as like I would try to be like, "You guys can come to me if like if there was a struggle you were in like" not necessarily a Black community struggle because that wouldn't be well, I don't know if it would be my business but I mean they might not I might not fit in that role, but like just a life role. I don't know how to explain what I'm saying but I'm just saying as a white person I think we could help. I don't know if that would help but I mean we could help them so much more than we do because we have more power. (S4)*

This idea that white teachers are the powerful ones who "help them" will be explored further in chapter six. What is necessary to understand here is the participants' construction of power as asymmetrical, advantaging one group over another, yet at the same time, legitimate as long as we, as whites, don't abuse it. Clearly there is a need for the participants to avoid problematizing the "multiplicity of power" (Griscom, 1992, p. 405). For example, if they unpack the underpinnings of white power, they would have to shed the veneer of benevolence that they associate with the power derived from membership in the dominant group. Instead of doing so, the participants find refuge in containing their power in a classroom and then using that power to educate their students "equally."

During session five, I tried to make connections between power, privilege, skin color, and the opportunities we, as white people, have to make changes—albeit small—in a society that advantages whites and disempowers people of color. I engaged the participants in a discussion of health care and women in the United States to illustrate the differential treatment of men and women in the health care system and then focused on the advantages I have, as a white woman, in gaining access to medical treatment. Space prevents me from including the discussion in its entirety, but it was particularly frustrating for me and illustrates how easily the participants shy away from acknowledging the power and privilege of whites. It also illuminates, once again, the hazards of whites talking to whites without substantial information, critique, or both. In addition, it illustrates how gender, age, and socioeconomic class filter how one experiences the world as white.

FAITH: *You can't change the policies of the insurance company.*

MARIE: *As a white woman who or white society like we, I have to start like instigating something to change[*

ELLEN: *What? What?*

MARIE: *I don't know.*

(ct)

ALICE: *Let's think critically for a minute because I also heard a lot of that last week. "But there's nothing I can do." "I don't know what I'm supposed to do." "It wasn't [my fault]." "I didn't do that." Some of you[*

ELLEN: *I was gonna say, do we start lobbying to the insurance companies about I mean how do we, as individuals, go about doing it?*

ALICE: *How do you [referring to Ellen] as an individual, as President of the Student Senate[*

ELLEN: *Don't put it on me. (laughter)*

ALICE: *Well, I'm just saying, you're president of an undergraduate association.*

ELLEN: *OK.*

ALICE: *How, I don't mean to put you on the spot but, you asked and it kind of dawned on me that I walk by and I see you in that office and what are some things you do to generate change and to reconstruct [the university] so that all of you feel like you have a voice or have a vote, have a say?*

ELLEN: *We gather people together who care about it. And then go to the appropriate authorities.*

. . . .

ALICE: *How do you get people to care about it?*

ELLEN: *. . . [We] decide what we want to get done so that we can talk to people who can actually do something about it. But it's people who care about, we don't have to go out and say, "Well, you should care about this because this this and this." People come to us and say, "This is a problem we're having. We're having a problem with this program. We don't like the way this is run." You've got a bunch of people saying they'd like to do something about it personally who then, in turn, get other people to do it and then, we're hoping that works.*

ELIZABETH: *But it's so hard. I mean you're talking about one program at one school in this entire country. And it's like the issue of racism just I mean to change the whole structure of society. I mean that's what you'd have to do I think to make it equal. Not so we lose privilege so they are equal you know[*

ELLEN: . . . *but with racism. There's no person. I'm not gonna say, "Excuse me, but this really needs to change[*

This discussion went astray and spiraled into a long discussion of voting rights and the Vietnam war and how demonstrations helped to wake up the White House to what was going on in the United States concerning that war. Eventually, it returned to the health care issue.

ELLEN: *Say our rates go up. Say we [white women] don't get as much money if we get breast cancer. Say they won't pay for as much. My health is more important than any stranger's to me. . . . I mean I don't wanna get you know, I don't wanna get breast cancer and have it go undetected and that that's me being selfish and wanting to preserve my own health[*

? *Yeah. We're all selfish.*

ELLEN: *It doesn't matter if that person person's Black or white[*

? *Yeah. Mhm.*

ELLEN: *If they're a stranger, of course, my health is gonna be more important than anyone else's. (S5)*

Again, I saw the face of American individualism and white privilege weave its way through the discussion disrupting what I had hoped would be a more critical discussion about power and privilege, individual and societal responsibility, and the opportunities we have to take action against injustice. I had also hoped that Ellen's experience as President of the Student Government would provide an example of how we, as individuals, with varying degrees of power, can work collectively to make institutional change. In the above conversation, I told her that I didn't mean to put her on the spot, but in reality I did. In one of my journal entries, I wrote:

> At one point . . . I turned to Ellen who was sitting next to me and I said, "Well, you're President of the Undergrad Senate . . ." and she turned red, blushed, put her head down and said, "Don't put this on me." And my reply was, "I'm not trying to put you on the spot, but . . ." I WAS trying to put her on the spot and I wanted her to share with us her experiences around being in that position. Now I knew at the time, right after I said it, that I was lying and that I thought it was a golden opportunity to use her daily life experiences to answer her question about "what can we do." (Oct. 15, 1994)

Unfortunately, it didn't have the effect I wanted. The participants shied away from thinking about strategies for understanding their power and privilege, and I engaged in poor modeling by telling Ellen that I wasn't putting her on the spot when, in actuality, I was. In the above journal entry I continued to write:

> The very same thing that aggravates me about what they do [being polite], I did. . . . If we are to make any sense of this experience, it has to come about through critical self- and collective reflection or we will be left with 14 individual stories of how I/we managed to marginally participate in a research experience about whiteness. But what did any of us learn if we do that? Did the time spent in talk only serve to affirm my assumptions and validate my feelings and beliefs or was I committed to opening dialogue that is painful and may cause me to be "impolite" in my contribution to this experience? (Oct. 15, 1994)

I opened the following session by explaining myself and informed the group that yes, indeed, I did want to put Ellen on the spot and that I thought it might be a good idea if we all tried a little of that with each other.

The ways we "put each other on the spot"—or didn't—are illustrated throughout this book and are related to the struggles I referred to in chapter three. Too much sameness, too much engagement with too little critique, too much resistance when thinking about "what to do," and way too much emphasis on not wanting to feel bad about being white were threaded throughout the discussions. These "natural" barriers to interrogating whiteness distanced us many times from engaging in the structural, institutional, and cultural language of power and privilege. My journal entry continued:

> I was kind of aggravated the other night at the session. At one point, I had to get up and go to the board. We were discussing privilege and I went up there to write what they thought it was. I don't think I really cared at that point. I just needed to move. In the talk about "what can we do about it? There's nothing we can do" I wanted to scream. In my head, I have this fantasy that they are going to be young, white, energetic, enthusiastic, self- and school reformers leading the battle against social injustice in their schools. Where I got this idea I am not quite sure. But I bought into it when I was younger. (Oct. 15, 1994)

WE'RE GOOD, THEY'RE BAD, AND DON'T BLAME US

As I mentioned in chapter three, I tended to think dichotomously about certain issues that emerged during the research project—a way of thinking that leaves little room for ambiguity and individual difference. I wasn't alone in that type of thinking. The participants spoke about whites in very dualistic terms throughout the research experience. There were the good whites and the bad whites—"us," the ones who are "average Joes" (Marie) and "they," the ones who have the power, for example. There were the whites who were seen as individuals and the whites who were members of a collective racial group. Lastly, there were the whites who were the oppressors and the whites who were the oppressed. These dualisms serve specific purposes for the participants as they try to gain a better understanding of their own racial and social locations. Implicitly, there is a sense that when it is in their best self-interest to be associated with the white race, the participants will align themselves accordingly. For example, when the participants reflect on their positions as white teachers, they recognize the possibilities they have to make a difference in the lives of their students—possibilities that have a great deal to do with the intersection of their racial, gendered, and classed identities. In contrast, when being a member of the white race requires that the participants reflect on the history of white racism and the consequences of racism for people of color *and* for their own individual and collective white psyche, they separate themselves from "those whites" and stress their individuality. Race then, becomes problematic and therefore, ignored or deemphasized as a factor in their lives. Lynn struggled with her white positionality in session five,

> You belong to that big [white] group. It implicates yourself and of course, no one wants to implicate themselves because as an individual I don't see myself wanting to or purposefully doing this [racism] but because I'm white and I'm in this group. It's difficult 'cause you don't want to implicate yourself and that's just about in anything. You don't wanna implicate yourself in that and it's, I don't know.... It's tough when it gets personal. (S5)

The tension between the personal and the collective was illuminated in a variety of contexts. The participants' stories, experiences, reflections, and struggles resonate with the question posed by David Wellman (1993) over 15 years ago in his analysis of white racism: "How do white Americans deal with the racial situation—the troubles and

aspirations of black people—without putting themselves at a disadvantage *and* thinking of themselves as sons of bitches" (p. 224)? The
participants of this research partially answered that question by creating
dualisms among whites. These dualisms seem to be sanctioned in a
society that continues to focus on people of color as the problem, ignoring the critical examination of the benefits of being white in this society.

GOOD WHITES VERSUS BAD WHITES

"Good whites and bad whites" was a dualism that I heard during
many of the participants' discussions.

FAITH: *Like when you're in a classroom and you're like, "Um, is that teacher
being racist because she's not calling on the Black girl or does she know
that the girl knows the material. She's trying to get somebody else who
knows the material?" You know what I mean? Sometimes I feel like it's a
racial something. I'm always like, "I bet they're a racist. Like I bet that
white person does not like Black people." I make this judgment on other
white people and it's so rude but I feel like I have to because there's so
many people, you know, who are so ignorant and I think that part of
being like . . . part of not being a racist is to be educated and to not be
ignorant about, like if you talk to people who are the die hard, white,
male hick redneck whatevers, they'll be like they don't even think. They
don't see race either because they'll just be like, "Nigger, whatever, let me
talk to you." You know what I mean? They're totally close-minded.
Whereas if you started to talk to someone who's open-minded and who's
been thinking about it, they're the people, if you think about it and you
try to make it a part of your life and you try and make yourself a better
person - and try to make the people around you feel better about themselves and I don't know how I could be a racist. I mean I know that I am
and well, I don't even know but I . . . (S5)*

Faith's struggle with whether or not she is a racist becomes
embedded in an all too common game that white people play with
themselves. We compare the various degrees of racism. On the other
hand, the participants conceptualize whites as rednecks, people with a
Ku Klux Klan mentality. On the other hand, the participants label some
whites as more open-minded and liberal, better educated, and trying to
be "better" people. And then there are the whites who are somewhere in
between those two extremes. The participants vacillated about their
own locations on this artificially constructed continuum of racism.

During session three, the participants were discussing the differences in thinking about racism between their parents' generation and the generation of young people today. As evidenced in the exchange, the participants see themselves as more enlightened than their parents. Some of the participants hesitate to define their parents as racist or as "bad" whites. Others, like Michelle and Gerry, speak openly about the racism in their immediate families. This conversation took place during session three.

ELIZABETH: *My Dad. I was talking to him the other night and I would not call him racist you know, like he's not gonna look at a Black person and just say things to him, you know? He's pretty cool, you know? And I I was telling him about this research and I said, "Well basically" I couldn't, I didn't know to explain it. "But basically we talk about racial issues and how we wanna try to solve them as teachers" and he's like, "Oh, that's something I'd wanna talk about ha, ha, ha" (laughter). I'm like I was just like, "What does that mean?" You know? And it's like you can just see like the generation gap.*

MICHELLE: *Yeah. Definitely.*

ELIZABETH: *It's amazing.*

ASHLEY: *I don't know what happened like why it seems like you go from the sixties to the nineties. . . . my parents grew up in the sixties and I don't see like I mean, I think my parents are very good people like I've never, ever heard any derogatory remarks from my parents ever and like they've always been so kind - but I mean they have never gone to like home homeless shelters but I mean they've never, ever brought me up to be like think anyone anything bad of anybody, anyone and but I've never I I thought it was like the sixties were like social action like do something. Love and all this. And now look at where we are. It seems like there's so much hate and it's like, I don't know. I guess the sixties weren't as cool as they looked like at Woodstock. (laughter)*

ELIZABETH: *But don't you wonder why we don't think that? You know what I mean? Like why are like I don't know where this change came from and maybe we're the only ones that think it but I don't know. Like it just I know what you mean like there's the people in between are so racist or so[*

MARIE: *I think it's deep seated. I think in the sixties I think everyone wanted to be like do the free love thing and it wasn't like it [racism] was never talked about . . . I just see it as a problem that like let's just not talk about this and it's like my parent's generation. . . .*

LYNN: *Yeah, sometimes I wonder like if it's taught if we learn it from our family.*

. . . .

MICHELLE: *Still now like my father always jokes about it, any of my friends here that are of color - any of my friends he always has something to say and now he says it 'cause he knows it pisses me off and he says it jokingly you know? He'll even say, "Oh what about your darky friend there?" or he'll like, it's so bad and like he does it to like make me mad and get me worked up - so I'm at the point where now I'll just tell him to be quiet and pass on and like I'll just pretend I didn't hear it you know? I mean he does it to be funny but it's not funny you know what I mean? And then I'll get into an argument with my parents and be like, "You're a racist. You're this, you're this." My Mom will sit there, "I have friends. I have Black friends." (laughter) Like it's so bad. I can't express to you how bad it is but I don't know. We argue about it a lot but they're my parents. I have to keep them so. (laughter)*

GERRY: *It's really interesting though like to look at 'cause I look at it and my grandparents are all very racist and very vocal about it and they know how much it bothers me and they still do it. My parents are more subtle about it but it's still there. I don't think that I have a lot of the opinions that my parents and grandparents have but I see them in my brother whose older than me. He's 23. We have the same education. We both lived in the house until we were 18 so we had the same amount of influence on each other that from my parents. Yet his ideas are so different and the way that he talks about them is awful - and he'll get my dad worked up and so it starts this whole family thing where we can't eat dinner together because we end up fighting because my opinions are so strong one way, theirs are so strong the other way, and my mother just sits there and goes, "Everybody be nice." (laughter) (S3)*

What becomes clear for me in this conversation is the confusion around what constitutes a white racist. On the surface, the good/bad dichotomy seems straightforward and rather palatable. Some people, and parents, are overtly racist. Some people, and parents, are more subtle. They are not all labeled as racist by the participants but rather are described as people who are not "gonna look at a Black person and just say things to him, you know?" (Elizabeth). As Marie suggested in session two when she described the poster her group made depicting racism: "We developed this big white guy as someone who could be in a position of power like in the government or someone who has the kind of the authority to pass on racism through laws and legislation and stuff like that. And the small white people are part of that group that promotes the racism but they're kind of like the average Joes who have these racist ideas but aren't really in a position to permeate it through society."

The participants perpetuate the notion that racism is located within the individual and that it can be defined on a continuum from good to bad, from the powerful to the "average Joes." The white people who never say anything derogatory or who never do anything that is overtly racist are "good whites," the "average Joes," and the ones that are "die-hard, white, male, hick, redneck(s)" (Faith) are the "bad whites." As noted in chapter one, typologists present various "white-types" as a way to relate types of white people to various levels of personal racism. Using such a paradigm is helpful *if* it is connected to, and seen in concert with, institutional and societal racism. The participants' categorizations frequently reflected a unidimensional perspective of racism, situating racism in the individual, and perceiving it as unrelated to a constellation of societal, institutional, and cultural factors. This limited definition of racism lets the "good whites" off the hook at the same time that it dilutes a critique of the multiple ways that white people perpetuate, and benefit from, white racism. It relieves "good whites" of taking any responsibility for the maintenance of white privilege and advantage and places the blame on "bad whites"—the ones who "would never consider like sitting around here talking like this" (Elizabeth).

"Sitting around here talking like this" meant a lot to the participants and indicated their commitment to looking at the problem of racism and their positionalities as white women and teachers. Yet, I struggled many times during the research project as I questioned the amount of time we were "sitting around talking" and the amount of time we were discussing individual, collective, or both forms of action— whether that action be in our personal or professional lives. If the participants considered themselves "good whites" because they were here and talking about it, then how were they going to "extend" that notion of themselves into their daily experiences and relationships? Furthermore, what was I going to do to help them understand the connection between talking and doing—something that was more difficult to do than I had originally thought.

I'M WHITE BUT I'M NOT THAT KIND OF WHITE

The participants repeatedly straddled the artificial boundaries they constructed between being white individuals and being members of the larger white racial group. This is not difficult to understand given their histories and the type of culture they/we live in. Bellah and his colleagues (1985) argue quite forcibly that "Individualism lies at the very core of American culture" (p. 142). I would add that individualism lies at the very core of a white patriarchal class-based culture that prides itself on pursuing individual rights and gaining material and political resources in order to maintain power and advantage. Not *all* Americans promote *all* facets of an ideology based on contemporary notions of individualism. Yet, most Americans *do* participate in forms of individualism and struggle with the contradictions inherent in a society that values individualism but "feel[s] the emptiness of a life without sustaining social commitments" (p. 151).

During the initial interviews, I asked the participants what it meant for them to be white. At that time, many of the participants had never been asked that question and responded with long silences and answers like:

> "--- Hmm --- to be white --- well --- I don't know (laughs). That's a tough question. I've never been asked that before or really thought about it" (Julie). Mary answers the question in much the same way: "--- Um, (laughs) I never really thought about that before. I guess it means that --- I'm the majority." Kerry hesitated for a few seconds and said: "--- Mmm. --- I don't really know. I mean it's kind of an odd thought. It's not something that usually I would think about. Um, --- I can't really say" (laughs).

This thread of ambivalence and "not knowing" was heard in many of the interviews and was clearly articulated throughout the sessions as the participants began to develop a sense of themselves as racial beings.

During session seven, the participants broke into small groups to discuss the question: "What does it mean for you to be white?" I proposed this activity for two reasons. First, prior to session seven, I had given the participants their original transcribed interviews so that they could spend a couple of weeks rereading them, interpreting them, and clarifying any statements and stories that they had shared with me during the interview process. In addition, we had spent six sessions together discussing myriad topics associated with whiteness and I wanted the participants to have the opportunity to go back and think the question through as a group. The beginning of session seven was spent in small groups sharing insights about the meaning of whiteness. The latter part of the session was spent with the small groups reporting back to the larger group. It was out of that sharing that the tension between being an individual white person and being a member of a racial group was highlighted.

MARIE: *Anyway, it was the three of us (Lynn, Kerry and Marie). We well, first of all very confused. When you asked us that question all three of us were like, "We just we don't know." It's just very vague. Then Lynn and I started talking about white privilege. In my own interview I was like, "Yeah, that's [white privilege] a theory." I even said like, "I don't put much stock into that." And at the end of the last session I was like, "OK. So, I've kind of like admitted that there's this thing but now I'm like no, I don't belong in that category. That's just not me." And so that's one thing we talked about. The other thing that we talked about was it's hard to get a sense of your own like self identity or like who you are as a white person without knowing what someone else might think of you. And so we were discussing the factors to whether or not if someone else who's not white looked at me and assessed me or evaluated me and said, "Well, these are the things that you do have and these are the things that you don't" would that change my self identity who I think I am as Marie or Lynn or whatever. And we couldn't really decide. It might change us and it might not.*

LYNN: *Like if we look at somebody who's not white, we see a kind of Black. . . . we identify things with them or who they are and we see them in a certain light by what they do or what they[*

MARIE: *They have ethnic or racial identities . . . and as a white person, I don't think that the white culture has a white identity. . . . Like that's me as a white person. Like a Black person or another person of another minority might think that I do have a white identity . . . they might think that they have an identity but they also might think that I, like that there's a Black identity and there is a white identity. That's what we talked about. (S7)*

The participants face a difficult task. They are attempting to find a sense of who they are as white individuals with very little knowledge of what exactly "white" means. As Marie so poignantly suggests: "and as a white person, I don't think that the white culture has a white identity." Without "knowing" about one's racial identity, it becomes all to easy to define oneself individually and/or in contrast to a particular race. Again, the idea that we only know ourselves in terms of our relationship to people of color is evident in the participants' discourse. Recognizing differences between and among people, in this case, between whites and people of color, is not in and of itself problematic.

What *is* problematic, and what occurred numbers of times throughout this research, was the participants' view that difference equals deficiency in the Other. Rather than focus on what difference *their own difference as white people makes* in our society, the participants tended to focus on difference as division and as in opposition to themselves (Reay, 1996).

In most of the interviews, on the one hand, the participants speak about the meaning of white in relationship to the meaning of Black. For example, Elizabeth states: "Um, I feel, well being white in this country is you're just thought of as superior to the other races which I think is horrible. Um, I would never think of myself as superior to a Black person sitting next to me. I mean they're just Black and I'm white. It's just their skin color."

On the other hand, my interpretation of the data suggest that we, as whites, also know our individual white selves, not just in relationship to people of color but in relationship to the larger white group. When the participants choose to define whites in dualistic terms, they rigidify their identities. They free themselves from the constraints of creating a racial image that is embedded in whiteness as a system of white supremacy. Instead, they step out of the collective white identity and define themselves individually as young white females who are "20 years old. We have so much time ahead of us. . . . We're still forming our thoughts and ideas and planning what we're gonna do . . . and what's really important to us" (Ellen). This forming of plans and ideas is constructed outside of an awareness of themselves as white women who are advantaged in many ways by their racial group membership. The dilemma for them is to position themselves as white females who both benefit from their skin color and at the same time, are implicated in the problem of racism and oppression. This proved to be an extremely anxiety producing dilemma for the participants.

During session four, Ashley told the group about an article she had just read in one of her classes about Rosa Parks and the day she was arrested on the bus in Montgomery. She commented on how she had never been told some of the more important details about Rosa Park's life and that maybe the absence of that information has led to a lack of respect by white people for many people of color in our nation's history. I present an excerpt from that conversation illustrating the difficulty the participants had in seeing themselves as members of a white racial group that "fail[s] to confront the racial, class, and gender inequities woven into our social fabric" (Bigelow, Christensen, Karp, Miner & Peterson, 1994, p. 4).

ASHLEY: *I should bring the article in. It was awesome. And it just shows you how a textbook is so biased and it doesn't give you the respect and maybe that's why we don't hold these people, like revere them the way we should because like from kids we were never taught to be like, "Ah, she's a great woman" you know? She [Rosa Parks] was supposed to move back and she refused and she had done that before and she had been like kicked off buses before and they never say this stuff and you don't, I never knew this. This was something I had never known and it just like maybe we if we portrayed things and gave them the respect they deserved we'd start building this respect and maybe the norm would come down, maybe our it wouldn't be such a white norm anymore if[*

MARIE: *But white people write it.*

ASHLEY: *I understand. Exactly.*

MARIE: *I mean not that it matters[*

ASHLEY: *But I have it and I'll bring it in and it's it's amazing how like he transformed everything and broke down every sentence that the textbook wrote and was like, "What does this mean?" You have no idea how you're learning things until you actually look into it. I don't know. It's really cool what we're doing right now is like looking at the textbooks and how they portray like Native Americans or just regular people and how they make such broad statements about people and[*

ALICE: *But who are* they?

ASHLEY: *Exactly and that's what we ask in classes and it's like[*

ALICE: *Who, who, who publishes? Who are the publishers? Who are[*

ASHLEY: *Big business . . . or like Texas schools (unint.)[*

ALICE: But who are they?

(ct) *"white people"*

ASHLEY: *Oh, white people, yeah.*

ALICE: *Who are these white people?*

MARIE: *Educators ---*

ALICE: *Who are we in relation to these white people?*

? *We are part of them. (laughter)*

CHRISTINE: *We are them.*

(ct) *"It's us."*

ELLEN: *We are the educators that may end up writing these biased stupid textbooks. (laughter)*

ELIZABETH: *It's not me. (unint./laughter)*

ASHLEY: *Yeah, you're right. It is us, I guess.*

ALICE: *I think the conversation is moving there but there's a tendency to think that "they," whether "they" are the Blacks, whether "they" are the Haitians, whether "they" are the [white] men[*

ELLEN: *You separate it from yourself.*

ALICE: *Exactly.*

ELLEN: *I'm an asshole. (laughter) Who's gonna say that? I'm biased. I can say history's biased. I I mean it's harder to say that it's me[*

ALICE: *Absolutely[*

ASHLEY: *But it's not really[*

GERRY: *No one wants to be a part of it[*

ASHLEY: *We didn't like we learned it that way, you know what I mean? Like I never knew, I never knew to question a textbook and that's the way I was brought up and I like now I would. Now I would say, "I don't think you can cover Native American history in three paragraphs." And I would make sure as a teacher I wouldn't just go by this textbook 'cause I would understand that this authoritative voice is mine or is my white culture and that's not fair to every other student that's not white.*

ALICE: *And I think that is what we need to do and ask how do you make meaning of it all as a white person and teacher. That is very difficult to do but somehow unless we do that, unless we interrupt this "we-they" as white people - we're constantly in that tension between "them" and "us" and where am I positioning myself as a white person in this whole dialogue about racism.*

This discussion, unlike some others, *did* push some of the participants to rethink their positionalities as white individuals who are members of a racial group. It challenged their core sense of themselves as white females, as college students, and as educators who want very much to make a difference in the lives of the students they teach. As future teachers they are "often simultaneously perpetrators and victims, with little control over planning time, class size, or broader school policies—and much less over the unemployment, hopelessness, and other 'savage inequalities' that help shape our children's lives" (Bigelow, et al., 1994, p. 4). They exist within a "conventional system of 'top-down' power structures" (Kenway & Modra, 1992, p. 143) that make it difficult for those who are committed to antiracist teaching to engage in transformative teaching practices. Though white females constitute the majority of the teaching force, they do not hold the same kind of "power over" the educational policies and programs as their mostly white male administrative counterparts do. This gendered imbalance provides less opportunity for broad based decision-making power to circulate among classroom teachers and provides fertile ground for dualistic thinking that pits "us"—as white individuals who are concerned teachers—against "them"—the whites who maintain power and make problematic the implementation of institutional change.

The challenge to think beyond dualisms is illustrated by the responses of some of the participants when they were asked to represent via drawing what they had learned about themselves as white people during the last session. (See accompanying photos.)

GERRY: —*like before I came into this I felt like, "Well, I know where I stand. Um, I know what I'm doing. I'll take responsibility for myself, my beliefs,*

PHOTO 5
GERRY'S DRAWING

my attitudes and that's that." . . . What I've learned is that no matter what I think and what my attitudes may be, I'm still part of the larger white population and I need to start taking responsibility for that too and as a part of that population, I have a responsibility to other people to start doing things - and just taking care of myself personally isn't good enough anymore. It has to go out and reach other people and so pretty much I've learned that as a member of this society there's a responsibility that comes with that - especially being a white person in this society.

MICHELLE: *This is mine. It's a web. I think being in this group, I think it's become increasingly clear to me that being white there are a lot of like connotations and implications historically, socially, institutionally, . . . and I think it's become clear to me that I'm never going to be free from those implications - and so I can't ignore them because if I ignore them, I'll just be stuck in that web like the little bug that the spider catches and just keep getting wound and wound and wound - unless I fight each*

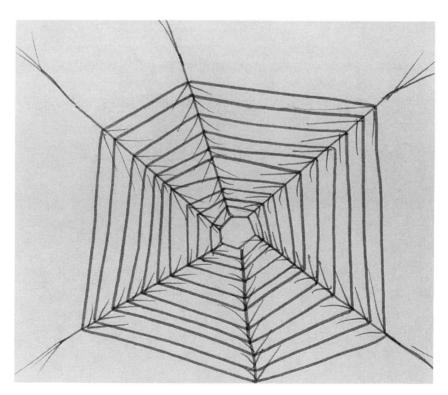

PHOTO 6
MICHELLE'S DRAWING

strand and each strand to me represents each level of racism on all aspects. So, until I do something, I think that I'm just going to keep getting wound up like the little bug. (S8)

Lynn: *. . . This sign, as a science major, three lines mean meaning, means definition. Um, and one of the big things is that I've developed more of a meaning for myself as an individual in a multitude of people. I thought I always had individuality but the whiteness part of my individuality has a lot more meaning now in a multitude of people . . . it is important and it does have meaning. I can't define it but it has developed a larger meaning in who I am and it's hard for me to explain that.*

These narrations suggest that Gerry, Lynn, and Michelle have begun to see the interrelatedness of being an individual white person and being a member of the dominant white racial group. The duality of the "good whites/bad whites" is muted. What I heard was more rele

PHOTO 7
LYNN'S DRAWING

vance being given to the notion that we, as white individuals, cannot disown ourselves from membership in the white race. This awareness was a starting point for a deeper analysis of the conflictual nature of white identity formation. Although the participants' multiple confusions, questions, denials, and insights were not fully answered within our research sessions, the dichotomous posture of the participants was highlighted, contributing to some of the participants rethinking their individual and collective positionalities as white people.

WHY SHOULD MY SKIN COLOR HAVE A NEGATIVE CONNOTATION?

The conservative political agenda of the 1980s and, thus far, the 1990s has weakened the more radical movement to address racism in the United States that some experienced in the 1960s. As was noted earlier, the participants wonder what happened to the values of the 1960s— the social action and the commitment to end racism and provide opportunities to *all* people. At that time, there seemed to be a clearer sense of who was the oppressed and who was the oppressor. Not so for today's generation who oftentimes thinks that civil rights were established for Blacks a couple of decades ago and now, if Blacks and other people of color would just work hard, then we would be free of racial problems. As Feagin and Vera (1995) suggest:

> A majority of white Americans in all social classes, including jurists, scholars, and commentators, now appear to believe that serious racism is declining in the United States; that black Americans have made great civil rights progress in recent decades; and that blacks should be content with that progress. Whites see widespread discrimination in most institutional arenas as a thing of the past. In particular, many whites believe that the black middle class no longer faces significant discrimination and is thriving economically—indeed more so than the white middle class. (pp. 2–3)

The participants have grown up during a time of backlash against the Civil Rights movement. For example, the current attacks on affirmative action are testimony to the kind of attitude that many white Americans hold, which is that "racial discrimination is no longer a serious problem in the United States" (Feagin & Vera, 1995, pp. 153–154). As Hacker (1995) suggests, "Most White Americans will say that, all things considered, things aren't so bad for black people in the United States. . . .

Some have even been heard to muse that it's better to be black, since affirmative action policies make it a disadvantage to be white" (p. 35). This myth that Blacks have it better than whites in our society situates whites as the victims. When whites cultivate such an unjust ethos, we contribute to the growing paranoia in this country that promises to anesthetize any kind of critical dialogue about race and white racism.

The research process provided opportunities for the participants to grapple with this false dichotomy—whites as the oppressors and whites as victims. In session two, Faith told a story that illustrates the degree to which some of the participants felt victimized by Blacks and distort the differential experiences between whites and Blacks in this society. This story highlights how quickly some of them identified with a victim status when it came to racism and how easily they blamed people of color for how they felt about themselves as whites.

FAITH: *OK. Um, I think that racism has to do a lot with everyday life and you know like I said that in my interview. I said that you know I was on the [subway] the other night and me and a couple of my girlfriends - and we were just sitting there talking about food or something and there was these Black girls and they were like mocking us and saying, "Ooh, look at those white girls talking about their white tuna melt" (laughter) - and I would call those girls a racist. I mean I would say that they have a big problem with white people and white girls and maybe they don't have economic or you know any other kind of power - but they had power over me and my friends that night on the [subway]. You know what I mean? They made us feel really uncomfortable.*

LYNN: *. . . people see racism as a white issue because white is the majority and we in our history have slavery. You've just had this predominance of racism coming from a white person. But today it may be from a smaller group but if that person, it's hard to explain but has a certain mentality. They're still being racist. I mean they were being racist against her because she was white. They were looking at her as a white person "She's eating a tuna melt." You know I mean?*

ELLEN: *Yeah but did they say that just because you were white or did they say that just because they wanted to make fun of you? You know what I mean?*

FAITH: *I would I be a racist if I said, "Ooh, look at those Black girls with her Black girl earrings." I would be racist.*

OTHER PARTICIPANTS: *"Yup." "Exactly."*

. . . .

MARY: *That'd totally be like[*

FAITH: *that you're a racist[*

MARY: *Mhm.*

FAITH: *but because they're Black and because they might be less of a population, then they're not a racist - even though they said those same things and meant them and had the same mind set and had the same ignorance. They, you know, like maybe they like tuna melts but they don't care. (laughter) You know what I mean?*

MARY: *Yeah.*

FAITH: *so I think they can definitely be racists.*

ELLEN: *Is that what racism is or you know 'cause I mean there's so many different things involved here but I feel like a lot of what happens first when you first see someone you're gonna see their skin color and what they look like and is racism stopping at their skin color and saying, "Oh, I already know what this person is like because of their skin color" and not going further in and finding out who they really are because that's where you find out like that's to me that's the most important part of someone. What they look like doesn't matter but that is always what you see first and no one can get by that.*

ELIZABETH: *I think it's such a fuzzy line and like I believe that I would call that racist you know what the girl said on the T but it's hard to define because our society is so[*

ALICE: *Well part of the problem I think you have is that you still can't get a definition of racism. . . . (S2)*

In this exchange Faith admitted that power is a salient aspect of racism and that "they" might not have certain kinds of power, but "they" had power over her and her friends that night on the subway. In her experience, she is the victim of racism. She becomes the oppressed which serves to take the focus off of her as a white person and keeps the focus on the Black girls. The naturalness with which the participants discussed "they" and the ease with which they agreed with Faith's interpretation of the story illustrates, once again, the power of embedded racist speech in the maintenance of white talk. Rather than explore the deeper dimensions of white racism and take seriously the historical domination of whites in this country *and* the underpinnings of power in the continuation of that domination, the participants constructed a version of whiteness that blamed Blacks and identified whites as victims.

At that point in the discussion—and as I mentioned in chapter four—I took to "teaching" the participants about the constitution of racism—a lesson that we learned and relearned throughout the research project, but one that we never collectively resolved.

During session seven, there was an exchange that occurred that again illustrates this notion of whites-as-victims. The exchange began with a discussion of the participants' interview question which was referred to above: "What does it mean for you to be white?" It spun off into a discussion of a book that Gerry had just read by Lorene Cary (1991) called *Black Ice*—an autobiographical account of the author's experience as a young, Black female attending a predominantly white prep-school.

LYNN: *They [Blacks] see the white privilege and they associate 'have' and 'have nots.' It's funny 'cause I kind of sometimes see the opposite. When they see my whiteness and I, I'm uncomfortable with what I'm gonna say because it's kind of I don't know, I'll just say it. That my whiteness is looked upon as negatively because I've associated my whiteness with a lot of the problems that have occurred in the past. So if somebody looked at me and looked at my whiteness, in some respects I think, this is hard for me to say but that it would be looked at as kind of a negative connotation. Does anyone[*

MARY: *I agree with that[*

ELLEN: *People are bitter against you towards what you achieve because you are white?*

LYNN: *Well, just could be negatively because of white privilege but negative in that just as the past is negative (sigh). I can't explain it.*

ASHLEY: *I know what you're saying.*

LYNN: *. . . I wonder sometimes if I'm associated with a negative thought because of my white skin and because of all the problems that have happened in the past between the white and African American individuals or, this is a question I'm asking you because I can't answer it and some of it would have to do possibly with white privilege - and some of it has to do with just not even just white privilege, just struggles between people of different ethnicities and cultures. Like I'm asking a question because I do see as a negativity, I don't know (laughs).*

GERRY: *I have something to say but I want to make sure I have the question right.*

MICHELLE: *I asked if Blacks look at whites and think of us in terms of our privilege. Do they have a basis to think that way?*

GERRY: *OK. Well, I don't know if this is really answering that or not but like sometimes I don't think that they do. I just read the book* Black Ice *and it's about this Black woman who's one of the only minorities to attend Philip's Exeter in New Hampshire. And as I was reading it, the thing that got me was everything that she talked about she kind of associated just with being a Black in this all white quote unquote rich school. And she clumped all the whites into one category and there were very few that she would let out of that category and it was really hard to read it because there would be passages, I went to a very similar school, and there would be passages that like I could completely relate to that I had felt while I was at my school. . . . I think that sometimes there are universal feelings but people tend to make them out to be Black or white issues. Does that make sense? I may have looked like every other student but internally I was having just as hard a time relating to half the students at this school as she probably was. They had lived completely different lives than I could ever have even like imagined and so in that respect, like I felt like an outsider at times too. But if you just looked at me, you would think that I fit in perfectly because of the color of my skin. Like sometimes, I just think that maybe that's used too much as an external factor and that things are really much more the same. People feel much more the same than everyone wants to kind of believe.*

ALICE: *But is it systematic for white people to experience that?*

CHRISTINE: *No.*

ALICE: *Don't lose sight of that. I mean on an individual basis, there's lots of individual stories that we use to contradict or to show that such and such is not happening. Does it systematically happen to white people what happens to that girl in that book?*

ELLEN: *. . . It happens to people regardless of their race. . . . Maybe that's the most externally obvious answer. "Well, it must be because I'm Black 'cause that's why I'm different."*

GERRY: *I mean it could have everything to do with her being a woman. Everybody chose to focus on her color like and she chose to make that the issue as to why things were happening. And I don't know.*

MICHELLE: *There's just like a fundamental history here that we can't ignore. I mean, our system privileges middle-class, upper-middle-class[*

ELLEN: *But once you're inside of an institution, you're inside of it. Then you're dealing on a personal level. . . .*

ASHLEY: *Her point was that in this particular book, she's putting her inner feelings and blaming it on white privilege. But I think the whole subject is that some people feel a negative connotation towards white. It's not, I don't feel like an evil or a bad or a negative person[*

MICHELLE: *Right, I don't think[*

ASHLEY: *but as a faceless person in a crowd of white people there is a negative connotation . . . I just don't see myself being like dying if I had to go in a all Black school. Like I would I would just go in and try to be myself. I'd be nervous but just because I'd be faceless first and then I'd be fine.*

. . . .

ALICE: *Well you know what I'm beginning to hear is that now you're victimized because you're white. I mean we have literally turned the question around (group laughter) to "Poor us. Boy, we have people who think negative of us because we're white and we have privilege"[*

(laughter)

? *I don't think I'm saying I'm a victim[*

ALICE: *I'm telling you though that's what I hear in the conversation is - if there's been a change in how we made meaning about being white [during the project] - it's now we make meaning of it as "Here we are, a group of white people and now we're victimized because we have privilege." It's a little disconcerting to hear that we're victims because we are the oppressors in this. . . . I think it's getting turned around to "How do they experience us?" Well, you said they experience us negatively and now again, it's about them. It's about how they, who have been historically discriminated against, individually, institutionally, and culturally, that now somehow we're re[*

ASHLEY: *We're the victim.*

ALICE: *We're the victim now because we're white.*

LYNN: *I don't think I'm portraying myself as a victim but[(S7)*

Within this exchange, the participants dispose of race as the salient factor in Lorene Cary's experience as a Black woman in an all-white preparatory school. Rather than take seriously Cary's presentation of the centrality of race as significant, the participants underplay her/it's power and neglect the history of race relations in this country. They disregard white people's cruel and unjust treatment of Blacks in educational institutions—not to mention within other dimensions of society—and position *themselves* as the victims, wondering why so much emphasis has to be put on race. Although "feeling like an outsider" may have some universal elements to it across race, class, and gender, the participants fail to recognize that what *causes* one to be marginalized mediates the resulting experience. They minimize the impact of racial marginalization, and the ramifications of white racism aimed at Blacks and other people of color, when they universalize "feeling like an outsider."

This type of victimization talk seems quite logical to the participants. They find it difficult to see any racism in their examples. Neither do they see that it is only from a position of power and privilege that one can subvert racism as the problem and instead, focus on minimizing the effects of being Black in this country. The participants identify with Lorene Cary's feelings, yet dismiss her beliefs and her own lived experiences that illustrate that race does indeed matter.

Like the exchange above, the same feeling of being victimized was illuminated in a story that Ellen and Kerry shared with the group at our last session. The previous evening, they had gone to hear an African American male—a member of the NAACP—speak about Black leadership. The event was taking place on campus and when the participants walked into the room where it was being held, they "looked around and there were all, we were probably two of ten white people in the whole room . . . and I felt really out of place" (Kerry).

KERRY: *. . . it didn't feel like he was talking to me and um I can't say but it did feel like he wasn't talking to me.*

ELLEN: *One of the things that the speaker said was that . . . he said to his brothers and sisters, which is a part of why we didn't feel really like we were being spoken to. Um, but, but African Americans were the only ones who could do anything about it [racism] and that's basically what he said and I looked at Kerry and we kind of looked at each other[*

KERRY: *. . . he just kind of looked at the few white people and he goes and he was saying that you know, "brothers and sisters, oh, and those who care" and that was supposed to be us because we were there because we were interested in what he was talking about. So, he really wasn't talking to us.*

ELLEN: *But basically . . . he was talking about leadership and how it was very important for these people, for the Black people, that he was talking to get out there and show some initiative and go to college and then go back to*

*their communities and you know, help the people who are still in the
communities. And he said you know, African Americans are the only
ones who can do anything about it and that really struck me 'cause I
had remembered us talking about, you know, well what can we do about
it and what are we going to do and I really feel like he was right. . . .
Sometimes I felt like well, why why do they think - the Black people who
came in and looked at us - 'cause we got some kind of looks, and I was
wondering what they thought our purpose was for going - why they
thought we were there and why these people who are looking at us
thought that we were there. (S8)*

Michelle Fine and her colleagues (1995) suggest that white people fail to understand the "experience of surveillance" undergone by
Black Americans as they live out their lives in this country. Kerry and
Ellen allude to the "kinds of looks" they got as they entered a room
where the majority of people were people of color. They were "kinds
of looks" that the participants are very unaccustomed to experiencing
in their daily lives. Kerry and Ellen were "under surveillance"—they
were the Other for a brief period of time. As they elaborated on their
description of the event, some of the other participants colluded in
the sense of victimization by retreating into white talk. They immediately began to admit their confusion about whether white people
should work with Black people against racism. As Ellen remarks:
"Well, what he was saying as a Black man is that white people can't
do anything about it and that we didn't really have any sort of a part
in it." Ellen agrees with the speaker: "I really feel like he was right."
In agreeing with her interpretation of what the speaker was saying,
she relieves the white population—and the participants of the
group—from "having to do anything." At the same time, she, and
the other participants, retain this image of themselves as the good
white individuals, as the ". . . 13 women who are trying to change it
[racism]" (Ellen).

During this session, I became frustrated with the direction of the
talk. We were in the last session of the research project. We had discussed myriad issues concerning racism and whiteness. We had examined a plethora of myths about the Black and white experience in the
United States. We had "broken new ground" in the institution by engaging in a research process that was aimed at change. And yet, here we
were fostering the continued growth of implicit and explicit racist
rhetoric. It was not one of my "aha" moments in the project. Rather, it
reminded me, once again, of how deeply embedded whiteness is in the
white psyche.

SUMMATION

Many of the words the participants used to construct their meanings of whiteness were racist, disturbing to me, and grounded in a dangerous ideology of oppression. Others were more hopeful and inserted themselves in different moments during the research project, sometimes in the sessions themselves; other times outside the group as we visited in my office, met in the hallways, or spoke on the phone. Those were the occasions that reassured me/us of what I mentioned in chapter three—that dialogue is not wasted. These participants showed a deep need for clarity about whiteness—a clarity that is difficult to find in a society—and in many educational institutions—fraught with deep racial divisions making it almost impossible to critique race in a way that interrupts the dominant ideology. This need for clarity about who they are as white women remains somewhat elusive for these young adults. Yet, in some highly cogent ways, these participants, however falteringly, engaged in a level of race talk which partially tells the story of how they, as young white women, made meaning of whiteness and of their positions of privilege in a deeply divided nation. The participants' engagement in difficult conversations and strained dialogue challenged them to address the relationship between their multiple white positionalities within our society. And rather than leave the conversation when the talk became too uncomfortable and too difficult, *all* the participants chose to remain at the table.

During session seven, in the midst of discussing what it means to be white, Lynn said: "We're . . . so boggled by everything. . . . Who am I? What am I? What am I supposed to do?" She said this with a good deal of humor and her remark was met with group laughter and identification. Yet, in that humor, and in that collective identification, were fundamental questions we had been addressing all along: Who am I? What am I? What am I supposed to do?

Engaging in critical dialogue about those questions was not easy. Nor did our eight sessions provide answers to those questions. It *did*, however, illuminate for the group some aspects of our own racism, some aspects of gender and social class, and also, some very important insights as to how we can continue the journey of finding out who we are, what we are, and what we are supposed to do.

In the following chapter, I illustrate another way that the participants make meaning of whiteness. I explore how "being a teacher" created a different, but not necessarily less paradoxical, understanding of what it means to/for them to be young, white, female student teachers.

CHAPTER 6

TEACHER IMAGE

Due to their educational backgrounds, and the ways in which they conceptualize the roles of teacher and student, the participants oftentimes looked to me for answers to the questions raised in the group sessions. They wanted some kind of "relief" from uncomfortable discussions—only they appeared to want that relief in the form of a lesson plan: "If you do A, B, and C you won't be a racist teacher." Although I was more than willing (sometimes) to challenge their assumptions, question their beliefs, provide them with historical information, suggest resources for them, discuss any and all of the issues that were brought up in the project, both inside and outside the group sessions, I wasn't willing to engage in a didactic relationship with them which would have undermined the tenets of PAR. Nonetheless, the long-standing perception of what it means to be a teacher in the United States weighed heavily on the group and it is that image— what it means to be a teacher—a "white" teacher, in particular, that we turn to now.

Over the years, many educators have critiqued the transmission model of teaching and learning and the impact such a pedagogical model has on the reproduction of the dominant discourse in our society (see, Britzman, 1986; Cochran-Smith, 1991; Gore, 1993; hooks, 1994; Macedo, 1993; Nieto, 1996; Sleeter & McLaren, 1995; Weiler, 1988). These educators argue that when teachers' positionalities, school curricula, and educational practices are left unproblematized and unchallenged, we run the risk of passively transferring unexamined knowledge, thus, reifying and maintaining oppressive structures that ensure the sanctity of the dominant group's power, privilege, and ideology.

As a white educator and an activist researcher, I take seriously the notion that teaching and research are political; the classroom and the research project, sites of social critique. This critique requires that we consider both the historical forces that (re)produce knowledge and the agency of teachers, students, and research participants in the problematization of such knowledge. With respect to this PAR project, and as noted in chapter one, I find the interplay between ideology, power, and the construction of knowledge most problematic in the field of multicultural education.

The invitation to participate in this PAR project stated that we would be discussing the "role of the white teacher in multicultural antiracist education." The majority of participants decided to participate in the research project because "it sounded interesting" (Mary) and because they were very concerned about the difficulties they were having, and might have, teaching minority students.

KERRY: *Um, Kerry. I'm Elementary Education. I got the thing in the mail too and I thought it was interesting and . . . I thought maybe it could help me keep from passing on stereotypes and the other things to the kids in my class.*

ELLEN: *My name is Ellen and I'm Early Childhood and I have always been interested in working in the inner city and there's been this big push lately for getting minority teachers in the cities and working with minority kids and I thought, "Well, I'm not a minority but I still want to work with minority kids and why am I being rejected? Just because of who I am?" So it's something that's concerned me and I've done a lot of work in the inner city and it's something that I just really enjoy and I feel like I need to understand better.*

GERRY: *Um, my name's Gerry. [I'm in] Elementary Ed. and when I got the thing in the mail I started to think about the environment that I'd grown up in and the schools that I'd attended and then my preprac last year which was [in the inner city]. Um, and I realized that there was a lot of stuff that I really had no idea about because of where I came from and it was just really difficult to be in my prepracticum and so I just wanted to do some more things to make myself better, improve what I'm doing.*

JULIE: *Um, my name is Julie and I'm in math in Secondary Ed. and I guess why really I'm here is . . . my mom is a kindergarten teacher in an inner-city school and she attended a class this summer and one of the professors, a Black professor said to the class that white teachers cannot effectively teach Black students. And, we were talking about it and then I got this [announcement] in the mail and I thought that's a very interesting topic. So that's why I pursued it.*

ELIZABETH: *My name's Elizabeth and I'm Early Childhood and when I got the thing in the mail I thought it sounded great. . . . We're all going to be white teachers [and] it doesn't get talked about that much and I think this opportunity will help all of us to be better teachers because we'll have a better perspective on how to teach minority students and um, just all that stuff. (laughs) (S1)*

"Being better teachers" was not just about pedagogy but also about how they would be perceived by their students of color. As Ashley stated: "I want them to look at me as someone who's there for them and I hope whether they're white or Black or Hispanic, whatever race they are, they can respect me because of who I am, not what color I am." These concerns about "being better teachers" and "being who they really are" were articulated throughout the research project in the multiple ways the participants conceptualized their roles as white teachers in our society. Their identities as white teachers were being formed in relation to other teachers—cooperating teachers they have worked with in their prepracticum sites, former classroom teachers, professors they have met at the university, as well as in relation to the "generic teacher" historically portrayed as the white overseer of everything that happens within the four walls of a classroom.

They also form their identities as white teachers around the belief that when they are teachers, they, as individuals, will be able to control racism in their classrooms, thereby, affording them a sense of manageability over a very difficult and complex issue. As previously discussed, the level of powerlessness the participants exhibited in relation to actively working against racism was often conceived as immobilizing. What offset their paralysis about "what to do" with such an overwhelming problem was to think about themselves as teachers. Teaching became the site of action—the one place that could provide a space for the participants to "do something," or at least, fantasize about "doing something . . . it's like it's like trying to find a cure" (Marie). Although the participants recognized their powerlessness as student teachers, they compensated for this feeling of powerlessness by constructing future narratives about themselves as "in-charge" classroom teachers. These future narratives served as strategies for creating the ideal classroom where the participants could keep "from passing on the stereotypes and the other things to the kids in my class" (Kerry).

TEACHERS AS (RE)PRODUCERS
OF THE DOMINANT DISCOURSE

Gerry represents the majority of the participants in this research project when, during her interview, she describes multicultural education as being about "awareness and exposure." Ellen suggests that multicultural education is "learning about other cultures . . . bringing all the cultures in and having all the cultures help learn." Others described multicultural education in their interviews in similar terms focusing on the need for all children to interact with each other, for teachers to look at history through a variety of lenses, and for cultures to be respected and celebrated. Although Michelle mentioned in her interview that multicultural education is "better in theory than it is in practice"—a good idea but not always practical—and Christine suggested that multicultural education fails to "deal with the topic of racism," the overall sense of what multicultural antiracist education is remained illusive to the participants and was grounded more in how they have experienced multicultural education in their own schooling.

The participants experienced moments of uncertainty as they began to examine the multiple dimensions of multicultural education. To decenter multicultural education as merely a tool of "awareness and exposure" and to center it around the issues of racism and white dominance was difficult. As mentioned in chapter one, when educational institutions fail to forcibly promote an antiracist approach within teacher education programs, they—and subsequently their students—have difficulty addressing a fundamental component of multicultural education. To attend to the underpinnings of multicultural education is to attend to the ideology of whiteness—an ideology that refutes the legacy of racism, dismisses the race inequities that exist in our schools, and resists the restructuring of educational institutions, making resources equitable for *all* students.

This resistance to critiquing whiteness distances white teachers from thinking that we are implicated in the kind of educational system that continues to privilege white students. We remain blind to our own positionalities within the institutions we inhabit and create. The participants of this project experienced a duality between seeing themselves as individual white student teachers and seeing themselves as individual white student teachers who are members of the larger dominant group and who are advantaged by and implicated in the maintenance of an educational system that advantages them and students who are like them. This duality resonates with previous dualisms presented in chapter five. It was easier for them to see themselves as individual actors—

separate from institutions, disconnected from the larger white race, and untouched by the history of whiteness. They protected themselves from a self-in-relation-to-society critique by locating themselves within their classrooms believing that "everything you say is influential especially to little kids and so I think it's really important for us to like to have a good attitude about [teaching values and beliefs]" (Faith). For them, teaching was a neutral and solitary act, individualized and removed from societal and cultural pressures. The participants' vision of teaching centered around values, attitudes, expectations, "loving kids," and creating safe places where students could feel protected from the outside world. What was striking in this vision of teaching was the participants' uncritical acceptance of their own sets of beliefs and values, attitudes and expectations, and their belief that teaching is an individualistic enterprise. They saw themselves as committed individuals, having good parents, good values, a good education, and a good sense of what is expected of them as teachers. In contrast, they saw students of color as not having— as somehow deficient. These perceptions provoked unsettling feelings for the participants that further reinforced the notion that the remedy for fixing racism in the classroom was to "share their wealth."

The participants reproduce a common refrain in the white American discourse—namely, "We had no control over who we are and how we were born" and "[l]ike there's nothing we can do . . . I don't think like any of us have to be you know [guilty]." As with their limited understanding of multicultural education, the participants limited understanding of the dialectical relationship between their belief systems and their teaching gave rise to an insular view of teaching and a disturbing view of what constitutes transformative classroom practice. The participants became (re)producers of the dominant ideology at the same time that they were fervently trying to construct images of themselves as "dedicated and committed white teachers." This myopic perspective lends itself to the further reproduction of a discourse that disclaims responsibility for current racism in this country. In addition, reproducing this kind of stance fosters the acceptance of a watered-down version of multicultural antiracist education since it resists the decentering of white racism as it was experienced *then* and as it is experienced *now*.

ELLEN: *But is it racism by making sure that you treat you know by maybe even giving people special treatment because they're of a different color or because they're minority in the classroom?*

FAITH: *No. Not at all.*

LYNN: *[Are you being] racist because you don't want to be racist. Does that make sense?*

ELLEN: *Yeah. That's that's exactly what I'm saying.*

FAITH: *Mhm. Like reverse racism.*

ELLEN: *Yeah.*

FAITH: *I mean like Ashley was saying last week how in her class she would want to make sure that she would open up the door for the minority students and everything else. And like that's great but if two kids come to me for one recommendation [for college], a Black kid and a white kid, and the Black kid is not working hard and isn't and now we go back to working hard but doesn't deserve my recommendation, I'm not going to give it to him and I'm not going to say, "I'll give it to you because you know, maybe you won't get into the other schools that you're applied to because you're Black." I that, for me, that's not the issue. For me, the issue would be giving my word, putting my name on something that I believe in. Do you know what I mean? And so I know people who do that and if they justify that and they feel good about it that's great. But that's just my personal feeling.* (S5)

In this excerpt, I heard the participants questioning racism and what constitutes racist teaching practice. The difficulty was sustaining this conversation with the hopes that it would lead the participants to question the underlying structures that maintain racial inequalities in our schools. The discussion veers quickly into "reverse racism" and then gets stuck in a "whites as victims" perspective. In addition, racist teaching practice gets defined as giving a recommendation to a Black student strictly due to his or her skin color when the white student really deserves it because he or she has obviously worked hard for it. In their eyes, that's antithetical to what they think their roles are as teachers. It's the students who "work hard"—regardless of skin color and prior educational advantage—that deserve the prizes we hand out in our schools and institutions of higher learning. Faith makes it clear that she is not going to give a Black student who isn't working hard her recommendation. Although she raises serious questions about how white teachers evaluate and assess white students and students of color, she also reifies a stereotype that Black students may not work as hard as white students do—a stereotype that went unchallenged in this exchange. Rather, she privileges the concept of "giving my word" as if people of color can put any trust in white people "giving their word."[1]

When I think of how these participants (as well as most of us who attended and/or attend our country's educational institutions) were—

and are—taught the history of race relations in this country, it's no wonder that they construct a discourse that mirrors the dominant ideology of whiteness. They have swallowed chunks of information about whites and Blacks that concretize stereotypes and easily lead them to believe in the myth that hard work and perseverance are intrinsic, equally distributed among the races, and equally available to all. What the participants find difficult to deal with is the information that rips open the veneer of racism as a past sin belonging to some anonymous white people, and forces them to take a good, hard look at the implications of being white teachers—something they both faced up to and hid from during our group sessions (see McIntyre, in press).

Teachers as "White Knights"

During a session where we were discussing the white students on campus and their relationship to UNITY (one student organization on campus that supports students of color) Michelle remarked, "Why do we have to go in there and support them, like we're some like white knights, that we need to support them in their endeavors?" This same characteristic—whites acting like white knights—was particularly salient in the participants' discussions about teaching "inner-city students." As "white knights" dressed in teachers' clothing, the participants enter their classrooms complete with a history of white dominance, privilege, and advantage. They also have high expectations of themselves as teachers, and this combination results in a skewed version of what constitutes multicultural education.

The participants' difficulty with understanding the interrelatedness of education and whiteness resulted in the participants viewing inner-city minority students as passive recipients of white teachers' goodwill. Their discussions about teaching in inner-city schools have this "going native" quality about them that is reminiscent of some historical anthropological writings in which the researcher entered a foreign culture and met the culturally deprived "Other." In session three, Marie described third-grade Haitian students: "The boys would come in and they wouldn't have eaten. They weren't um, showered. Their uniforms weren't clean. They were very like unkompt. They had um, they were slow learners." Lynn told us about a high school student in her class. "He was minority . . . and could not read or write. . . . The teacher says, 'I can't do anything about him. Just let him just do whatever and he'll get by.'" Elizabeth taught school in an inner-city school and she stated: "I was a little scared just because I didn't know what to expect. But going in there it was like so amazing how much more the kids need you, know what I mean? This little girl everyday at recess . . . she'd just wanna sit and like not necessarily tell me her problems but she just like wanted a friend to talk to." Mary shared a similar story. "These little kids they like look at you . . . and when you come to them they're . . . so psyched and they show you what they're doing. Some of them just didn't even have a clue. They just looked at you like, 'Please talk to me.'" She continued telling us about the inner-city school in which she taught: ". . . some of them come to school in like November, no coat. They don't even realize what's going on and like I just look at them like, 'Oh my God.' . . . It was a really difficult situation 'cause I didn't know whether or not I should just be like, 'I wanna take them all home' . . . I didn't know how to relate to them."

"Relating to them" manifested itself in wanting to "save them" both from their personal lives and from the bad white teachers who are part of "the problem" (Gerry). Gerry went on to tell us that "If I can give them like 6 months of someone caring about them, I'm gonna do that." Faith followed that up by saying: "I think it's funny how when we talk about little kids, it's like they need you so much and like I taught in [the inner city] last year and it was awesome." For the participants, being needed and being wanted by "these poor kids" (Gerry) was an "awesome" feeling.

The observations that are made by the participants reveal several stereotypes located under a canopy of caring that enveloped the discussion of teaching "inner-city" students. The participants easily saw themselves as warm and personable, friendly and loving, even to the point where Mary suggests that "I wanna take them all home." What's missing in their desire for positive interpersonal relationships with their students of color, is a shared desire to think more radically about *why* they feel this way about teaching students of color.

The participants' talk, embedded in a "caring and sharing" storyline, propels them further into the maintenance of myths, while simultaneously it distances them from thinking more critically about a system that allows such gross inequities to flourish in our schools (Eaker & Van Galen, 1996). Rather than expressing anger and rage at racist practices, this sense of urgency about a fundamental restructuring of educational institutions is absent from the participants' discourse. The participants conceptualize the problem as being internal to their students. The solution then is to "save" them.

These discussions were disconcerting, highly uncomfortable at times, and reveal the complexities of trying to unravel our racial positions within the discourse of teaching and racism. Together, we grappled with the participants' potential roles as active agents of change in their classrooms and schools, *but agents of change who are intimately tied to societal structures.* It was evident, (and from a veteran teacher's point of view) admirable, that the participants saw themselves as actively working *for* students. What was not so evident to the participants was their inability to see their complicity with the (re)production of knowledge, values, beliefs, and racist myths that have their genesis in a white, Eurocentric, class-based system of privilege and authority.

"WHITE" TEACHERS

Britzman (1986) discusses how teachers' personal histories are created and maintained by the valorization of three myths that create a teacher. These myths are (1) teachers are self-made, (2) teachers are experts, and (3) everything depends on the teacher. Couched in these myths is the notion that one is a natural teacher—a myth that promotes an essentialist notion of what makes a good teacher. In addition, believing that teachers are experts demands that teachers should know everything. Therefore, a teacher's "job" is controlling all aspects of knowledge creation and dissemination. Britzman describes the third myth as "Everything—student learning, the presentation of curriculum and social control—is held to be within the teacher's domain, while the teacher's isolated classroom existence is accepted as the norm" (p. 449).

Although Britzman offers a powerful critique of the educative process and illuminates the mechanisms for controlling educational discourse, she fails to explicitly connect such practices with the racial and/or gender identities of the teachers she describes. Nonetheless, I share her analysis as a framework for discussing how these participants' identities, as white female student teachers, are embedded in these myths and how both—the myths and the identities—are fundamentally grounded in their positionalities as members of a privileged racial group.

There is an interdependency between whiteness and educational reproduction, between whiteness and control of discourse, and between whiteness and teaching. The participants dabble in those interdependencies when they talk about themselves as being *white* teachers—not just as being generic teachers who sound very much like Britzman's historical, mythical figures. I heard the participants discuss their prepracticum experiences particularly within inner-city schools and the tension they feel as they enter into unfamiliar environments and interact with unfamiliar students. They enter into these experiences deeply influenced by Britzman's observations: they think they have to "know" everything and they think they have to be "experts" on school culture. What becomes problematic for them is their lack of knowledge—not only about the Other's racial and cultural identities, but about their own as well. This exchange occurred during a conversation regarding the participants' anxieties about teaching in an inner-city school.

FAITH: *You know what I mean? "Like you're my white teacher and you went to a $25,000 college and you're trying to be my friend. Get out of here," you know what I mean?*

LYNN: *It's funny you said that 'cause I called my cooperating teacher that I'm gonna be working with and that's the first question I asked her. I said, "Your class is what, at least 90 percent Black or minority." She said, "Yeah." I said, "Um, I guess there's one hesitation I have." I said, "Do they think I'm some white girl comin' in from a $25,000 a year school," like you said, "thinking that I'm gonna change the world?" She says, "They're not gonna think that. They're gonna love you. . . . Believe me. It's not going to be an issue unless you make it an issue with them. As long as you're cool, as long as you don't think you're the biggest shit that ever hit this place." (S3)*

Lynn's belief that race isn't going to be an issue is understandable in light of the participants' conceptualizations of the nature of racism as they have been presented in previous chapters, as well as how they frame "being a teacher." In addition, her cooperating teacher is supporting the notion that race doesn't matter and won't be a factor in Lynn's teaching as long as she doesn't act like she's "the biggest shit that ever hit this place." The participants' tendency to be "colorblind" resonates with how many whites, including white teachers, tell the story of race in our country. Deciding that "skin color shouldn't matter," relieves whites of accepting the "value imputed to being white" (Hacker, 1995, p. 66). Being colorblind allows white people to both ignore the benefits of whiteness and dismiss the experiences of people of color. For these white participants, their classrooms become a microcosm of the larger society that needs to believe that skin color isn't an issue. By minimizing the importance of their students' skin color, the participants accept the fallacy that "kids are just kids." Unfortunately, the participants' way of thinking negates the essentiality of recognizing and valuing the lived experiences of their students, and understanding the relationship between those experiences and the bifurcation of racial equity in our schools and in our society.

The dualisms presented in chapter five are also present in the discussions the participants had about teaching and teachers. The participants are white teachers but they are "good white teachers." They see themselves as embodying an understanding of the highest principles of teaching: caring for students, increasing students' self-esteem, and creating safe places for students to learn. As Ellen commented during session six, "We're all optimistic teachers who plan on not having racism in our classroom." Not having racism in their classrooms meant not succumbing to the pressures of teaching and not colluding with the "bad white teachers" who have given up on students of color and who treat them like they are "just there" (Faith).

The participants are armed with idealism, youth, intelligence, and a clear willingness to work hard. They are more hopeful than some veteran teachers they have met and clearly have a refreshing optimism that some veteran teachers lack. At the same time, they fear their own "hardening" as they struggle with the notion of how to avoid becoming insensitive to students of color. How do they remain optimistic? How do they keep from being disenchanted with the complexities of teaching in inner-city schools? Are they going to be able to make a difference?

LYNN: *My teacher was there [inner-city school] for 26 years and you listen to them talk and you would be appalled at what they say and how they talk about their students and the relation to race or academic level - and their expectations of them and they said, "You know, we didn't come into this believing these things or thinking these things . . . but after being in urban schools for over 26 years. . . . She said this is the first time she ever felt prejudiced or developed stereotypes about certain races and I fear that. After being in there for so many years that I'm gonna be overwhelmed by the urban school. I mean I just gave a test last week that four people passed and my fear is going into these schools and after 26 years of that, it's really developing low expectation of students. I don't want to. I don't think it's the best way to go about your teaching. I think you should have all these high expectations for your students but there's the fear that because you're in an urban setting, there's a lot going on in these kids lives, that it drains you and it gets very discouraging and I just fear being like those teachers are now. They said, "You probably think we are probably some of the meanest teachers in the world but you have to realize where we've been for 20 years. We still love these kids. We still care about these kids' education. We still want to give them the best, best education but you will be very surprised at how your attitude changes from the first day you walk in there 'til the last day." I think that's what I fear.*

ELLEN: . . . *Do you develop these low expectations and discriminative feelings as a defense mechanism for yourself - so you save yourself the heartache of watching these kids fail that you have such high expectations for - that you almost see a failure in yourself because these kids have failed and is that why we go into it with high expectations and then after 10 years, 20 years, we start thinking, "Well, these kids just can't do it - and it has no reflection on me and it has no reflection on what I'm doing but I can't do anything about it" - and is that so that we don't so we don't hurt as bad inside?*

MARY: *Do we think we're gonna all go gung-ho, "Oh, I can teach these kids. The other teachers just don't have expectations" and then after awhile - if you're not producing the results you want to you feel that it's not because I'm a bad teacher. It's just because these students obviously can't do it like I mean after 26 years.*

ELLEN: *Or just having hopes for these kids and seeing your hopes get crushed, you know? Some of them are gonna fail and some of them aren't gonna make it to the second grade and some of them are gonna drop out of school and it hurts, you know and I think that after 20 years you kinda get hardened.*

MARY: *If after 26 years if you take it all so hard as you did the first couple of years, you're gonna be a mess.*

ALICE: *Well, I disagree. I think if you recognize your role in that school and in the institution, and if I may do a little drawing because of what you said.*

[The following bold print is an excerpt from my field notes.]

Again, I hit the board for a good part of the session as I wanted to depict a story of two schools which Faith was telling us about. I wrote a couple of things on the board that they had said to use as a reference point. These are things they said in the conversation that I wrote on the board. "We are influenced by racism, but we are not racist." "IT drains you." "IT'S overwhelming." "IT hurts." "You can't change institutional racism." I was trying to relate the individual teacher in the classroom (them), to the institutions/schools they are in, with the society these institutions are part of. (Oct. 28, 1994)

ALICE: *One of you said that you have to harden yourself to "it." So, my question is, what is "it"? What causes this [the differential treatment of students] to happen?*

ELLEN: *Family and students.*

LYNN: *I think it's the whole society[*

? *The system.*

ALICE: *What kind of system would cause that?*

(ct) *"Racist." "Racism in education"*—

ALICE: *Does that make sense to all of you?*

ELLEN: *That it's racism?*

. . . .

KERRY: *I think it is the students continually failing and ending up disappoint-
ing you.*

CHRISTINE: *Not meeting the expectations of the teacher or the administra
tion. . . .*

ALICE: *Which come from where?*

(ct) *"Society" "Institutions"*

ALICE: *OK. . . . So, there's you down here in your classroom trying to do your
thing, but do you see how this is all connected [pointing to board]?*

ELLEN: *But the higher the expectations you have the more likely the kids are
gonna fail at meeting our expectations.*

ALICE: *What is causing them to fail though is what I'm trying to say.*

(ct) *"Unequal opportunities"*

ASHLEY: *The poverty.*

MARY: *Poor resources, poor community support, bad schools[*

ALICE: *And some of that or lots of that or most of that, depending on where you
are in how you're thinking about it, stems from what someone already
said. That. [pointing to the word 'racism'] Do you see that there's a
strong connection between racism and what you're talking about?*

(ct) *"Yes." "Yeah"*

. . . .

CHRISTINE: *We're all influenced by racism but we're not necessarily racist.*

ALICE: *Is that a general feeling?*

(ct) *"Mhm." "Yeah." (S6)*

This discussion continued along the lines of teacher expectations and student performance. The participants found it extremely difficult to make connections between societal structures, institutions, and their own positionalities as white teachers. And when they did make those connections, there was a tendency to minimize the resulting oppression for students of color, blame other whites for the damage done, or both. In order to examine the intersection of the individual and societal systems and structures, I tried to link the above discussion to sexism and the power differentials that exist between women and men in education, from the textbook publishers to the classroom teachers. In my field notes later that evening I wrote:

> At one point, I tried to connect racism to sexism hoping that sexism would be a way for them to think about racism. I was so frustrated by the responses that I got, that I literally turned my back on them and put my head against the wall. They had no problem seeing that I was totally flabbergasted by their quick defense of white male dominance and their ability to excuse oppression - no matter how it manifests itself. I was thinking later that they do not feel oppressed. Not in any way, shape, or form that I can see do they experience any kind of oppression so they have no reference point, no experience. Ashley shared her frustration in her prepracticum teaching experience with being treated less than by the males in her department and I was glad to hear it. At least one of them felt discriminated against and knew - at least a little bit - how disempowering it feels to be ignored because of her sex. She certainly didn't get the support I thought she might from the others but then again, I am confronted with my own assumptions that they are "up on" sexism and the effects of a sexist system on all women. I was mistaken. (Oct. 28, 1994)

In the above exchange the participants created a "caring without critique" discourse that uncritically accepts the status quo that is rigidified in our educational institutions. Couched in uncritical caring, it became difficult for the participants to stare at the discriminatory practices that are played out against Blacks and other students of color in our school systems—by white teachers—and point to racism in education as one of the contributors to that experience. As Eaker-Rich and Van Galen (1996) suggest,

> well-intended teachers who may invest much of their relational work with students may, nonetheless, manifest caring in culturally

bound ways that limit, rather than support, students' personal and academic growth. Van Galen contends that disempowering relationships couched in a rhetoric of care may ultimately render the differential treatment of students invisible and unspeakable. (p. 7)

The participants are caught up in a rhetoric of care that fails to address the fact that no amount of caring—if that caring is situated in hugs, pats on the back, and stickers on tests—is going to dismantle the foundations of racism that hold our schools intact. The participants' paternalism mutes a critical discussion of racism and teaching. Instead, it frees them, as white teachers, to "love" *all* students, while at the same time, relinquishing them from taking responsibility for confronting the conditions that keep people in poverty and ignorance.

SUMMATION

ELIZABETH: *I came into this like happy great, this'll be a great, not that it's not a great group, but (laughter) like we're gonna solve the world you know and then at some at one point, I felt sad 'cause it was like I guess 'cause I realized then like you have to we have to really own up like we do have privilege and we have to face that. . . . It is so overwhelming and . . . me teaching, I feel like that's the where I can at least start to try to change my little aspect of the whole picture. (S8)*

This chapter illustrates the inherent challenges that face the participants of this project as they complete their teacher education programs and enter into a long-term process of developing a racial awareness that will assist them in creating a multicultural antiracist praxis. The participants bring to their conceptualizations of teaching a perspective rooted in their social locations as white middle- and upper-middle-class females. The participants are not accustomed to examining the intricate web of racism as it exists in the educational systems of this country. Thus, many of them tend to reproduce the dominant discourse through the uncritical acceptance of myths and stereotypes, as well as through unreflective teaching practices. In addition, many of the participants had difficulty examining the richness, subtly, and vitality that "inner-city" students bring to their classrooms. The participants seemed "more comfortable" when viewing these students as wanting of white teachers' attention, care, and love—concepts that were taken for granted as remedies for "dealing with the racism in my classroom." These concepts led the participants to invoke an ethic of care in order to "deal with it," while simultaneously locating racism within individual teachers who had become "hardened." Lastly, a number of the participants embraced a doctrine of colorblindness when it came to thinking about students of color, and about themselves as "white" teachers. Although they admit to being white, many are not so willing to name themselves as "raced." By "raced," I refer to acknowledging the implications of being white and calling attention to the relationship between skin color and societal positionality and more specifically, to the privileges and opportunities we experience as whites. Entertaining the idea that they are "raced," challenged the participants to alter the fundamental ways that they view themselves as teachers and resulted in an uncertain and unsettling experience.

The data suggest that these young, white, female student teachers have constructed a set of ideas, images, and strategies for teaching that raise fundamental questions about the discourse of race in education. These constructions are illusory, limited, full of possibilities and pitfalls. They reveal the complexities of addressing race issues in our schools and within ourselves as white teachers. Notwithstanding these complexities, the participants clearly have many opportunities to insert antiracist pedagogy in their classrooms. As noted in chapter one, these young teachers are capable of being agents of change and of influencing and informing teaching practices on a number of levels. What becomes increasingly difficult for them is understanding the chasm that exists between their antiracist ideals and their tendency to appropriate long-standing strategies for teaching that benefit the dominant group (e.g., treating all students equally, individualism, hard work, "loving" students). What is also very disturbing for me in that scenario, is that they also don't appear to have many white cooperating teachers who can assist them in developing that kind of understanding. Thus, the participants felt confused and uncertain about "what to do next."

I concur with Cochran-Smith (1995a) who suggests that:

> Constructing uncertain knowledge about race and teaching meant feeling doubtful, confused, angry, and surprised . . . by new realizations. These are psychic conditions that are difficult and very different from the conditions successful students are used to feeling in school where the point, as we know, is often to get the right answer, summarize the major points, or, in college, restate the teacher's point of view. . . . It is not surprising that this process sometimes explodes in unpredicted, off-putting, and even harsh directions. (p. 553)

This research project illustrates the unpredictable nature of creating an antiracist discourse that deals with white racial identity and pedagogical practice. Though complex and disconcerting, engaging in this research of critique provided the participants with a basis for learning about themselves as white educators, and assisted them in constructing new forms of knowledge about race and racism. It is to be hoped that the participants' continued commitment to meaning-making will lead to the types of individual and collective change they envision for themselves—and that can happen for them (and for all of us)—even in the midst of paradox and uncertainty.

CHAPTER 7

IMPLICATIONS FOR
RESEARCH AND TEACHING PRACTICE

The story of how this group of white female student teachers made meaning of whiteness is a story that ended, in many respects, on the last day of the research project. It is a story that *never* ends, in many respects, for those of us who are still finding ourselves challenged by the roadblocks and detours of our own racial histories, lived experiences, and positionalities in the system of whiteness. The roadblocks and detours presented in this book seem intractable, entrenched in a history of inequality and privilege that resists interrogation. Their resistance to move without a great deal of sustained pressure has far-reaching implications for teachers and researchers committed to antiracist praxis.

In this chapter, I present the implications of this PAR project for developing research methodologies and pedagogical practices for decentering whiteness. In addition, I discuss the implications of this research experience for the participants, and for white people who are interested in teaching and research that is aimed at changing the face of racism and whiteness. I advocate for a PAR methodology that provides opportunities for white researchers and educators to expose the dynamics of racism among white people, and the need for such a methodology in our institutions of higher learning. The emphasis on lived experiences, the subjectivity and activist stance of the teacher and researcher, and the emphasis on social change are characteristics that have considerable potential to challenge aspects of racist thinking and practices in our research experiences. The data also suggest that we need to continually define and redefine "action" and "social change" within PAR projects aimed at transformation.

Along similar lines, I suggest that all white educators must critique our pedagogy and infuse our teaching practices with the same characteristics described above. The data suggest that when our teaching fails to illuminate the past, present, and future consequences of white racism, we limit the construction of knowledge and privilege the dominant discourse. By reimagining our praxis and locating it within the tradition of PAR and Freirean knowledge creation and transformation, white educators have the opportunity to disrupt racist teaching practices and reinvent teacher education programs.

REPRESENTATIONS OF WHITENESS

The results of this research imply that for these young white females, being white is normal, typical, and functions as a standard for what is right, what is good, and what is true. The data indicate that these participants experience an unvarying conformity with the dominant white Eurocentric discourse that underlies white society's ways of thinking, living, and relating with people of color. The participants experienced definite feelings of guilt, fear, and anger about what happened to Blacks "back then." Yet, given the "culture of niceness" described earlier, and the participants' gendered and classed locations, it was difficult for them to muster up enough rage and anger at contemporary white racism to decenter their privileged racial positions *now*. Instead, when they entered into the discussion of racial inequities in the United States, they oftentimes shifted to a hallmark of U.S. culture—the individualistic myth that, no matter what your color, if you work hard and stick to your goals, you, too, can achieve the American Dream.

The data also suggest that the participants reify whiteness by consciously and unconsciously transmitting the official pronouncements of white society. Oftentimes, their discussions resonate with an ideology of separateness and a perspective that intimates that "difference is deficient." The explicit and implicit racism that was laced throughout many of the discussions highlights the pervasiveness of white racism, the lack of sensitivity of white people to our own racism and that within U.S. society, and the ease with which whites "talk about" people of color. The conversations that took place in our group sessions suggest that these participants have had very little—if any—opportunity to "talk *with*" the Other. Rather, they have learned about people of color from the media, their parents, teachers, texts, peers, and the evening news.

It was in the classroom that these white participants felt most able to imagine themselves as confronting racism, and thereby, felt they could undo the damage of hundreds of years of oppression and "make a difference" for their students. "Caring" for students, being colorblind, sympathizing with the plight of students of color, and being couched in the suffocating world of altruism made it difficult for the participants to keep the focus on them, as white people, who benefit in a racist society. Their continued "fixed gaze" (Fine, 1995) on people of color interfered with the participants taking their own racial inventories.

Faced with being beneficiaries of white racism, and yet, shuddering at the thought of "being racist," resulted in the participants having to live with contradiction—a state of dissonance that many whites find unwilling to accept, choose as a way of life, or both. My personal experience and my experiences teaching white students, along with the analysis of the participants' talk, suggests that the dissonance caused by critically investigating whiteness, the history of racism, the untold stories of white supremacy, and the advantaged positionalities of white people in our society immobilize many whites, thereby, distancing us from engaging in critique. The data suggest that refusing to examine whiteness is not just about white self-interest, white power, and white gains—although they are certainly cemented into the face of racism—but also about the ability of whites to live with ambiguity, contradiction, and personal and collective responsibility for racial injustice. The average white person is not exposed to daily harassment, stereotyping, marginalization, and living "under surveillance" (Fine, 1995). Therefore, when the spotlight shone on us, as white people, and we were asked to critically examine and confront our own lived experiences, many of us ran for cover.

To some readers, the above observations may suggest that making meaning of whiteness with young, white, female student teachers is an exercise that ironically leads to the legitimation of whiteness, rather than the dismantling of it. Although this is a tempting conclusion, it falls into the same dualistic thinking that characterized much of the participants' discourse and some of my own tendencies. Rather, the data lead me to conclude that how these participants make meaning of whiteness is more complex and therefore, more disturbing, and, most definitely, needs to be attended to by white people who are committed to developing strategies for understanding the "white psyche" and its relationship to the realities of racism. Yet, like Feagin and Vera (1995), I am

> not interested in labeling particular white Americans as "bad" or "good," for this name-calling [as the data suggest] will not lead to meaningful remedial action. The examination of white thinking as racialized, racist, or antiracist is of interest only as it aids the understanding of the system of white racism in the United States. (p. 168)

Oftentimes during our sessions, I felt like the door to thinking more critically about racism was firmly closed. Yet, my experience suggests that there were times when the participants were willing to open the door to reconceptualizing the complexities of white racism. Although their feelings of defensiveness, fear, frustration, powerlessness, and privilege slammed the door shut, as they frequently do for white people, the participants oftentimes managed to reenter the discourse with a desire to better understand themselves as white people, thus, gaining a different perspective about the multifaceted world of racism as it is experienced by people of color.

Many white people have been the irrepressible promoters of a hierarchical racial order, and they benefit from that hierarchy. The participants are no exception. Considering this factor, it is no wonder that our sessions were infused with tension, anxiety, denial, and racist jargon that was difficult to unravel. Nonetheless, short as our time together was, the faulty foundations of white and Black life in the United States were shaken. The contrast between the lives of people of color and the lives of white people that illuminated the sessions challenged the participants to reconstruct their understandings of race, racism, and what it means to be white in this country today.

LIMITATIONS OF CONDUCTING WHITE-ON-WHITE PAR

I addressed a number of personal and methodological limitations of this PAR project in chapter three. I explored the limitations of being a white participant-researcher attempting to conduct a PAR project for her dissertation, and the tensions that arise when one has to "work the intersections" of multiple roles. I also addressed the time factor of the project and the restructuring of the research design to accommodate the schedules of the participants. In this section, I elaborate further on the significance of "time" as it relates to the process of consciousness-raising. In addition, I address the limitations of "living in a white bubble" while engaging in a PAR project aimed at puncturing that bubble. Lastly, I explore the limitations of white-on-white research, questioning the exclusion of people of color from the white racism dialogue.

The Question of Time

As noted in chapter three, once the participants rearranged the schedule for our group sessions, there was little time to visit the participants at their classroom sites and then relate those visits to our discussions about whiteness, racism, and education in a meaningful and productive way. Reorganizing the schedule led to changes in the original proposal and shifted the research agenda. More important than that, the short period of time we had together (the fall semester with only two follow-up meetings in the spring semester) limited the degree to which we could engage in what is a long-term process of critiquing ourselves as white people in the system of whiteness.

The amount of time allotted for a PAR project varies according to the characteristics of the particular project. In terms of this PAR project, the fact that we met for only eight sessions suggests the possibility that we may have just scratched the surface of what it means to be white. The participants spent many hours describing the experiences of whites and Blacks, questioning deeply ingrained assumptions, investigating racism and whiteness in ways that were new to them, and basically, telling their racial stories for the first time. Yet, my experience in this project leads me to believe that we required more time for examining what is often submerged and hidden in the white psyche. I remember feeling at one point that "a little whiteness" could be dangerous. That when we scratched the surface, the participants would mistake that for "knowing all the answers." I was concerned that rather than realize that they had just begun the process of recognizing themselves as white, the participants would jump on a bandwagon of designating themselves "white antiracists" without undergoing a substantial transformative consciousness-raising experience.

Participatory action research is a powerful tool for consciousness-raising and as a methodology it was instrumental in disrupting the white worlds that the participants brought to the sessions. Yet, I hesitate to promote a project such as this if it does not entail a long-term commitment to the process of a self- and collective white critique. Among other things, lack of time for white people to process the kinds of issues that are raised around the multiple aspects of white racism militates against critical reflection. The issue of time is most notable in university structures where one semester courses make it difficult to "continuously interrogate" (Reay, 1996) particular issues. Similar problems arise within PAR, which is a methodology that requires flexibility and concentrated attention—over time—to reflection and action around specific problems and situations. Without critical reflection, action—if it occurs—becomes problematic in both instances. As noted in chapter one, "there is no authentic praxis outside the dialectical unity, action-reflection, practice-theory" (Freire, 1985, p. 156). And without action—whether that be in the classroom, at the university, individual, and/or collective—racism remains solidly grounded in the white psyche and persistently played out against people of color.

Living in a White Bubble

Another limitation of this project was the lack of connection the participants had to the realities of Black life. The monocultural environments that they live in—and the predominantly white university this project took place in—make it difficult for the participants to grasp the lived experiences of people of color. Some of the participants had engaged in practice teaching in urban schools working with multiethnic, multiracial students. Others shared their experiences of working with children of color in summer camp or in afterschool programs. These experiences provided the participants with a glimpse of how children of color live. Yet, it is important to note that the data suggest that these "glimpses" were loaded with racist assumptions and that the participants' experiences with people of color were driven by a hidden agenda that focused on saving "them." The paternalism that was evident in the notion of "how much more the kids [students of color] need" (Elizabeth) reifies stereotypes and legitimates acting "like white knights" (Michelle).

My experience suggests that PAR projects developed to facilitate white people investigating whiteness must include a predetermined action component that adds to the reeducation of white people. Entering a PAR project with a predetermined agenda seems antithetical to the underlying assumptions of many PAR projects. Yet, due to the nature of white-on-white research, I think it essential that we advocate for some types of "structured immersion experiences" (Sleeter, 1993, p. 169) so that white participants spend time with people of color. Coupled with those experiences would be "instruction about racism and the history and culture of that group, as well as the development of some emotional bonding with members of the group" (p. 169). Whites need to take responsibility to educate ourselves about "the Other" which means reading about people of color—their histories, their lived experiences—*in their own words*. It means *not* relying on people of color to teach us about themselves, or about ourselves, or about racism and the impact of racism on their/our lives. That's *our* responsibility and it's been my experience that if we take that responsibility seriously, then, and only then, will there be opportunities for "emotional bonding" with members of other racial groups.

There is no talking cure for racism. As white activist researchers, we have a responsibility to link our theory and practice, reflection and action, talking and doing. Although some of the participants chose to become actively involved in antiracist political action on campus following this project (something addressed later in this chapter), a limitation of this research was that the participants had no ongoing process of connecting with people of color—a component that has the potential to create a richer and more critical dialogue among white people.

Creating Dialogue with People of Color

The above conclusion leads to my final suggestion for those of us interested in conducting white-on-white PAR. The data suggest, and my experience confirms, that white people talking to white people about racism is a necessity. At the same time, encapsulating ourselves in our own white worlds raises questions about how far we can go in our critique. I worry that "on our own," we, as whites, will too easily slip into "white lies" (Fine, 1995), justifications, and fall victim to purposeful forgetting. Ensconcing ourselves in everything white with an occasional adventure to visit the Other, muffles the realities of "living in a complex, multifaceted world that is rent by racism directed toward Black Americans" (Gaines and Reed, 1995, p. 99).

I continue to advocate for whites talking to whites, but my experience offers a perspective that also includes opportunities for talking to and acting with people of color. People of color bring profoundly different life experiences and perspectives to the table than white people. "Although Americans of color express a wide range of analyses of racism, the strongest critiques of racism tend to come from communities of color. The life experiences of people of color can be politicized to challenge racism . . . more readily than can those of white people" (Sleeter, 1993, p. 169).

Whites who are committed to interrogating whiteness realize that our old attitudes, beliefs, feelings, and assumptions need to undergo drastic revisions. In an effort to attend to those underlying "ways of being white," I suggest that we, as whites, develop strategies for examining whiteness alongside allies of color who will risk making the journey with us. Coupled with white-on-white discussions, discussions and actions that foster mutual accompaniment with people of color, provide whites with a better chance of developing new states of consciousness. Examining whiteness can then be viewed—not as something to be endured or mastered—but in a very real sense, as a continuing discourse and struggle to enact liberation and justice.

IMPLICATIONS: METHODOLOGY, PEDAGOGY, AND MEETING THE WHITE SELF

I present the above limitations, not to deter others who are committed to addressing racism with white people. Rather, I suggest that we learn by doing. The unfinished outcomes of this project provoke possibilities for white educators and researchers to rethink the meaning of whiteness, thus creating liberatory pedagogies and methodologies in hopes of dismantling it. In addition, the implications of this project are far-reaching for the lifelong (re)creation of the white identity.

PAR: Provoking Possibilities for White-on-White Research

When I began this project, I defined PAR as a methodology for the

> social investigation of problems, involving participation of oppressed and ordinary people in problem posing and solving. It is an educational process for the researcher and participants, who analyze the structural causes of named problems through collective discussion and interaction. Finally, it is a way for researchers and oppressed [and ordinary] people to join in solidarity to take collective action, both short and long term, for radical social change. (Maguire, 1987, p. 29)

I also recognized that participatory action research is more than a set of research techniques. It is a "philosophy of life as much as a method" (Fals-Borda & Rahman, 1991). This philosophy embodies a set of assumptions about social action and people's lives that, by their very nature, call into question the system of whiteness and the responsibility of white people within that system. Subsequently, infusing the principles of PAR with members of the dominant racial group raises important methodological questions: Why would white people want to examine white racism? What investment do white people have in engaging in a critique about a system we benefit from and in? How does being a member of the dominant group affect one's commitment to "radical social change"? Questions like these need to be asked, and the answers need to be heard.

It is my experience that the *possibilities* of conducting PAR with the dominant group need to be the focal point of our research. The inherent contradictions need to be acknowledged, but they need not result in researchers *rejecting* PAR as a resource for understanding social problems and for engaging in critical dialogue. Rather, the complexities can be catalytic, challenging white people to reflect on the causes of racism and the system of whiteness "as being rooted in human actions, [thus coming] to realize that things do not have to remain the way they are and that they can engage in actions to transform the reality. Critique thus turns into will to action and action itself" (Park, 1993, pp. 7–8). As Feagin and Sikes (1994) suggest:

Until whites recognize that they have been raised in a racist soci- ety and harbor its hidden influence even when they deny it, until whites recognize that they too must take action to deal with per- sonal and societal racism, no matter how subtle, and to eradicate it, the racial situation in the United States will only worsen. . . . The task of educating white Americans will not be easy, but it is pos- sible. Once the problem is admitted, the solutions can at least be envisioned and implemented. (p. 321)

My experience in this project suggests that gauging the extent to which individuals and groups both act and change within a PAR project is related to the particularities of the research project itself. "Transformation" was a difficult thing to gauge in this research pro- ject. "However," as Maguire (1993) suggests,

transformation, social and personal, is not an event. It is a process that we are living through, creating as we go. . . . We never know when we begin where the work will take us and those involved. Perhaps that is what allows us to begin. . . . The point is to learn and grow from doing, and to celebrate the doing, no matter how flawed, small-scale, or less than ideal. (p. 176)

Implications of PAR for participants. Action *within* a PAR project is possible when the participants are involved in multiple aspects of the PAR process. The participants and I shared some decision-making powers regarding the structure of this project, the formation of the dis- cussions, and the analysis of the data. As noted in Appendix C, I invited the participants to register for an independent study the semes- ter following the completion of the project, thus providing an oppor- tunity for the participants and I to collaborate in the analysis of the data that was gathered during the eight group sessions. Although not all of the participants were able to collaborate in this aspect of the PAR project due to other commitments, Julie, Christine, and Michelle par- ticipated with me in analyzing and interpreting the data. The advan- tages of being able to engage on a deeper level with the data, was that Christine, Michelle, and Julie reread the transcribed sessions, listened to all the tapes, and delved more meaningfully into readings about racism and whiteness. They situated themselves more critically in the discourse, critiquing both their individual talk, and the talk that was generated by the group. During the group analysis meetings, they made frequent references to the changes they had undergone in their thinking about whiteness and racism.

At the close of our eight sessions, the campus where this project was developed experienced a level of racial unrest that resulted in the formation of several new undergraduate student groups that were committed to addressing racism within the university. Although many of the participants resisted taking collective action at the culmination of the group sessions, the public identification of racist behavior on campus, coupled with the raising of consciousness experienced within the project, led five of the thirteen participants to join in the formation of undergraduate student groups to address racism at the university. Others have spoken to me about insights they have had into their own positionalities as white people since the project ended and how they have been able to "have conversations about race—something I just couldn't do before without feeling uncomfortable" (Marie). Still others have made changes in both their personal and academic lives since the project ended.

I had the opportunity to speak with many of the participants as they completed their final year at the university. In particular, I was able to informally reinterview four of the participants before they graduated. Both the participants and I were eager to revisit the project and discuss the ways in which participating in the research project influenced—or not—their/our lives as white females and/or as white teachers. Since meaning-making takes place within particular historical times and under shifting conditions, I imagined that the participants would have a different understanding of the research experience having had "time away" from the intensity of our group sessions. In addition, I was curious to see if the participants had moved beyond their own understandings of whiteness and if so, how these new understandings were being constructed and lived out in their daily lives.

What emerged from those conversations—and from the many that I had over the course of a year and a half with many of the participants—was a clear sense that most of the participants "had come a long way" (Gerry) in understanding the multiple dimensions of whiteness and the multiple ways in which their racial locations give them access to resources and opportunities that are not so readily available—if at all—to people of color. Oftentimes throughout our conversations, I heard the participants say things like: "The first word that I would link with being white now would be privilege and before, I don't know what I said" (Gerry). Faith commented on the fact that the research project had "done a lot" for her. "It's gotten me to . . . be more aware. It's kept me awake at nights, too." Ashley stated that she was more aware now of institutional racism and her "part in it," something she was unaware of prior to becoming a participant in the project. She added that, "I think it's given me a lot more responsibility as a white person that I didn't know I had." Michelle discussed how she now saw whiteness as something real and concrete. Whereas before the research experience she had never heard the word, Michelle now believes that whiteness is "very alive as opposed to being invisible. . . . I've come to the conclusion that I am privileged and I need to act on that knowledge." Michelle has taken steps to further her understanding of whiteness and the ways in which education intersects with systems of privilege and oppression. She made conscious choices about the schools she would student teach in, deciding to put her energy into both working with students of color for one semester, so as to "gain a better understanding of their lives" and become "more cognizant of my own whiteness . . . so that I'm not pushing or imposing my privileged background or my values on them" and working with white privileged students "like myself" the following semester because she felt she could identify with the assumptions they were bringing into the classroom. The assumptions are "already there," she said, "so that then we can begin to deconstruct it from that point."

Ashley made changes in her program of studies and decided to take courses in Black History stating that, "I love African American history. I think they are so much more real [than readings from European-American history]. You see so many parts of the world that I've never experienced . . . and I was never taught any of this stuff in my history courses."

Gerry was hired as a teaching assistant for a course in feminist psychology during her senior year. Her professor was impressed with how Gerry was able to facilitate critical and self-reflective discussions with her all-white students about racism and oppression. Gerry commented that her view of racism has changed dramatically after "all our weeks of trying to figure it out."

Faith participated in and codeveloped a year-long research project with the psychology department examining the multiple ways in which undergraduates identify themselves (i.e., racially, academically, socially). She and her peers hypothesized that the white students would be less likely to identify as white and more likely to identify with their ethnic backgrounds than students of color. On completion of the research project, Faith and the other researchers presented their findings and the implications of their work at a university-sponsored symposium.

These small individual steps contribute to keeping the conversation alive and are significant reminders to the participants that they *can* take action in their personal lives to alleviate various forms of racism. They continue to struggle with their whiteness and realize that they are only just beginning to unravel the complexities of their racial locations. I think Ashley speaks for all the participants when she says: "I also think I have so much further to go."

In a research paper that Julie wrote for our analysis group, she stated: "Many times we were just beginning to form our beliefs on the issues of oppression and so our views may have changed several times throughout the sessions." I concur with Julie's observation. PAR, as a methodology for examining white racism among white people, afforded us the opportunity to be involved in a process, to allow our views to change over time, both individually and collectively. Unlike more traditional approaches to studying racism (e.g., surveys, attitudinal scales, and questionnaires), PAR provides a framework for examining the lived experiences of the participants—in all their complexities and contradictions—thereby, stretching the limits to which research can impact the lives of those involved.

Implications of PAR for critical research. A key component of this PAR project is the participant-to-participant and participant-to-researcher dialogue. Through the sharing of our "white lives" and the examination of the meaning of whiteness, there is a possibility for both the researcher and the participants to experience consciousness-raising, which—in the ideal PAR project—gives way to transformative action.

In addition, PAR provides the researcher with the opportunity to be what Denzin and Lincoln (1994) call a "bricoleur."

> The researcher-as-bricoleur-theorist works between and within competing and overlapping perspectives and paradigms. . . . The bricoleur understands that research is an interactive process shaped by his or her personal history, biography, gender, social class, race, and ethnicity, and those of the people in the setting. . . . The bricoleur also knows that researchers all tell stories about the worlds they have studied. (p. 3)

Traditional positivist research paradigms would not have allowed me the opportunity to "tell stories" about the lived experiences of the participants and relate those stories to the meanings of whiteness generated by the participants. Nor, would it have allowed me the opportunity to incorporate my personal politics and activism within the research design. Claiming that they are implicitly apolitical, positivist paradigms deemphasize social change as an aspect of the research process. Thus, to examine whiteness and to problematize racism—without also stressing the importance of changing the systems themselves—

would be antithetical to one of my original goals for this PAR project.

Guba and Lincoln (1994) suggest that ontological, epistemological, and methodological questions should serve as the major foci of any research paradigm. My experience suggests that PAR is "a" way to address those questions in a provocative, reflexive, and transformative way. Ontologically, a participatory action researcher "studying" the meaning of whiteness can ask: What is the nature of whiteness? How does whiteness manifest itself in the "real" world? What can we know about it by examining it through "white eyes"? Epistemologically, the researcher and participants can question "the nature of the relationship between the [white] knower or would-be knower and what can be known [about whiteness]?" (p. 108). From a methodological viewpoint, the researcher and participants can develop strategies for discovering what we know about ourselves as white people and how we have come to know such things. Using a PAR methodology allowed us to touch on those questions during our group sessions, leading some of us to move toward a more comprehensive and critical perspective about ourselves as white people and about the overall system of whiteness of which we are an integral part.

Politicizing Pedagogy and Reimagining Praxis

This project illuminates how white students respond to critical, transformative approaches to (re)learning about themselves as whites. The participants felt threatened—their white identities called into question, their identities as teachers, challenged. The participants' avoidance is representative of many white students who recoil from deconstructing racism (see, e.g., Ahlquist, 1991; Ellsworth, 1989; Roman, 1993; Sleeter and Grant, 1988; Tatum, 1994). Precisely because we need to question and confront our white identities and challenge the meaning of being a "white" teacher, we, as educators, must continue to actively pursue teaching practices that significantly alter the way white students are "educated" about themselves and about multicultural antiracist education.

Thinking about the (re)construction of a transformative educational praxis among a homogeneous group of white females required a breadth and depth of imagination that sometimes eluded me. As noted in chapter one, many teacher education programs in this country tend to minimize—if not totally ignore—racism in the development of their multicultural courses. At the university where this project was conducted, there is a diversity course requirement for all undergraduates. This course falls under the canopy of "anything multicultural" and does not necessarily entail a critical, sustained perspective that challenges the underlying social order in U.S. white society. This is highly problematic for those of us who are attempting to create more comprehensive and sustained strategies for antiracist education in our educational institutions.

There are many antiracist educators and scholars who have eloquently addressed ways to develop those strategies—many of whom I have referred to in this book. Although they come at it from differing perspectives, and although each may highlight a particular strategy, in general, they agree on the following: the need for multiculturally antiracist curriculum in our schools; populating the teaching force with people of color; planning long-term learning and teaching experiences that expose white students to the lives of people of color; rewriting the history of race and whiteness into our texts; and requiring that white teachers develop awareness of their racial identities so as to support, challenge, and (re)educate their students.

My engagement with these participants strongly supports the idea that we, as white educators, need to do all of the above—and more. The data from this project suggest that schools of education need to "interrupt the multicultural silences existing in the student teaching experience" (Grant & Zozakiewicz, 1995, p. 269). Grant and Zozakiewicz argue that student teachers, cooperating teachers, and supervisors have been silenced—and themselves silence   a multicultural education orientation that "encompasses democratic principles such as equality, justice and equity" (p. 269.) They suggest a number of strategies for making "social justice noise" such as more effective screening and interviewing of cooperating teachers and supervisors, a more systemic focus on multicultural education throughout the teacher education program as well as in the larger institution, short-term and longitudinal research that measures the effectiveness of multicultural education in the student teaching experience, and "professional development time to foster . . . awareness, acceptance and affirmation of multicultural education" (p. 271). The data presented in this book supports those recommendations. Just as time was a limitation in this research project, teaching a course for only one semester becomes problematic as well, making it difficult to implement long-term processes that lead to self- and collective reflection and action. Thus, it would appear that we, as educators, need to think more holistically about our teacher education programs and work collaboratively to design interdisciplinary courses under the rubric of multicultural antiracist education.

In addition, schools of education need to prepare preservice teachers to "teach against the grain" by placing them in classrooms with "experienced teachers who are themselves struggling . . . in their class-rooms, schools, and communities" (Cochran-Smith, 1991, p. 279). Being in the company of cooperating teachers, and supervisors, who are committed to politicizing their pedagogy and reimagining their praxis is integral to teacher preparation programs dedicated to restructuring inequitable systems of teaching and learning within our country's schools.

In addition, and as discussed in chapter three, I believe that we, as white educators, need to make our whiteness public. With white colleagues and colleagues of color, we need to engage in critical dialogue *and*

> develop a discourse of tactical insurgency . . . that seeks to construct counterhegemonic pedagogies, oppositional identity formations, and social policies that refuse, resist, and transform existing structures of domination primarily in school sites but also in other cultural sites within the [global] arena. (Sleeter & McLaren, 1995, p. 28)

Many white teachers in the United States teach in areas where there are no teachers or students of color. Such an arrangement does not preclude one from developing antiracist pedagogy (see, e.g., the ABC film, *Eye of the Storm*, 1985, for an example of how a white teacher examined racism and prejudice in an all-white third-grade classroom). White teachers—no matter where they teach—can "do our homework." We can investigate our own backgrounds and use our own histories as starting points for gaining a more realistic perspective of what it means to "become white" and "be white" in this country.[1] We can make changes in our curricula focusing on pedagogies of/for equity and justice, teaching our students that racism and "oppression are not merely *painful*; [they] are *wrong*, and wrongs should be denounced" (Lebacqz, 1987, p. 88). We can support professional development activities that help us to practice what we, as educators, teach (see, e.g., Martin, 1995). As the data in this book suggest: we can move beyond just "talking about it" and "engage systematically in changing institutions that reproduce equality, including [our] own educational institutions" (Sleeter, 1992, p. 221).

I believe that the greatest challenge for teachers who are committed to antiracist pedagogy is confronting the teaching profession itself. As white educators, we need to address our own complicity around issues of educational racism and be accountable for some of the exclusionary and racist practices that exist in our schools. It is unwise for us to theorize and reflect on the need to teach multicultural antiracist education if we ignore our own construction of what it means to be white and if we refuse to examine the ways in which we are implicated in the continued oppression of people of color in white society. We need to take responsibility for our actions—and inactions. What is our responsibility as white teachers? What can we do "with the privileged positions we currently occupy" (Sleeter & McLaren, 1995, p. 22)? What wrongs do we need to make right? are questions that must guide our pedagogies and inform the choices we make about how we want to engage in the world as "white" teachers.

When I was just beginning my dissertation, I wrote a letter to Patricia Maguire—a participatory action researcher whose work (along with others) inspired me to conduct this project. Her reply to my tension-filled questions about conducting a PAR project around the issues of whiteness and racism was: "As I say to my students, when I get especially discouraged, I imagine the Grand Canyon—after all, it is merely the result of a little pressure applied over a long period of time. And collectively we can be like that pressure" (personal communication, May 16, 1994). My experience suggests that only by remaining committed to transformative pedagogy, can we, as white antiracist educators, "be like that pressure" and work to form "communities in which the dangerous memory of [white] injustice and of [our] response to injustice is kept alive" (Lebacqz, 1987, p. 149).

SUMMATION

My aim is not to generalize the findings of this research to all young, white, female student teachers or to essentialize whiteness and imply that all white teachers and people are the same. Neither am I suggesting that what I presented are the only "lessons to be learned" from a project aimed at examining whiteness. Rather, I suggest that conducting this PAR project can assist white educators and researchers in our quest to make meaning of whiteness with and among other whites, so as to further develop theoretical and practical strategies for research and educational praxis, thus, liberating us from our own suffocating discourse and helping us to disrupt the sanctification of whiteness.

I experienced a reconstruction of my own meaning of whiteness as a result of participating in this project with these 13 participants. It was a transformative experience for me. The participants have their own stories about how this project impacted their lives. Some of the participants didn't always agree with my analyses. Some did. Some valued the experience of "seeing" themselves in print. Some weren't so sure. Some welcomed the opportunity to learn from my critique. Some found aspects of my critique wanting. Patai (1991) suggests that, "Ultimately, we have to make up our minds whether our research is worth doing or not, and then determine how to go about it in ways that let it serve our stated goals" (p. 150). I am convinced this research was "worth doing" and can only hope that it served its stated goals and that the participants "learned by doing."

In closing, I quote Freire (1994) once again: "Let me put it this way: you never get *there* by starting from *there*, you get *there* by starting from some *here*. This means, ultimately, that the educator must not be ignorant of, underestimate, or reject any of the 'knowledge of living experience' with which the educands come to school" (p. 58). By beginning "here" and by initiating a conversation about whiteness as it related to the participants lived experiences, we *did* manage to begin the process of unpacking the "white lies" (Fine, 1995) that underlie the pervasive and destructive system of whiteness. We began at "some *here*." Through our mutual engagement in the continuing struggle subsequent to this PAR project, I hope we planted seeds that assisted us in arriving at a more just *there*.

APPENDIX A

SEMISTRUCTURED INTERVIEW QUESTIONS

SEMISTRUCTURED INTERVIEW QUESTIONS:

1. Tell me a little bit about what brought you to the School of Education.
2. Tell me why you want to become a teacher.
3. Tell me about the neighborhood you grew up in and the school(s) you attended. Are there any other features about the neighborhood/school that you'd like to tell me about?
4. Do you remember the first time you noticed that somebody else was different than you?
5. What does it mean for you to be white?
6. Please describe your interactions with individuals from other racial and ethnic groups?
7. Are your friends primarily in your same racial group or ethnic group?
8. Can you think of an experience of prejudice, racism, and/or discrimination? Tell me about it.
9. How would you define racism? Does this relate to the example you just described? In what ways?
10. Tell me what you think multicultural education is all about.

APPENDIX B

DATA ANALYSIS

My analysis really began when the project began. Throughout the research project, I listened, and relistened, to the session tapes, identifying the codes (i.e., themes) and concepts that I heard each week. For instance, how the participants perceived themselves as teachers was a code reflected in the group talk. Some of the concepts that informed that code were: caring for students, committed to equal education for all students, and self-image as a white teacher. I continued to develop and organize preliminary concepts and codes that began to frame my initial analysis. I then offered these as reflections to the participants and to Brinton during our weekly meetings. They became the basis for helping me to think through the process of meaning-making.

Once the research sessions were over, I transcribed the taped sessions. I am committed to the perspective shared by other researchers (see e.g., Mishler, 1986; 1991; Reissman, 1990; Tannen, 1984) that transcription is an aspect of interpretation and that the way that I transcribed the interviews and the group talk reflects and supports the theoretical aims and perspectives that I have regarding the relationship between language and how the participants make meaning of whiteness. Regarding the analysis and interpretation of "white talk"—talk that serves to insulate white people from examining their individual and collective role(s) in the perpetuation of racism—I was particularly interested in documenting the interruptions, overlaps, silences, and ways that the participants both challenged one another, and colluded in uncritically accepting problematic race talk. The appearance of words, phrases, and clauses, and where and how they determine lines, was set by the margins on the computer. Like Mishler (1991), "lines served no analytic purpose in my approach" (p. 271). I *was* concerned with transcribing every word, nonlexical expression, pause, and demonstrative expression. Since there was an abundance of emphasis placed on the group speech by the participants, highlighting emphatic stress with italics or bold print would make for an arduous read. Instead, when it was necessary, I parenthesized the emphasis after the participant's statement(s).

Following the completed transcriptions, I read, and reread, the texts multiple times. During these initial readings, I defined concepts (e.g., powerlessness), identified codes (e.g., teaching; constructions of the Other; white image), and described the participants' talk in the margins of the transcripts. Some of those concepts were descriptive (I would write "anger" if a participant said: "I'm angry"); others were less defined by the participants' exact words (I used the term "powerless" to conceptualize how the participants spoke about being unable "to do anything" about racism). During numerous read-throughs, I began to link the various concepts and codes that I developed across the session texts. Out of that process, I created a number of categories to represent the concepts and codes that were generated by this analysis. For example, I created a category called "Constructions of Whiteness" to illustrate the many-sided perspectives the participants had about what it means to be white. I originally created seven categories which, after numerous writes and rewrites, I synthesized into three major categories: White Talk, Constructions of Whiteness, and Teacher Image, each consisting of subcategories and various characteristics that are listed below:

White Talk
> Subcategory 1—Constructing Difference
>> Characteristic 1—Defining Racism
>> Characteristic 2—Zero-sum Thinking
> Subcategory 2—Reconstructing Myths
>> Characteristic 1—Myth of Inclusion
>> Characteristic 2—"Exceptions to the Rule"
> Subcategory 3 - Privileged Affect
>> Characteristic 1—Powerlessness
>> Characteristic 2—Fear and Defensiveness

Constructions of Whiteness
> Subcategory 1—Whites as Living a Fairy Tale
>> Characteristic 1—The Idealization of Whites
>> Characteristic 2—Whites as Normative
> Subcategory 2—Whites as Keepers of the American Dream
>> Characteristic 1—"White" Equals Power and Privilege

Subcategory 3—Whites as Dualistic
    Characteristic 1—Good Whites/Bad Whites
    Characteristic 2—Whites as the Oppressors/Whites as the
        Oppressed
    Characteristic 3—Whites as Individuals/Whites as Members
        of a Racial Group

Teacher Image
Subcategory 1—Teachers as (Re)producers of the Dominant
    Discourse
    Characteristic 1—Teachers as "White Knights"
Subcategory 2—"White" Teachers

My decision to transcribe the texts in such detail is also related to the examples of discourse analysis that I present in Appendix D. There, I highlight two sections of text that illustrate the underlying structures of the group talk. Discourse analysis allowed me to systematically analyze the underlying structures of the group talk. I then relate these structures to the discourse of whiteness. Through this relationship, I show how the participants created multiple discourses about teaching, racism, whiteness, and racial identity within our group sessions. (The transcription code can be found in Appendix C.)

MEMOS, WRITING, AND REWRITING

As mentioned above, I began writing my interpretations of the talk early on in the research project. As the analysis became more situated in the transcripts, I began to accumulate numbers of memos—written records that documented the seemingly endless thoughts and reflections, questions and ideas that were produced for me during the analysis. These memos contained a variety of features: some were brief one-liners; others were more formalized and were used to formulate conceptual relationships among the categories. Some of the memos were reminders to recheck my analysis or to retrieve a piece of data that would either substantiate a concept or illustrate a deviant or exceptional piece of text. All the memos, no matter their particularities, helped me to move in and out of the data and assisted me in what Charmaz (1990) calls the "extended on-going dialogue with self" (p. 1169).

The memos continued to be helpful even as I was beginning the more formal writing stage—a stage that is more processual than it is stagelike. "[W]riting and rewriting actually become crucial phases of the analytic process. Through writing and rewriting, a researcher can identify arguments and problems, make assumptions explicit and sharpen the concepts" (Charmaz, 1990, p. 1169). The writing and the rewriting also forced me to make decisions about what aspects of the talk I would present. Within a PAR project, those kinds of decisions are problematic. It was in the writing that I began to understand the difference between writing a document *with* the participants and writing a document *about* the participants.

During the writing and rewriting, I reworked categories, reorganized conceptual relationships, and began to theorize in a much more critical way how the participants made meaning of whiteness. I was also very fortunate in that Brinton critically reviewed my writings as we went along, providing me with helpful insights, incisive comments, and important suggestions. Conducting a PAR project, especially as a doctoral student within a university setting, required "passionate mentoring." My experience suggests that being accompanied by a trusted, and trusting, advisor is *essential* if one is to engage in this type of research.

PARTICIPANT ANALYSIS

PAR provides the participants with opportunities for making decisions about data analysis. This collaborative approach to data analysis raised questions about who controlled the data and who made the analytical and interpretive decisions—questions that I addressed throughout the research project with the participants, my advisor, Brinton, and my dissertation committee, as well as with other colleagues.

To operationalize the tenets of this PAR project, the participants were offered a number of opportunities to engage in the analysis of their interviews and their group talk. The participants were presented with their transcribed interviews and had the opportunity to provide clarification, elaboration, and critique. All of the participants took advantage of the chance to respond to their interviews.

In order to involve the participants in the analysis of the group talk, I invited the participants to register for an independent study the semester following the completion of the project, thus providing an opportunity for the participants and the researcher to collaborate in the analysis of the data that was gathered during the eight group sessions. Although not all of the participants were able to collaborate in this aspect of the PAR project due to other commitments, there was a subgroup of three participants: Michelle, Julie, and Christine, who worked with me in analyzing and interpreting much of the data. They embarked on individual research questions within the analysis group (which are found in the reference list), while simultaneously working with me to clarify interpretations and sharpen their individual analyses as well as my own analyses of the overall data. Despite their important contributions to the analysis, I am solely responsible for the interpretations that are contained within this manuscript.

I also met with the full group of participants twice during the semester following the project. During those two group sessions, we reviewed the overall analysis and continued thinking about issues related to whiteness. I invited the participants to take time to listen to the session tapes, review the transcripts of the sessions, come to the weekly subgroup analysis meetings, and/or meet with me individually if they wanted to discuss any aspect of the research project. These are the kinds of transformative actions that can be included within the PAR design and that provide opportunities for the participants to be actively engaged in the data analysis of the research.

This PAR design provided an opportunity for what Lykes (1989) refers to as "engaged" or "passionate scholarship"—a scholarship that attempts to capture the essence of how we, as subjects living out our individual and collective stories, make meaning of our realities and discover connections among the multiple and contradictory forces that shape our daily lives. This "engagement" required that both the participants and I develop a kaleidoscopic lens in viewing the processual nature of analysis and interpretation within a PAR project.

APPENDIX C

TRANSCRIPTION CODE

TRANSCRIPTION CODE

(unint.) unintelligible.

(ct) crosstalk, which is defined as two or more persons in the sessions talking over a speaker or among themselves while a speaker is talking.

demonstrative expressions are included in parentheses. For example, (sighs), (laughter), (coughs), (clears throat).

--- hesitations, silences, pauses. Each hyphen represents one second.

[interruptions, overlapping speech, or both.

- the participants often speak in run-on sentences. I inserted one hyphen to help the reader understand the intended meaning of the sentence.

, comma indicates end of a clause or phrase.

. period indicates end of a sentence.

. . . . four periods indicates omission between speakers.

. . . three unspaced ellipses indicate omission within or between sentences.

? question mark *within* the transcript indicates a question either by intonation or syntax. Question mark *preceding* a line of text indicates an unidentifiable participant.

S with a number after it (1–8), indicates session number.

APPENDIX D

EXEMPLARS OF WHITE TALK

To contextualize my interpretation of white talk, I present two exemplars that explicate different strategies for either maintaining white talk or trying to interrupt its formation. I chose the first exemplar (maintaining white talk) because it represents a recurring phenomena within the sessions. It illustrates how the participants avoided the topic of whiteness by using a number of white talk strategies: avoidance, interruptions, overlaps, silences, and an uncritical acceptance of each other's biased comments and stereotypical thinking. It illuminates how easily—and how quickly—a conversation aimed at critiquing whiteness turned into a conversation that significantly derailed that critique. The second exemplar represents an attempt by some of the participants to interrupt white talk. I chose the second exemplar because it was one of the few times that the participants overtly clashed over issues of racism and privilege. It shows how some participants challenged what they heard as racist comments and disrupted the flow of unexamined white talk. Interrupting white talk in the group sessions, although episodic, is crucial for understanding the participants' meaning-making. The participants found it very difficult to challenge one another, to question one another's assumptions and to risk critique. In analyzing the disparate, yet intimately related aspects of white talk, I developed a better understanding of "how voices *in safe and challenging conversation* can change and be changed by collective talk, inquiry and revision" (Macpherson & Fine, 1995, p. 186). I sought to explicate both the benefits and the dangers of collective talk among the white participants as they/we shifted positions within the discourse of whiteness. (See Appendix B for a detailed account of how I analyzed the group talk.)

Exemplar One: Avoiding Whiteness

The first exemplar illustrates a moment during session three when the participants were faced with an opportunity to critically examine the role of white people in the racist history of the United States. Within minutes, this opportunity was subverted and the participants decided to focus instead on how African Americans shouldn't "get mad at [us]" (Faith) for what happened in the past. The participants avoided a direct assault on whiteness choosing instead to claim their innocence in the history of racism in this country. This exemplar illustrates how these white participants sanctioned racist values, beliefs, and practices. It also shows how easy it was for the participants to collude in the uncritical, unexamined creation of white talk.

01 ASHLEY: *(unint.) going into high school, I just get nervous 'cause*
02   *like as a history teacher, I'm gonna be teaching like Civil War*
03   *and stuff like that where like if I'm in like the inner city, I'm like*
04   *how do I say like all these horrible things that we did like me as*
05   *a white person that we have the history of doing and I just,*
06   *I'm gonna be like like we're doing that in my class for um,*
07   *history of methods. We're talking about um, reconstruction*
08   *and stuff and to me it's it's like my favorite part of history but*
09   *I'm just like what what happens when these kids just start*
10   *getting angry and are like, "This is so bad," you know like what*
11   *do I tell them? Sometimes I'm just like I just wanna be like,*
12   *(unint.) (laughter) I don't know. I'm like I get so worked up and*
13   *I'm just[*

14 (laughter/ct)

15 ASHLEY: *I don't like I want them to know that they should be*
16   *angry you know and like they should but I don't wanna sit*
17   *there like I don't wanna incite a riot my God.*

18 (laughter/ct)

19 ? *I agree. I'm just as angry about it as you are because I don't*
20   *I mean I would be like[*

21 LYNN: *if I was teaching it I would be just as angry.*

22 ? *Yeah.*

23 ASHLEY: *I just want them to know like[*

24 (ct)

25 FAITH: *But you didn't do it. But you just have to tell them. Be*
26   *like, "You know guys if you are gonna get all worked up about*
27   *what happened to your great, great grandfather or what*
28   *happened whenever" be like, "That's great." But be like, "I*
29   *didn't do it. And you didn't do it. We're just studying and*
30   *it's history and it's the past and we're studying it because*
31   *we're gonna change it?" You know what I mean? Like they*
32   *can't get mad at you.*

33 ASHLEY: *I know. And also with all this like like political*
34   *correctness. It's not as bad anymore but I used to be like, I*
35   *always say Black and now I have to say African American and*
36   *now I'm gonna be like, "OK when the African Americans were in*
37   *the slave" you know and I'm gonna be like[*

38 (ct)

39 KERRY: *Actually, actually I have a problem with that term because I*
40   *feel really clumsy saying it. Like I think it's not that it's easier.*
41   *I know there's that connotations that go along with saying*
42   *someone's Black but no one describes me as you know, an*
43   *English Irish Czechoslovakian white person. (laughter) I think*
44   *it's the most ridiculous thing because they [African Americans]*
45   *were like most of them were born in America. I was born in*
46   *America so they you know, I'm an American.*

47 ? *Mhm.*

48 ? *Yeah.*

49 KERRY: *They don't I mean OK I'm white. So if you need to*
50   *describe me my color is white but it has nothing to do with*
51   *you know, like my my heritage coming from Europe.*

52 ? *Yeah.*

53 ASHLEY: *The thing is they'll [African Americans] argue is that you*
54   *came here on your own will probably.*

55 KERRY: *I didn't.*

56 ASHLEY: *Well, I mean that your relatives came here they were[*

57 KERRY: *Not all of them.*

58 ASHLEY: *Well[*

59 FAITH: *Well, now they [African Americans] have they want to go*
60   *back? Go. You know what I mean? It's like everybody's*

61   *we're all here you know, and you this is where you were born*
62   *and if you're you know, if you're an Irish American or if you're*
63   *English American or African American, you're all in the same*
64   *class you know? You're all here in you know, in [the city] or*
65   *whatever and you know, like my theory is there's nothing we*
66   *can do about the past. There's nothing, we can't say, "I'm*
67   *really sorry that we took your family as slaves. That I didn't*
68   *do it and my parents didn't do it to your parents and you*
69   *know, in particular but this is the situation now and this is how*
70   *we have to deal with it you know?" I don't know. I that's just*
71   *the way I feel. (S3)*

Ashley brought up a very salient point to/for these participants, especially the few participants who were teaching high school students and who may be teaching "in like the inner city." (By teaching "in the inner city," Ashley, and the other participants, mean teaching students of color. In this particular segment, Ashley was referring to Black or African American students. The participants use both terms interchangeably to describe students of color.) Ashley's question in lines 10 and 11: "What do I tell them?" was embedded in a complicated segment of text where she shared her anxiety about teaching Black students about the "horrible things that we [whites] did" in this country. Accompanying Ashley's anxiety was her struggle to make sense of herself as a white person/teacher. To complicate her situation even further, Ashley was attracted to that particular aspect of history—"it's it's like my favorite part of history." During numerous playbacks of the tapes, I heard the strong affect that accompanied Ashley's talk. Her delivery substantiated her claim in line 12 that "I'm like I get so worked up."

The multiple anxieties that Ashley shared at the beginning of this excerpt about teaching "like the Civil War and stuff" were handled with comic relief by the time she finished her narrative. Using humor as a way to diffuse participant anxiety was employed by Ashley (and others of us) during the group sessions. It was both a strength and a weakness for all of us and one that created a sense of camaraderie at the same time that it shielded us from the self- and collective exposure of our fears, doubts, and confusions.

After Ashley exposed her feelings of anxiety and vulnerability in lines 1 to 17, she made a brief remark that was unidentifiable on the tape. This was due to the fact that it was simultaneously accompanied by screams of laughter and a high pitched crosstalk that reached a point of collective hilarity. Ashley still had the floor and continued to explain that she wanted them [Black students] "to know that they should be angry." At the same time, she didn't "wanna incite a riot." Again, in listening to the tapes, there was a nervous humor that accompanied that comment. And again, Ashley's use of humor was met with collective laughter by the participants who joined her in assuming that if she allowed her Black students to get angry, she might "incite a riot."

There was a great deal of "movement" during this segment. Lots of laughter, crosstalk, "mhms," "yeahs," which made it difficult to identify all the speakers. In lines 19 and 20, an unidentified participant agreed with Ashley's assessment of the situation but before she could fully explain her reasoning for such an agreement, she was interrupted by Lynn. Lynn taught science to high school students, but assured Ashley that if she was teaching it [Civil War] she "would be just as angry." Another participant joined in the discussion as well agreeing that she, too, would be angry if she was in a similar predicament. What I heard in their exchange was that the participants were somehow identifying with the Black students' anger. What is disconcerting, is that the participants express a racially privileged anger—an anger that bonds them with their students, at the same time that it protects them from having to take responsibility for white racism. They share in the Black students' anger, only the participants' anger is directed at anonymous white people "back then" as opposed to *real* white people "here and now." More crosstalk ensued, which added to the affable rapport that was being created around Ashley's dilemma. The more affable the rapport, the more difficult it was to curtail the white talk.

At this point in the conversation, the participants began to rally around Ashley in support of her desire to solve this "problem." How was she going to teach about the Civil War knowing that whites had done horrible things and that her Black students might get angry? It was an important question and one that could have led to a direct assault on the privileging of whiteness in our history books, the positionality of white teachers in our country's schools, the responsibility of whites for the history of our country, the silencing of Black anger by white educators, or a whole host of other issues that would have kept the spotlight on the participants as white teachers in an educational system that privileges them. Instead, the laughter, the crosstalk, the privileging of Ashley's feelings, the perpetuation of the extant theory that "it's not our fault" wove its way into the discussion and opened the door for Faith to directly interrupt an already tenuous discussion.

In line 25, Faith rescued Ashley from her overriding dilemma and reassured Ashley that she "didn't do it [enslave Blacks]." Faith refocused the dialogue excusing Ashley—and, I would suggest, all white teachers—from having to interrogate ways to suspend the kind of fabricated history about slavery (and other issues of dominance and oppression) that are posited by many of our country's educators. Instead, Faith told Ashley, "Like they can't get mad at you." Ashley immediately agreed with Faith and then colluded in the further refusal to keep the focus on "us." Instead, Ashley inserted the problematic of ". . . all this like like political correctness." Ashley stated in lines 34 and 35, "I always say Black and now I have to say African American. . . ." Bringing up the subject of political correctness, a term that has polarized discourses of race and power, led to more affable crosstalk and a statement by Kerry that further distanced the participants from critically examining Ashley's original question. White talk was reinforced and maintained as Kerry argued that "it's the most ridiculous thing [wanting to be called African American] because they were like most of them were born here." Her comments moved the conversation a step closer to the racist jargon that permeates much of the race talk in this country—a discourse that situates all Americans under the canopy of sameness due to place of birth. Kerry was buoyed in her statements by her fellow participants who willingly agreed with her position. Kerry then inserted the relationship between ethnicity and race into the conversation, a relationship that she saw as nonexistent.

In lines 53 and 54, Ashley used "them" to challenge Kerry's position. "The thing is they'll [African Americans] argue that you came here on your own will probably." Kerry and Ashley interrupted each other as they negotiated who came here [to America] and who didn't. At that point in the exchange, Faith interrupted Ashley asserting, "Well, now they [African Americans] have they want to go back? Go. You know what I mean?" (lines 59 and 60). Faith reinserted the "we're all here [in America] you know?" approach to understanding race relations, suggesting that since we are all "here," we should all identify as Americans. In addition, Faith's "theory" that "there's nothing we can do about the past" was a recurrent theme within the group sessions and one that resonated with the larger societal rhetoric espoused by many white Americans (see, e.g., Feagin & Vera, 1995; Wellman, 1993; Hacker, 1995). Faith's comments trivialized "the past" at the same time that they relieved white people from having to challenge existing forms of individual, institutional, and societal racism. Faith's statement that "This is how we have to deal with it" (lines 69–70) was never investigated. "Dealing with it" was framed around ignoring "it" and abdicating responsibility for "it." Faith concluded her commentary by saying, "I don't know. I that's just the way I feel" (lines 70–71).

These types of culminating sentences were aspects of white talk that I heard repeatedly in the group sessions. Generally speaking, if the participants argued a certain point, or presented an opinion, or told a personal story, they usually ended their contribution with a partial disclaimer or, if not a disclaimer, a request for support and solidarity. Many times the participants concluded narrations with statements like, "I don't know," "Do you know what I mean?" and/or "Like you know." These markers were usually cues that the participant was finished with her turn. They were also delivered in muted tones and tended to trail off into a muffled silence or an unfinished sentence. Repeated use of these types of comments suggested an uncertainty about some of the topics we discussed—topics that were new to the group and that the group was not always comfortable talking about. I suggest that those uncertainties were the exact points of entry into which the participants could have engaged in a more critical discussion of race. Yet, instead of uncovering the fabric that bound the participants' uncertainties together and secured their need for group support, the participants became ensconced in white talk.

In the above exemplar, I have shown how quickly the participants created a discourse that prevented them from examining their/our individual and collective role(s) in the perpetuation of racism. By privileging camaraderie, by fantasizing about future teaching anxieties, and by colluding in the macronarrative of whiteness, the participants ensured that whiteness would not be compromised.

In the next exemplar, I present an example of more self-conscious and critical talk that challenged the participants' assumptions about whiteness, race, and racism. I show how two participants refused to let white talk shape the discussion about white privilege. White talk was certainly not ameliorated in the following exchange, but it was momentarily suspended.

Exemplar Two: Disrupting White Talk

At the beginning of session seven, the participants were asked to form small groups and discuss the question: What does it mean for you to be white? They had answered that question individually during their interviews. This was an opportunity for them to discuss it in a group and to think about what changes—if any—they had experienced over the past 2 months in light of that particular question. The participants received their transcribed interviews 2 weeks prior to session seven. During that time, they had the opportunity to read the text, provide clarifications and/or feedback, as well as make additions and/or deletions.

Marie was the first participant to present her group's summation. During that brief presentation she mentioned the fact that she, Kerry, and Lynn had wondered how Black people "assess me or evaluate me [as a white person]." This query initiated a very complicated and contentious discussion about what Blacks think about whites—and about white privilege. Some of the participants felt that many Blacks think of whites in negative terms. Michelle then asked the group, "Do you think they have a basis for that?" What ensued was a discussion that ultimately spiraled downward to the point where some of the participants were feeling victimized because they were white (see chapter five for a further discussion of whites as victims). The participants had a difficult time getting a handle on white privilege. They were confused about the relationship between whites as individuals and whites as members of institutions. They were distracted by their own assumptions about people of color and how people of color experience whiteness in this country. Yet, within these complicated discussions, there were moments of disruption that suspended the group's white talk.

01 MICHELLE: . . . *we all in this room have been granted so much power*
02   *being white like in every facet of our life, on a personal level,*
03   *institutional level, cultural level. Anywhere you want to look at*
04   *it we have all been granted some kind of privilege or power. I*
05   *don't know if everyone's ready to admit that . . . because all five*
06   *or six sessions that we've been here no one has been, like it*
07   *seems like everyone is like avoidant, like scared to admit that*
08   *they have privilege and scared to see it. . . .*

09 LYNN: *I think most of us have admitted white privilege.*

10 ? *But why do you have to admit it?*

11 MICHELLE: *But have we?*

12 (ct)

13 ELLEN: *(unint.) That's my question. Is is, why are you trying to get*
14   *all of us to say, "I am privileged because I'm white." Why are*
15   *you[*

16 MICHELLE: *Because if you don't really think you're privileged than*
17   *how can you change anything? (said emphatically)*

18 ELLEN: *I can't[*

19 MICHELLE: *Like I, like in our little session [the small group discussions]*
20   *we talked about it and I don't, if I misquote you just say it, but*

21   *basically, after we talked what I understood is that you don't*
22   *think that your race informed your socioeconomic standing*
23   *and[*

24 ELLEN: *Personally. On a personal level[*

25 MICHELLE: *. . . on a personal level? But can you separate your*
26   *personal from your institutional? Can you? Do you know*
27   *what (sigh).*

28 ASHLEY: *Yeah. I know.*

29 ? *I can see what you're saying.*

30 (silence ---)

31 ELLEN: *I can't tell you how institutions have affected my life*
32   *because I don't know.*

33 MICHELLE: *But you live in an institution. I mean like everything you*
34   *do was within the structure of an institution.*

35 LYNN: *But you haven't separated yourself from the institution so*
36   *you don't can't[*

37 ALICE: *Well, let her answer.*

38 (silence ---)

39 ELLEN: *I don't have an answer.*

40 MICHELLE: *You don't? (said in a whisper)*

41 ELLEN: *Michelle, you're not going to get me to say, "I am privileged*
42   *because I'm white." You're not going to get me to say that right*
43   *now because that's not how I feel. It's[*

44 MICHELLE: *I don't want to, I'm not asking you to say that. I'm*
45   *asking you to think of I'm just asking you to think about it.*

46 ELLEN: *I have and I am thinking about it. It's it's not that it's it's a*
47   *question I don't have an answer to because I can't say in*
48   *absolute fact I have seen how the underlying institutions of this*
49   *nation, I mean I can see how the nation does it favors people*
50   *of the white race, of the European-based race. I see that and*
51   *I know that and we can see it from all the Presidents in our*
52   *country. There has not been a minority. But, aside from all of*
53   *that, aside from what the nation has done in the, in my little*
54   *world, in my world in [an upper-middle-class town on the West*
55   *Coast], in my house, race is just not an issue.*

56 MICHELLE: *That's what's wrong. That's why we're never gonna*
57 *change anything is 'cause it's not an issue. I can sit in here*
58 *and say it's not an an issue. I can go on living my life and*
59 *nothing will change for me. (S7)*

In this excerpt, the question that gets raised is: Had the participants really admitted their privilege? My analysis indicates that in previous sessions some of the participants *had* begun to recognize and admit the privileges they are afforded in this country due to their skin color. Yet, instead of referring back to previous conversations in which the participants specifically dealt with problematizing privilege, the participants talked over each other (line 12) and avoided any direct response to Michelle's query. The crosstalk ended when Ellen took control of the conversation and asked Michelle why she was so intent on getting "me to say, 'I am privileged because I'm white.'" Listening to the tapes, I heard the frustration in Michelle's voice as she emphatically stressed the fact that unless the participants admitted their privilege (lines 56–57), they would not be able to change anything.

Michelle then reported on the conversation that she had with Ellen and Mary in their small group session where they had discussed the question: "What does it mean to be white?" During that discussion, Ellen suggested that her race had nothing to do with her socioeconomic status. Ellen posited that her socioeconomic status had to do with her parents' employment opportunities—opportunities which she felt were unrelated to their racial identities. Although the leaps from socioeconomic status, to Ellen's personal life, to the relationship between the individual and the institution seem like disjointed logic, when situated within the larger text(s), Michelle and Ellen's exchange in lines 19–27 makes sense. This exchange highlights how white talk was maintained. A strategic way for the participants to avoid whiteness, even if it was an unconscious occurrence, was to produce a convoluted discourse that confused instead of illuminated. The dissonance that resulted from the ambiguity of the topics and the multiple disparities that were embedded in the dialogues, invoked a number of conversational retreats and withdrawals.

Michelle refused to retreat from her initial inquiry and remained persistent in her line of questioning. Her "sigh" in line 27 signified her frustration at being unable to rally any support for the discourse she was trying to develop. Although Ashley and another participant "hear" what she said, neither elaborated on their perspectives. A noticeable silence lingered in the group. Ellen intervened and ended the collective discomfort by self-disclosing her inability to understand the relationship between her own personal life and "the institution." Michelle refused to waiver in her pursuit of problematizing the various topics that emerged and, in lines 33 and 34, forced Ellen to think about how "everything you do was within the structure of an institution."

By this time in the discussion an obvious tension arose between Ellen and Michelle. This type of overt face-to-face confrontation was rare in the group and there was a definite feeling of unease as the two participants negotiated unfamiliar terrain. In order to force them to remain in the messiness of critique, I interrupted Lynn (line 37) telling her that Ellen needed to answer Michelle. As has already been mentioned, interrupting each other was fertile ground for the augmentation of white talk.

Again, there was a noticeable silence as the group waited for Ellen to respond. Ellen explained that she didn't have an answer. As was noted in the previous exemplar, "I don't know" suggests uncertainty—an uncertainty that arose out of ignorance (sometimes the participants just didn't know) as well as out of moments of uneasiness and confusion. Most times, the participants ignored the "I don't knows," left them unchallenged, and accepted them as part of the dialogue. In line 40, Michelle provoked an explanation when she whispered, somewhat incredulously, "You don't?"

As a participant in this exchange—and the many that led up to this particular one—I suggest that Michelle *did* want Ellen (and the other participants) to admit that there was white privilege and that they all benefited from it. I suggest that what was frustrating for Michelle was the abundance of "thinking about it [privilege]" as opposed to the lack of a critical problematization and critique of it.

Ellen refuted Michelle's implicit claim that she was not thinking about the issue. "I am thinking about it. It's it's a question I don't have an answer to. . . ." Ellen then proceeded to cloak her quasi-answer in a stream of white talk. Ellen admitted that she had seen "how the underlying institutions of this nation . . . favor the white race. . . ." She even presented an example of this favoritism when she mentioned that there had never been a "minority" President. Beyond that "incidental" consequence of racism, Ellen minimized the historical dimensions of racism and dismissed the legacy of minority oppression and marginalization. She obfuscated the relationship between her own lived experiences as an upper-middle-class white female and the lived conditions of people of color in "the nation." In line 55, Ellen declared that "in my house, race is just not an issue." The other participants did not join Ellen in expressing similar perspectives, but neither did they intervene in her narration.

After a brief withdrawal from a highly frustrating discussion, Michelle continued to advance her assault on white talk. In line 56, Michelle named "what's wrong"—something that was difficult to achieve within the polite protocol that was established within the group. She reminded Ellen—and the rest of us—that we, as racially privileged participants, *have a choice* as to whether we want to make "it" (the multiple aspects of racism and white privilege) an issue or not. Michelle's closing comment invited a discussion about what the group could do about changing the current state of race relations—a discussion that concluded with the participants feeling somewhat immobilized and unsure of what their responses should be.

Presenting these two divergent exemplars illustrates the complicated set of devices the participants used for manufacturing—and dismantling—white talk. They reveal to/for us the multiple aspects of white talk that we, as white educators and researchers, need to be aware of as we create spaces for white-on-white dialogue.

NOTES

INTRODUCTION

1. I use the upper case "B" for Black and the lower case "w" for white in reference to racial identity because, as Harris (1993) argues, both have "a particular political history. Although 'white' and 'Black' have been defined oppositionally, they are not functional opposites. 'White' has incorporated Black subordination; 'Black' is not based on domination . . . 'Black' is naming that is part of counterhegemonic practice" (p. 1710).

2. Many biologists, physical anthropologists, social scientists, and educators recognize that "Race is more of a social category than a reliable biological classification. . . . The danger," as Campbell (1996) suggests, ". . . is not race, but racism, the oppression of a group of people based on their perceived race" (p. 49). The term "race"—as well as other terms used in this book—are particularly important for understanding how the participants made meaning of race, racism, whiteness, and multicultural education. The definitions used in this book are more a tool for providing a point of entry for thinking through the issues that emerged in the group discussions than definitive explanations with fixed meanings. These terms were problematized throughout the research as the participants began to define, for themselves, the language through which they could best describe their lived experiences as white females. Therefore, the terms I use throughout this book are to be seen as assisting in the development of my own goal of constructing a framework from which to study whiteness and white racial identity. The terms I use (e.g., "race," "people of color," "whiteness," "racism") will be presented with the recognition that "Language is always changing. It responds to social, economic, and political events and is therefore an important barometer and descriptor of a society at any given time" (Nieto, 1996, p. 23).

3. In this research, the focus is on the meaning of whiteness and the ways in which it informs both the participants' daily lives and their conceptualizations of what it means to be a white teacher. Thus, I highlight aspects of multicultural education that have to do with race and racism, recognizing that they are only one aspect of a truly emancipatory multicultural educational philosophy. In order to eradicate the various forms of privilege and advantage, neglect and oppression that exist in our educational institutions, we must embrace a holistic multicultural education that speaks to the multiple ways people are discriminated against in our schools and in our society. For a comprehensive overview of multicultural education as a social movement, see Sleeter (1996).

4. A focus on white teachers and how their racial identity relates to multicultural education is a piece of a larger question about the effectiveness of multicultural education as a discourse for educating a culturally diverse teaching force. See Montecinos (1995) for a discussion of how education programs can move beyond their emphasis on "'What can we do for white teachers to prepare them to work with children different from themselves?'" (p. 107) and focus more effectively on preparing multicultural minority teachers to teach to diverse ethnic groups.

5. I present a detailed account of how I analyzed the group's discourse in Appendix D. In chapters four through six, I illustrate the content of that discourse.

CHAPTER ONE

1. I don't use "discourse" to mean merely the discussion of a subject and/or people's verbal and written exchanges. Discourse encompasses the multidimensionality of language and represents the ways in which language is created, shaped, reproduced, and contested.

2. Hacker (1995) suggests, "having a white skin does not immunize a person from misfortune or failure. Yet even for those who fall to the bottom, being white has worth" (p. 35). Though I am not dismissing the significance of ethnicity, gender, social class, and differences to access to wealth and power among white people, I am calling attention to the relationship between skin color and the privileges and opportunities afforded whites in this country. Thus, I chose to focus my analysis on the worth of being white.

CHAPTER TWO

1. I had the good fortune to hear Paulo Freire speak as I was writing my dissertation. He spoke eloquently about a pedagogy of critical consciousness that is applicable to/for *all* people. Like other educators, I am concerned about Freire's work being misused in educational settings and through a series of

manipulations advantaging the oppressor at the expense of the oppressed. But it has been my experience that Freire's (1970) discourse on power, dialogue, and the idea of *conscientizacao is* a possibility with/for the oppressors. My hope is that Freire's philosophy can assist us in rethinking our positionalities as white educators and assist us in developing ways to disrupt educational practices that perpetuate racism and oppression.

2. All white undergraduate female prepracticum students at the university where this research took place were sent an announcement informing them about the research project prior to the fall semester, 1994. Students who met the requirements for participation in this project (being white and practice teaching in the fall semester), and were interested in participating, were asked to contact me by phone or through the University's Field Placement Office. Those students who decided to participate were presented with a more detailed letter explaining the goals of the project, along with an accompanying informed consent form.

3. Each participant chose a pseudonym that was used throughout the research project.

4. As a way for the participants to make meaning of racism and whiteness, they created collective representations of racism during session two and group collages representing whiteness during session four. In addition, we ended the research project (session eight) with an activity that invited the participants to create a group flower. Each participant was given a precut petal and was asked to write something that they were going to take with them from the research project on the petal. They then shared their petals with the large group and hung the completed flower on the wall. These activities were adapted from Brinton's work in Guatemala (see, e.g., Lykes, 1989; 1994a; 1994b; Lykes & Liem, 1990). See Lykes (1994a) for a discussion of the creative techniques she and other mental health promoters use in working with survivors of organized violence and oppression.

5. I conducted a detailed and systematic analysis of the talk from the eight group sessions, modifying Charmaz's (1990) version in two particular ways. First, she, and other grounded theorists (see Strauss & Corbin, 1990; Orona, 1990, for examples) posit that grounded theory method can assist the researcher in theorizing about certain sociological and psychological issues *directly from the data*. In other words, the use of technical and nontechnical literature can be problematic if the aim is to "explain phenomena in light of the theoretical framework that evolves during the research itself" (Strauss & Corbin, 1990, p. 49). They argue that "unrecognized assumptions" that researchers acquire through interacting with existing literature may constrain the investigation and skew the researcher's ability to theorize about her or his data. Although I agree, in theory, that one could be easily distracted by preexisting theoretical frameworks for understanding phenomena, I suggest that the knowledge I acquired in familiarizing myself with the much understudied field of white racial identity and the

limited literature on conducting participatory action research in educational contexts, stimulated my thinking and allowed me to enter into this PAR project with a much needed sensitivity to the topics the project generated.

Second, Charmaz (1990) continues the tradition of theoretical sampling suggested by Strauss and Corbin (1990) in her work. Theoretical sampling is an occasion to compare developing concepts among different samples of people. For example, Charmaz collected data on how chronic illness affects people's self-concepts with a particular sample of chronically ill people. She defined key concepts and checked those concepts with other samples of chronically ill people to clarify her interpretations. I suggest that conducting PAR—as opposed to one-to-one interviews—adds another dimension to the idea of theoretical sampling. Rather than checking the concepts that I created with other white female interviewees, or other groups of white female student teachers, I chose to immerse myself in the talk of the participants and to engage in a recursive process of analysis and interpretation *with* the participants of the study. This choice ensured methodological thoroughness within the PAR paradigm and gave "analytic power and conceptual grasp [with] which [to] synthesize, explain, and interpret the data" (Charmaz, 1990, p. 1163).

CHAPTER THREE

1. Due to the schedule change, an important piece of understanding the relationship between consciousness-raising dialogue and teaching practice was lost. As the manuscript illustrates, the participants spoke often about their prepracticum experiences. These examples gave the group dialogue a more experientially based feel to it, yet, as a researcher-educator, I regret the missed opportunity for connecting the participants' theorizing about whiteness and race with their actual teaching practice. Many scholars have addressed the variables needed in teacher education programs for teaching to diversity (see, e.g., Banks & Banks, 1993; Campbell, 1996; Diaz, 1992; Grant & Gomez, 1996; Larkin & Sleeter, 1995b; Nieto, 1996; Sleeter & McLaren, 1995). In keeping with that tradition, I believe that further research is needed in the area of how *white* teachers make meaning of racism, whiteness, multicultural education, and their racial identities and how that meaning-making is directly linked to their teaching practices (see, e.g., Cochran-Smith, 1991; 1995a; 1995b; Paley, 1979; Sleeter, 1992; 1993).

CHAPTER FOUR

1. I present an exemplar which illustrates how intercommunicative strategies functioned to maintain white talk in Appendix D. By conducting a line-by-line analysis, I show how the participants colluded in the formation of uncritical, racist talk. In addition, I present an exemplar that shows how some of the participants tried to interrupt white talk and engage in a more self-conscious critique of whiteness.

Chapter Five

1. I borrow this title from Christine Sleeter's (1992) book: *Keepers of the American Dream*, a book chronicling a 2-year multicultural education staff development program which she and her colleagues conducted with 30 mostly white teachers. Sleeter states: "*Keepers of the American Dream*, however, is more than a study of staff development. It is an examination of social relations and social meanings about cultural and racial diversity at a particular time in the history of the United States" (p. 5). I, too, discuss what the American Dream means to the participants of this project and how their conceptualization of that Dream informs their own understandings "of social relations and social meanings about cultural and racial diversity."

Chapter Six

1. See James W. Loewen's (1995) *Lies My Teacher Told Me: Everything Your American History Textbook Got Wrong* for a cogent analysis of the twelve most popular history textbooks used in this country. Loewen presents disturbing facts that illustrate how easily, and how often, whites have "gone back on their word" in the history of the United States.

Chapter Seven

1. One activity that may help many white European-Americans to understand the differential experiences of our foremothers and forefathers and those of people of color in this country is to learn about how ethnic groups "became white" as a way to "become successful" (see, e.g., Ignatiev, 1995). In addition, it is helpful for white people to be able to identify with other whites who have reflected on their own racial identities and who have committed themselves to engaging in antiracist activities (see, e.g., Dees, 1991; Frankenberg, 1996; King, 1972; Segrest, 1994; Smith, 1994; Stalvey, 1970; Terry, 1975; Thompson, 1996).

References

ABC News (1985?). *Eye of the storm.* [Film]. ABC Media Concepts, Mount Kisco, NY: Center for Humanities.

Ahlquist, R. (1991). Position and imposition: Power relations in a multicultural foundations class. *Journal of Negro Education, 60* (2), 158–169.

Banks, C. A. (1992). The leadership challenge in multicultural education. In C. Diaz (Ed.), *Multicultural education in the 21st century* (pp. 204–214). Washington, DC: National Education Association.

Banks, J. A. (Ed.). (1996). *Multicultural education, transformative knowledge, and action: Historical and contemporary perspectives.* NY: Teachers College Press.

———. (1995). *Multicultural education and development, dimensions and challenges.* Paper presented at Winter Roundtable on Cross-Cultural Psychology and Education, Teachers College, NY.

———. (1992a). African American scholarship and the evolution of multicultural education. *Journal of Negro Education, 61* (3), 273–286.

———. (1992b). Multicultural education: Nature, challenges, and opportunities. In C. Diaz (Ed.), *Multicultural education for the 21st century* (pp. 12–22). Washington, DC: National Education Association

———. (1991). A curriculum for empowerment, action, and change. In C. E. Sleeter (Ed.), *Empowerment through multicultural education* (pp. 125–142). Albany: State University of New York Press.

Banks, J. A. &. Banks, C. A. (Eds.). (1993). *Multicultural education: Issues and perspectives* (2nd ed.). Needham Heights, MA: Allyn and Bacon.

Bellah, R. N., Madsen, R., Sullivan, W. M., Swidler, A., & Tipton, S. M. (1985). *Habits of the heart: Individualism and commitment in American life.* NY: Harper and Row.

Bigelow, B., Christensen, L., Karp, S., Miner, B., & Peterson, B. (1994). *Rethinking our classrooms: Teaching for equity and justice.* Milwaukee: Rethinking Schools Limited.

Block, C. J., Roberson, L., & Neuger, D. A. (1995). White racial identity theory: A framework for understanding reactions toward interracial situations in organizations. *Journal of Vocational Behavior, 46* (1), 71–88.

Britzman, D. (1986). Cultural myths in the making of a teacher: Biography and social structure in teacher education. *Harvard Educational Review, 56* (4), 442–456.

Campbell, D. (1996). *Choosing democracy: A practical guide to multicultural education.* Englewood Cliffs, NJ: Prentice Hall.

Carter, R. T. (1993). Does race or racial identity attitudes influence the counseling process in Black and white dyads? In J. E. Helms (Ed.), *Black and white racial identity* (pp. 136–145). Westport, CT: Praeger.

———. (1990). The relationship between racism and racial identity among white Americans: An exploratory investigation. *Journal of Counseling and Development, 69,* 46–50.

Carter, R. T., Gushue, G. V., & Weitzman, L. M. (1994). White racial identity development and work values. *Journal of Vocational Behavior, 44* (2), 185–197.

Cary, L. (1991). *Black ice.* NY: Random House.

Charmaz, K. (1990). 'Discovering' chronic illness: Using grounded theory. *Social Science Medicine, 30* (11), 1161–1172.

"Christine" (1995). *Avoidance strategies encountered while making meaning of whiteness.* Unpublished manuscript.

Claney, D. & Parker, W. M. (1989). Assessing white racial consciousness and perceived comfort with Black individuals: A preliminary study. *Journal of Counseling and Development, 67,* 449–451.

Cochran-Smith, M. (1995a). Uncertain allies: Understanding the boundaries of race and teaching. *Harvard Educational Review, 65* (4), 541–570.

———. (1995b). Color blindness and basket weaving are not the answers: Confronting the dilemmas of race, culture, and language diversity in teachers education. *American Educational Research Journal, 32* (3), 493–523.

———. (1991). Learning to teach against the grain. *Harvard Educational Review, 61* (3), 279–310.

Collins, P. H. (1990). Women's studies: Reform or transformation? *Sojourner: The Women's Forum, 10*, 18–20.

Corvin, S. A. & Wiggins, F. (1989). An antiracism model for white professionals. *Journal of Multicultural Counseling and Development, 17*, 105–114.

Dees, M. with S. Fiffer (1991). *A season of justice: The life and times of civil rights lawyer Morris Dees.* NY: Charles Scribner's Sons.

Denzin, N. K. & Lincoln, Y. S. (1994). Introduction: Entering the field of qualitative research. In N. K. Denzin & Y. S. Lincoln (Eds.), *Handbook of Qualitative Research* (pp. 1–17). Thousand Oaks, CA: Sage.

Diaz, C. (Ed.). (1992). *Multicultural education for the 21st century.* Washington, DC: National Education Association.

Eaker-Rich, D. & Van Galen, J. (Eds.). (1996). *Caring in an unjust world: Negotiating borders and barriers in schools.* Albany. SUNY Press.

Elder, J. (1974). *White on white: An anti-racism manual for white educators in the process of becoming.* Doctoral dissertation, University of Massachusetts.

Ellsworth, E. (1989). Why doesn't this feel empowering? Working through the repressive myths of critical pedagogy. *Harvard Educational Review, 59* (3), 297–324.

Essed, P. (1991). *Understanding everyday racism: An interdisciplinary theory.* Newbury Park, CA: Sage.

Ewick, P. (1994). Integrating feminist epistemologies in undergraduate research methods. *Gender & Society, 8* (1), 92–108.

Ezekiel, R. S. (1995). *The racist mind: Portraits of American Neo-Nazis and Klansmen.* NY: Viking.

Facundo, B. (1984). *Issues for an evaluation of Freire-inspired programs in the United States and Puerto Rico.* Latino Institution. (ERIC Document Reproduction Service No. ED 243 998.)

Fals-Borda, O. & Rahman, M.A. (Eds.). (1991). *Action and knowledge: Breaking the monopoly with participatory action-research.* NY: Apex Press.

Feagin, J. R. & Vera, H. (1995). *White racism.* NY: Routledge.

Feagin, J. R. & Sikes, M. P. (1994). *Living with racism: The Black middle-class experience.* Boston: Beacon Press.

Fine, M. (1995). *White noise: Re-thinking race and privilege.* Paper presented at Winter Roundtable on Cross-Cultural Psychology and Education, Teachers College, NY.

——— . (1994). Working the hyphens: Reinventing self and other in qualitative research. In N. Denzin & Y. Lincoln (Eds.), *Handbook of qualitative research* (pp. 70–82). Thousand Oaks, CA: Sage.

——— . (1992). Passions, politics, and power: Feminist research possibilities. In M. Fine (Ed.), *Disruptive voices: The possibilities of feminist research* (pp. 205–231). Ann Arbor, MI: University of Michigan Press.

Forester, J., Pitt, J. & Welsh, J. (1993). *Profiles of participatory action researchers.* Einaudi Center for International Studies and Department of City and Regional Planning, Cornell University.

Forester, J. & Pitt, J. (1993). Introduction. *Profiles of participatory action researchers.* Einaudi Center for International Studies and Department of City and Regional Planning, Cornell University.

Frankenburg, R. (1996). When we are capable of stopping, we begin to see: Being white, seeing whiteness. In B. Thompson & S. Tyagi (Eds.), *Names we call home: Autobiography on racial identity.* NY: Routledge.

——— . (1993). *White women, race matters: The social construction of whiteness.* Minneapolis: University of Minnesota Press.

Freire, P. (1994). *Pedagogy of hope: Reliving pedagogy of the oppressed.* (R. Barr, Trans.). NY: Continuum.

——— . (1985). *The Politics of Education: Culture, Power, and Liberation* (D. Macedo, Trans.). South Hadley, MA: Bergin and Harvey.

——— . (1973). *Education for Critical Consciousness* (M.B. Ramos, Trans.). NY: The Seabury Press.

——— . (1970). *Pedagogy of the Oppressed* (M.B. Ramos, Trans.). NY: The Seabury Press.

Gaines, S. O. & Reed, E. S. (1995). Prejudice: From Allport to DuBois. *American Psychologist,* 96–103.

Gay, G. (1993). Ethnic minorities and educational equality. In J. A. Banks & C. A. Banks (Eds.), *Multicultural education: Issues and perspectives* (pp. 171–194) (2nd ed.). Needham Heights, MA: Allyn and Bacon.

——— . (1983). Multiethnic education: Historical developments and future prospects. *Phi Delta Kappan,* 560–563.

Glaser, B. & Strauss, A. (1967). *The discovery of grounded theory.* Chicago: Aldine.

Golden, M. G. (1995). Introduction. In M. G. Golden & S. R. Shreve (Eds.), *Skin deep: Black women and white women write about race.* NY: Doubleday.

Gore, J. (1993). *The struggle for pedagogies: Critical and feminist discourses as regimes of truth.* NY: Routledge.

Grant, C. A. & Gomez, M. L. (1996). *Making schooling multicultural: Campus and classroom.* Englewood Cliffs, NJ: Prentice Hall.

Grant, C. A. & Zozakiewicz, C. A. (1995). Student teachers, cooperating teachers, and supervisors: Interrupting the multicultural silences of student teaching. In J. M. Larkin & C. E. Sleeter (Eds.), *Developing multicultural teacher education curricula* (pp. 259–278). Albany: SUNY Press.

Grant, C. A. (Ed.). (1995). *Educating for diversity: An anthology of multicultural voices.* Boston: Allyn and Bacon.

Greene, M. (1992). The passions of pluralism: Multiculturalism and the expanding community. *Journal of Negro Education, 61* (3), 250–261.

Griscom, J. (1992). Women and power: Definition, dualism, and difference. *Psychology of Women Quarterly, 16* (4), 389–414.

Guba, E. G. & Lincoln, Y. S. (1994). Competing paradigms in qualitative research. In N. K. Denzin & Y. S. Lincoln (Eds.), *Handbook of Qualitative Research* (pp. 105–117). Thousand Oaks, CA: Sage.

Hacker, A. (1995). *Two nations: Black and white, separate, hostile, unequal.* NY: Ballantine Books.

Hall, B. (1993). Introduction. In P. Park, M. Brydon-Miller, B. Hall & T. Jackson (Eds.), *Voices of change: Participatory research in the United States and Canada.* Toronto: Ontario Institute for Studies in Education.

Hardiman, R. (1982). *White identity development: A process oriented model for describing the racial consciousness of white Americans.* Dissertation Abstracts International, 43, 104A, University Microfilms No. 82-10330.

Harris, C. (1993). Whiteness as property. *Harvard Law Review, 106* (8), 1709–1791.

Helms, J. E. (1994). The conceptualization of racial idendity and other "racial" constructs. In E. J. Trickett, R. J. Watts, and D. Birman (Eds.), *Human diversity* (pp. 285–311). San Francisco: Jossey-Bass.

———. (Ed.). (1993). *Black and white racial identity: Theory, research and practice.* Westport, CT: Praeger.

Helms, J. E. & Carter, R. T. (1991). Relationships of white and Black racial identity attitudes and demographic similarity to counselor preferences. *Journal of Counseling Psychology, 38* (4), 446–457.

hooks, b. (1994). *Teaching to transgress: Education as the practice of freedom.* NY: Routledge.

———. (1990). *Yearning: Race, gender, and cultural politics.* Boston: South End Press.

Hurd, T. & McIntyre, A. (1996). The seduction of sameness: Similarity and representing the other. *Feminism and Psychology, 6* (1), 86–92.

Ignatiev, N. (1995). *How the Irish became white.* NY: Routledge.

Jones, J. M. (1972). *Prejudice and racism.* Reading, MA: Addison Wesley.

"Julie" (1995). *The use of gender in making meaning of whiteness.* Unpublished manuscript.

Katz, J. & Ivey, A. (1977). White awareness: The frontier of racism awareness training. *The Personnel and Guidance Journal, 55* (8), 485–489.

Katz, J. (1978). *White awareness: Handbook for anti-racism training.* USA: University of Oklahoma Press.

Katz, P. A. (Ed.). (1976). *Toward the elimination of racism.* NY: Pergamon Press.

Kenway, J. & Modra, H. (1992). Feminist pedagogy and emancipatory possibilities. In C. Luke. & J. Gore (Eds.), *Feminisms and critical pedagogy* (pp. 138–166). NY: Routledge.

King, J. E. (1991). Dysconscious racism: Ideology, identity, and the miseducation of teachers. *Journal of Negro Education, 60,* (2), 133–146.

King, L. (1972). *Confessions of a white racist.* NY: Viking Press.

Larkin, J. M. & Sleeter, C. E. (Eds.). (1995). *Developing multicultural teacher education curricula.* Albany: SUNY Press.

Lebacqz, K. (1987). *Justice in an unjust world: Foundations for a Christian approach to justice.* Minneapolis: Augsburg.

Lenzo, K. (1995). Validity and self-reflexivity meet poststructuralism: Scientific ethos and the transgressive self. *Educational Researcher, 24* (4), 17–23.

Loewen, J. W. (1995). *Lies my teacher told me: Everything your American history textbook got wrong.* NY: The New Press.

Lopez, I. F. H. (1996). *White by law: The legal construction of race.* NY: New York University Press.

Lykes, M.B. (1994a). Terror, silencing, and children: International, multidisciplinary collaboration with Guatemalan Maya communities. *Social Science and Medicine, 38* (4), 543–552.

———. (1994b). Speaking against silence: One Maya woman's exile and return. In C. E. Franz & A. J. Stewart (Eds.), *Women creating lives: Identities, resilience, and resistance* (pp. 97–114). Boulder: Westview Press.

———. (1989). Dialogue with Guatemalan Indian women: Critical perspectives on constructing collaborative research. In R. Unger (Ed.), *Representations: Social constructions of gender* (pp. 167–185). Amityville: Baywood.

Lykes, M. B. & Liem, R. (1990). Human rights and mental health in the United States: Lessons from Latin America. *Journal of Social Issues, 46* (3), 151–165.

Macedo, D. (1993). Literacy for stupidification: The pedagogy of big lies. *Harvard Educational Review, 63* (2), 183–206.

Macpherson, P. & Fine, M. (1995). Hungry for an us: Adolescent girls and adult women negotiating territories of race, gender, class and difference. *Feminism & Psychology, 5* (2), 181–200.

Maguire, P. (1993). Challenges, contradictions, and celebrations: Attempting participatory research as a doctoral student. In P. Park, M. Brydon-Miller, B. Hall & T. Jackson (Eds.), *Voices of change: Participatory research in the United States and Canada* (pp. 157–176). Toronto: Ontario Institute for Studies in Education.

————. (1987). *Doing participatory research: A feminist approach.* Amherst: The Center for International Education, University of Massachusetts.

Mallory, B. L. & New, R. S. (Eds.). (1994). *Diversity and developmentally appropriate practices: Challenges for early childhood education.* NY: Teacher's College Press.

Martin, R. J. (Ed.). (1995). *Practicing what we teach: Confronting diversity in teacher education.* Albany: SUNY Press.

McCarthy, C. (1994). Multicultural discourses and curriculum reform: A critical perspective. *Educational Theory, 44* (1), 81–98.

McIntosh, P. (1992). White privilege and male privilege: A personal account of coming to see correspondences through work in women's studies. In M. L. Anderson & P. H. Collins (Eds.), *Race, class, and gender: An anthology* (pp. 70–81). Belmont, CA: Wadsworth.

McIntyre, A. (in press). Constructing an image of a white teacher. *Teachers College Record.*

"Michelle." (1995). *White deliverance.* Unpublished manuscript.

Minh-Ha, T. T. (1996). *Gender and cultural politics.* Paper presented at National Association of Women in Catholic Higher Education, Boston College, MA.

Mishler, E. (1986). *Research interviewing: Context and narrative.* Cambridge: Harvard University Press.

Mishler, E. (1991). Representing discourse: The rhetoric of transcription. *Journal of Narrative and Life History, 1* (4), 255–280.

Montecinos, C. (1995). Multicultural teacher education for a culturally diverse teaching force. In R. Martin (Ed.), *Practicing what we teach: Confronting diversity in teacher education* (97–116). Albany: SUNY Press.

Moore, R. (1973). *A rationale, description and analysis of a racism awareness program for white teachers.* Doctoral dissertation, University of Massachusetts.

Naidoo, B. (1992). *Through whose eyes? Exploring racism: Reader, text and context.* Staffordshire, England: Trentham Books.

National Education Association (1992). *Status of the American public school teacher, 1990–91.* Washington, D.C.

Ng, R., Staton, P., & Scane, J. (Eds.). (1995). *Anti-racism, feminism, and critical approaches to education.* Westport, CT: Bergin & Garvey.

Nieto, S. (1996). *Affirming diversity: The sociopolitical context of multicultural education* (2nd ed.). NY: Longman.

———. (1994). Lessons from students on creating a chance to dream. *Harvard Educational Review, 64* (4), 392–426.

Orona, C. (1990). Temporality and identity loss due to Alzheimer's disease. *Social Science Medicine, 30* (11), 1247–1256.

Paley, V. (1995). *Kwanzaa and me: A teacher's story.* Cambridge: Harvard University Press.

———. (1979). *White teacher.* Cambridge: Harvard University Press.

Pang, V. O. (1992). Institutional climate: Developing an effective multicultural school community. In C. Diaz (Ed.), *Multicultural education for the twenty-first century* (pp. 57–71). Washington DC: National Education Association.

Park, P. (1993). What is participatory research? A theoretical and methodological perspective. In P. Park, M. Brydon-Miller, B. Hall & T. Jackson (Eds.), *Voices of change: Participatory research in the United States and Canada* (pp. 1–20). Toronto: Ontario Institute for Studies in Education.

Park, P., Brydon-Miller, M., Hall, B. & Jackson, T. (Eds.). (1993). *Voices of change: Participatory research in the United States and Canada.* Toronto: Ontario Institute for Studies in Education.

Patai, D. (1991). U.S. academics and Third World women: Is ethical research possible? In S. B. Gluck. & D. Patai (Eds.), *Women's words: The feminist practice of oral history* (pp. 137–154). NY: Routledge.

Ponterotto, J. G. (1988). Racial consciousness development among white counselor trainees: A stage model. *Journal of Multicultural Counseling and Development, 16,* 146–156.

Pope-Davis, D. B. & Ottavi, T. M. (1994). The relationship between racism and racial identity among white Americans: A replication and extension. *Journal of Counseling and Development, 72,* 293–297.

Reay, D. (1996). Dealing with difficult differences: Reflexivity and social class in feminist research. *Feminism and Psychology, 6* (3), 443–456.

Reissman, C. K. (1990). *Divorce talk: Women and men make sense of personal relationships.* New Brunswick: Rutgers University Press.

Roediger, D. (1994). *Towards the abolition of whiteness: Essays on race, politics, and working class history.* London: Verson.

Roman, L. (1993). "On the ground" with antiracist pedagogy and Raymond Williams's unfinished project to articulate a socially transformative critical realism. In D. L. Dworkin & L. Roman (Eds.), *Views beyond the border country: Raymond Williams and cultural politics* (pp. 134–158). NY: Routledge.

Ryan, W. (1976). *Blaming the victim* (rev. ed.). NY: Vintage Books.

Sabnani, H. B., Ponterotto, J.G., & Borodovsky, L.G. (1991). White racial identity development and cross-cultural counselor training: A stage model. *The Counseling Psychologist, 19*, 76–102.

Scheper-Hughes, N. (1992). *Death without weeping: The violence of everyday life in Brazil.* Berkeley: University of California Press.

Segrest, M. (1994). *Memoir of a race traitor.* Boston: South End Press.

Shor, I. & Freire, P. (1987). What is the "dialogical method" of teaching? *Journal of Education, 169* (3), 11–31.

Sleeter, C. E. (1996). *Multicultural education as social activism.* Albany: SUNY Press.

Sleeter, C. E. (1995a). *Racism and multicultural education.* Paper presented at Winter Roundtable on Cross-Cultural Psychology and Education, Teachers College, NY.

————. (1995b). Reflections on my use of multicultural and critical pedagogy when students are white. In C. E. Sleeter & P. McLaren (Eds.), *Multicultural education, critical pedagogy, and the politics of difference* (pp. 415–437). Albany: SUNY Press.

————. (1994). *Multicultural education, social positionality, and whiteness.* Paper presented at the American Educational Research Association, New Orleans.

————. (1993). How white teachers construct race. In C. McCarthy & W. Crichlow (Eds.), *Race identity and representation in education* (pp. 157–171). NY: Routledge.

————. (1992). *Keepers of the American dream: A study of staff development and multicultural education.* London: The Falmer Press.

Sleeter, C. E. & McLaren, P. (1995). Introduction: Exploring connections to build a critical multiculturalism. In C. E. Sleeter & P. McLaren (Eds.), *Multicultural education, critical pedagogy, and the politics of difference* (pp. 5–32). Albany: SUNY Press.

————. (Eds.). (1995). *Multicultural education, critical pedagogy, and the politics of difference.* Albany: SUNY Press.

Sleeter, C. E. & Grant, C. A. (1988). *Making choices for multicultural education: Five approaches to race, class, and gender*. NY: Macmillan.

Smith, L. (1994). *Killers of the dream* (rev., originally published in 1949). NY: Norton.

Stalvey, L. M. (1970). *Education of a WASP*. NY: Morrow.

Stewart, A. J. (1994). Toward a feminist strategy for studying women's lives. In C. E. Franz & A. J. Stewart (Eds.), *Women creating lives: Identities, resilience, and resistance* (pp. 11–36). Boulder: Westview Press.

Strauss, A. & Corbin, J. (1990). *Basics of qualitative research: Grounded theory procedures and techniques*. Newbury Park, CA: Sage.

Tannen, D. (1984). *Conversational style: Analyzing talk among friends*. Norwood, NJ: Ablex.

Tatum, B. (1994). Teaching white students about racism: The search for white allies and the restoration of hope. *Teachers College Record, 95,* 462–476.

Tatum, B. (1992). Talking about race, learning about racism. *Harvard Educational Review, 62* (1), 1–24.

Terry, R. W. (1981). The negative impact on white values. In B. P. Bowser & R. G. Hunt (Eds.), *Impacts of racism on white Americans* (pp. 119–152). Beverly Hills: Sage.

———. (1975). *For whites only* (Rev. ed.). Grand Rapids, Mich.: Wm. B. Eerdmans.

Thompson, B. (1996). Time traveling and border crossing: Reflections on white identity. In B. Thompson & S. Tyagi (Eds.), *Names we call home: Autobiography on racial identity*. NY: Routledge.

Tripp, D. (1993). *Critical incidents in teaching: Developing professional judgment*. London: Routledge.

Watkins, W. (1994). Multicultural education: Toward a historical and political inquiry. *Educational Theory, 44* (1), 99–117.

Weiler, K. (1988). *Women teaching for change: Gender, class and power*. South Hadley, MA: Bergin & Garvey.

Wellman, D. (1993). *Portraits of white racism* (2nd ed.). NY: Cambridge University Press.

West, C. (1994). *Race matters*. NY: Vintage Books.

Yang, J. (1992). *Chilly campus climate: A qualitative study on white racial identity development attitudes*. Shippensburg University (ERIC Document Reproduction Service No. ED 352 576).

INDEX

A

action, 21, 23, 71–72, 76, 136, 138, 140–41, 144, 149, 156; collective, 20, 69, 99, 141, 143, 147; individual, 20, 69, 99, 139, 147; social, 97, 108, 141

activism, 22, 33, 145; activist, 21, 36, 38, 44, 118, 134, 139

affirmative action, 2, 109

African Americans (*see also* Blacks; people of color), 5, 9, 11, 37, 42, 74, 111, 114, 144, 159–61, 163

Ahlquist, R., 12, 146

American Dream, 61–62, 79, 88, 135, 175n. 1Ch.5

analysis: data, 4, 6, 25, 27–28, 61, 136, 142, 150, 152–56, 158, 167, 172n. 5, 173n. 5, 174n. 1Ch.4; interpretation, 6, 26, 28, 102, 110, 152–56, 158, 173n. 5; participant, 80, 100, 142, 155–56, 173n. 5

anger, 42, 74, 78, 124, 132, 135, 153, 159, 162; Black students', 159–60, 162–63

antiracist education (*see also* multicultural antiracist education) 21, 105, 120, 147

assimilation, 61–62

B

Banks, C. A., 11–13, 174n. 1Ch.3

Banks, J. A., 11, 174n. 1Ch.3

Bellah, R. N., 68, 100

Bigelow, B., 102, 105

Blacks (*see also* African Americans; people of color), 16–17, 43, 49–53, 59–64, 66–68, 74–76, 83, 85, 87, 90, 93, 96–98, 101–102, 104, 108–15, 119, 122, 126, 130, 135, 137–40, 160, 162–63; children, 1, 31, 53, 85; identity, 15, 17, 101; students (*see also* minority students; students of color), 70, 118, 122, 161–63

Block, C. J., 18

Borodovsky, L.G., 18

Brydon-Miller, M., 20

Britzman, D., 117, 125

C

Campbell, D., 5, 90, 171n. 2, 174n. 1Ch.3

caring, 46, 124, 127, 130–31, 152

Carter, R. T., 18

Cary, L., 111, 113–14
change, 5–6, 115, 142; collective, 26,
    135; individual, 26, 41, 135; insti-
    tutional, 41, 93, 105; social, 9, 14,
    21–22, 35, 38, 41, 134, 141, 145
Charmaz, K., 28, 154–55, 173n. 5
Christensen, L., 102
Civil Rights movement, 9, 108
Claney, D., 18
Cochran-Smith, M., 3, 5, 12, 18, 117,
    132, 148, 174n. 1Ch.3
collage, 26, 40, 73, 80, 82, 85, 87,
    173n. 4
Collins, P. H., 4
colorblind, 15, 126, 132, 136
conscientizacao, 19, 172n. 1Ch.2
consciousness, 16, 22, 36, 46, 140;
    collective, 19, 35; critical, 20–22,
    36, 172n. 1Ch.2; individual, 19,
    35
consciousness-raising, 21, 24–25, 27,
    30, 34, 36–37, 39–40, 42, 47, 52,
    71, 78, 137–38, 143, 145, 174n.
    1Ch.3
Corbin, J., 173n. 5
Corvin, S. A., 16
critique, 5, 7, 10, 13, 27, 30, 32–33, 37,
    39–43, 46–47, 50, 77–78, 91, 94, 99,
    116, 118, 121, 125, 130, 133, 136,
    138, 140–42, 150, 155, 158, 168
culture, 5, 9–10, 13, 99–100, 111, 126,
    139; of niceness, 40, 46, 135;
    United States, 5, 15, 61, 100, 135;
    white, 14, 62, 100–101, 104

D

data analysis. See analysis
data collection, 24–27
Dees, M., 175n. 1Ch.7
defensiveness, 42, 69, 74, 77, 137
deficient: difference as, 9, 87, 102,
    121, 135, 137
denial, 38, 71
Denzin, N. K., 145

dialectic: of critique, 35–41, 43–45,
    51, 94; of engagement, 35–41,
    43–45, 51, 94
dialogue, 6, 19–22, 24, 27–28, 36–37,
    39, 41–43, 57, 66, 78, 94, 104, 109,
    116, 137, 140–41, 145, 148, 154,
    167–69, 174n. 1Ch.3
Diaz, C., 11, 174n. 1Ch.3
discourse, 12, 23, 27–28, 30, 32,
    39–40, 43, 46, 55, 66, 121–22, 125,
    130, 137, 140, 142, 149, 167, 172n.
    1Ch.1, 172n. 1Ch.2; dominant,
    12, 117, 120, 131, 135, 154; edu-
    cational, 4, 7, 12, 125; partici-
    pants' 35, 52, 65, 78, 101, 124,
    164, 172n. 5; racial, 2, 59, 132,
    163; whiteness, 6, 45–46, 58, 121,
    158
discrimination, 2, 5, 11, 14, 48, 87,
    108, 113, 128, 130, 151, 172
diversity, 5, 10–11, 13, 146, 174n.
    1Ch.3, 175n. 1Ch.5
dominant group, 6, 17, 44, 48, 52, 68,
    91, 117, 120, 132, 141

E

Eaker-Rich, D., 46, 124, 130
educational: institutions, 6, 9, 13, 71,
    114, 116, 120, 122, 124, 130,
    147–48, 172n. 3; system, 2, 10,
    12–13, 67, 120, 130, 162
educators (see also teachers):
    antiracist, 11–12, 39, 147, 149; of
    color, 11–12, 68, 148; white,7,
    12–14, 16, 55, 118, 134–35, 141,
    148–49, 162, 169
Elder, J., 16–17
Ellsworth, E., 12, 146
equal opportunity, 60–62, 66–68
Essed, P., 52
ethnicity, 1, 10, 13, 75, 101, 111, 145,
    163, 172n. 2; ethnic group, 9–12,
    15, 60, 67, 85, 151, 172n. 4, 175n.
    1Ch.7

Ewick, P., 6
Ezekiel, R. S., 54

F

Facundo, B., 29
Fals-Borda, O., 20, 141
Feagin, J. R., 16, 50, 57, 60, 108, 136, 141, 163
fear, 60, 69, 73–74, 77, 123, 127, 135, 137, 153, 161
feminism, 10; research, 21; theorizing, 3–4
field notes, 6, 27, 128, 130
field sites (see also practicum experiences), 2, 27, 33, 34, 137
Fine, M., 21–22, 29–30, 52, 87–88, 115, 136, 140, 150, 158
Forester, J., 20, 34
Frankenburg, R., 3, 22, 175n. 1Ch.7
Friere, P., 19–22, 27, 30, 35–37, 39, 41, 47, 78, 135, 138, 150, 172n. 1Ch.2

G

Gaines, S. O., 140
Gay, G., 9, 11
gender, 1–2, 4, 10, 12–13, 22, 29, 78, 87, 91, 95, 102, 105, 114, 116, 125, 135, 145, 172n. 2; males: African American, 114; Black, 74–75; white, 1, 12, 96, 105, 130
Glaser, B., 28
Golden, M. G., 43
Gomez, M. L., 174n. 1Ch.3
Gore, J., 117
Grant, C. A., 11, 146–47, 174n. 1Ch.3
Greene, M., 25
Griscom, J., 29, 88, 91
grounded theory, 28, 173n. 5
Guba, E. G., 146
guilt, 48, 50, 74, 76, 121, 135
Gushue, G. V., 18

H

Hacker, A., 16, 61, 75, 108, 126, 163, 172n. 2
Hall, B., 20, 23
Hardiman, R., 16–17
Harris, C., 171n
Helms, J. E., 3, 15, 17–18
history, 27, 87, 89, 104, 113, 120, 139, 144–45, 159–60, 171n. 1, 175n. 1Ch.6; of Blacks, 52, 144; Native American, 104; of racism, 11, 37, 89, 95, 136, 159; of slavery, 89, 109, 159, 163; United States, 11, 37, 89, 102, 104, 109, 112, 159, 162, 175n. 1Ch.5; and whiteness, 121, 123, 134, 147, 162
hooks, b., 13, 16, 117
Hurd, T., 30

I

ideology, 52, 60, 100, 110, 116–18, 135; dominant, 47, 116, 121, 123; of whiteness, 3, 7, 22, 40, 47, 120
Ignatiev, N., 175n. 1Ch.7
inclusion, 10, 62, 64–65, 153
individualism, 61, 65, 93, 100, 135
inner city, 118, 124, 159, 161; schools, 2, 118, 123–27, 131
interviews, 24–26, 28, 79, 100, 102, 109, 111, 120, 143, 151–52, 155, 164
invisibility, 1–2, 14, 16, 131, 144
Ivey, A., 14, 16

J

Jackson, T., 20
Jones, J. M., 18
journals, 6, 27, 32–34, 38–39, 71, 75, 93–94

K

Karp, S., 102
Katz, J., 14–16

Katz, P. A., 16–17
Kenway, J., 105
King, J. E., 36, 78
King, L., 175n. 1Ch.7

L

Larkin, J. M., 11, 174n. 1Ch.3
Lebacqz, K., 148–49
Lenzo, K., 34
Liem, R., 173n. 4
life experiences, 12, 21, 31, 33, 36, 42,
   78, 134, 136; of participants, 5,
   21–22, 26, 32, 36, 80, 87, 134, 136,
   145, 150, 171n. 2; of people of
   color, 9, 47, 76–77, 126, 139–40
Lincoln, Y. S., 145–46
Loewen, J. W., 175n. 1Ch.6
Lopez, I. F. H., 3
Lykes, M. B., 23, 156, 173n. 4

M

Macedo, D., 117
Macpherson, P., 158
Maguire, P., 7, 20, 22, 27, 44, 141–42,
   149
Mallory, B. L., 11
Martin, R. J., 11, 148
McCarthy, C., 11–12
McIntosh, P., 16, 26, 50, 57
McIntyre, A., 30, 123
McLaren, P., 11, 117, 148–49, 174n.
   1Ch.3
Miner, B., 102
Minh-Ha, T. T., 18
minorities, 9, 54, 58, 63, 66–67, 90,
   101, 166, 168; students, (see also
   Black students; students of color),
   90, 118–19, 121–23, 126; teachers,
   10, 118, 172n. 4
Mishler, E., 152
Modra, H., 105
Montecinos, C., 172n. 4

Moore, R., 16–17
multicultural antiracist education
   (see also antiracist education), 5–6,
   9, 12–14, 18, 26, 118, 121, 146–47,
   149
multicultural education, 3, 9–14, 18,
   38, 118, 120–21, 123, 147, 151,
   171n. 2, 172n. 3, 172n. 4
multiethnic education, 9–10
myths, 9, 32, 45, 47, 57, 60–62, 64, 65,
   68, 77, 109, 115, 123–25, 131, 135,
   153

N

NAACP, 114
Naidoo, B., 43
Neuger, D. A., 18
New, R. S., 11
Ng, R., 11
Nieto, S., 3, 11, 13, 32, 117, 171n. 2,
   174n. 1Ch.3

O

oppression, 2–7, 13, 17, 19, 20, 23, 37,
   50, 71, 84, 95, 102, 108–10, 113,
   116–17, 130, 136, 141, 144–45,
   148–49, 171n. 2, 172n. 3, 172n.1
   Ch.2
Orona, C., 173n. 5
Ottavi, T. M., 18

P

Paley, V., 3, 12, 174n. 1Ch.3
Pang, V. O., 12
parents: participants', 24, 57, 82,
   97–98, 121, 135, 161, 167
Park, P., 20, 141
Parker, W. M., 18
participatory action research (PAR),
   3, 6–7, 18–24, 26–28, 30, 33–39, 41,

44, 46, 78, 117–18, 134–35, 137–42,
    145–46, 148–50, 155–56, 173n. 5
Patai, D., 12, 44, 150
pedagogy (*see also* teaching prac-
    tices), 3, 7, 19, 22, 41–42, 55, 117,
    119, 132–33
people of color (*see also* Blacks;
    African Americans), 3, 6, 9, 13,
    16–17, 41–43, 45–47, 52, 56–57,
    59–66, 68–69, 73–80, 83, 85–87,
    90–91, 95–96, 101–102, 108–109,
    114–15, 122, 126, 135–37, 139–40,
    143, 147, 149, 165, 168, 171n. 2,
    175n. 1Ch.7; Arab Americans, 5;
    Asian Americans, 11–12, 17, 62;
    Asian/Pacific Americans, 51;
    Chinese, 66–67; Haitian students,
    123; Hispanic, 62, 119; Latinos/as,
    5, 11, 17; Native Americans, 5, 62,
    103–104
Peterson, B., 102
Pitt, J., 20, 34
Ponterotto, J. G., 17–18
Pope-Davis, D. B., 18
power, 9–13, 16, 19, 23, 42, 44, 48, 52,
    55–56, 62, 64, 79, 82, 84, 88–91,
    93–95, 100, 105, 109–10, 113–14,
    117–18, 130, 136, 163, 165, 172n. 2,
    172n. 1Ch.2
powerlessness, 69, 71–72, 76–77, 119,
    137, 153
practicum experiences (*see also* field
    sites), 24, 26, 33, 54, 118–19, 125,
    130, 139, 173n. 2, 174n. 1Ch.3
prejudice, 48, 67, 76, 127, 148, 151
privilege, 2–5, 56–59, 64, 69, 76,
    79–80; white, 15–16, 22, 37, 48, 52,
    57–58, 65, 76–77
professional development, 147–48,
    175n. 1Ch.5

R

race, 2–3, 5–6, 10–16, 21–22, 24,
    26–29, 31, 35, 37–38, 40, 42–43, 46,
51–53, 56, 58–59, 61, 63–64, 67–68,
    71, 73, 77–79, 84, 88–90, 95,
    101–102, 108–109, 112–15, 119–20,
    123, 126–27, 132–33, 137, 143, 145,
    147, 152, 163–64, 166–69, 171n. 2,
    172n. 3, 174n. 1Ch.3
racial advantage, 15–17, 48, 52, 59,
    61, 65, 79, 83, 86, 91, 99–100, 105,
    120, 123, 136
racial group, 3, 9–12, 15, 60, 65–67,
    75, 85, 95, 100–102, 104, 107, 125,
    139, 141, 151, 154
racial identity, 3, 5, 13, 16–18, 101,
    125–26, 154; white, 3, 5–6, 14,
    16–18, 20–22, 24–25, 28–29, 36,
    46–47, 77–79, 95, 133, 147, 167,
    171n. 1, 172n. 4, 173n. 5, 175n.
    1Ch.7
racial locations, 4–5, 48, 65, 95,
    143–45
racism, 2–3, 6–7, 11–14, 16–18, 21–22,
    25–29, 31–32, 37–38, 41–43, 45–50,
    52–57, 59–61, 65, 67–69, 71–73,
    76–77, 87–90, 92–93, 95–99, 102,
    104, 107–11, 114–16, 119–24,
    126–29, 131–32, 134–46, 148–49,
    151–54, 158–59, 162, 164, 168–69,
    171n. 2, 172n. 3, 173n. 4, 174n.
    1Ch.3; cultural, 9, 14, 87; and edu-
    cation, 129–31, 148; individual, 7,
    14, 46, 55–56, 68, 78, 87, 99, 132,
    142, 163; institutional, 9, 14, 48,
    56, 67, 78, 87, 99, 128, 143, 163;
    history of, 11, 37, 89, 95, 136, 159;
    and multicultural education, 13,
    18, 120–21, 146; and participants'
    families, 97–98; representation of,
    47–48, 83–84, 173n. 4; "reverse,"
    122; societal, 56, 78, 99, 142, 163;
    and teaching practices, 7, 14, 26,
    121–22, 127, 148
Rahman, M. A., 20, 141
Reay, D., 102, 138
Reed, E. S., 140
reflective practice, 7, 20, 27, 36, 42, 71,
    138–39; collective, 3, 27, 30, 94,

reflective practice *(continued)* 147; participant, 5–6, 25, 33–34, 36–37, 46, 77, 80, 95; researcher, 25, 30, 34, 39, 152, 154; self-, 3, 7, 14, 25, 27, 30, 41, 46, 94, 144, 147; and white teachers, 6, 14, 30, 95, 149; and whites, 41, 142, 175n. 1Ch.7

Reissman, C. K., 152

research methodology, 6–7, 20–23, 32–33, 37, 134, 137–38, 140–41, 145–46, 173n. 5

researcher, 4, 18, 20–22, 26–30, 34–35, 37–39, 44, 118, 123, 134, 141, 144–46, 149, 152, 154–55, 173n. 5, 174n. 1Ch.3; participant, 21, 23, 25, 27, 29–30, 32–33, 35–36, 38, 41, 118, 137, 145; white, 4, 6–7, 33, 36, 38, 41, 118, 134, 137, 139, 141, 149, 169

resistance, 32, 39–40, 46, 48, 52, 56, 59, 73, 75, 77, 79, 87, 94, 120–21, 134

responsibility, 16, 37, 45, 47, 61, 64, 69–70, 72, 76, 93, 99, 105–106, 121, 131, 136, 139, 141, 144, 149, 162–63

Roberson, L., 18

Roediger, D., 3

Roman, L., 31, 39, 68, 76, 146

Rosa Parks, 102–103

Ryan, W., 16

S

Sabnani, H. B., 18

sameness. *See* similarities

Scane, J., 11

Scheper-Hughes, N., 30

Segrest, M., 175n. 1Ch.7

Shor, I., 20

Sikes, M. P., 141

silence, 19–20, 22–23, 33, 37–38, 40, 46–47, 68, 73, 75, 100, 147, 152, 157–58, 162, 164, 166–68

similarity: researcher and participant, 7, 29–30, 31–33, 44–45, 58

skin color, 1, 59, 62–63, 91, 102, 108, 110–12, 122, 126, 132, 167, 172n. 2

slavery, 89, 109, 160–63

Sleeter, C. E., 3–4, 7, 11–13, 15–16, 71, 87, 117, 139–40, 146, 148–49, 172n. 3, 174n. 1Ch.3, 175n. 1Ch.5

Smith, L., 175n. 1Ch.7

social class, 1–5, 10–12, 22, 24, 29, 56–57, 59, 66, 78, 80, 83, 87, 91, 95, 100, 102, 108, 112, 114, 116, 125, 131, 135, 145, 166–68, 172n. 2

Stalvey, L. M., 175n. 1Ch.7

Staton, P., 11

Stewart, A. J., 3

Strauss, A., 28, 173n. 5

stereotypes, 31–32, 49–50, 53, 56, 66, 76–77, 118–19, 122–24, 127, 131, 136, 139, 158

student teachers, 5, 73, 119, 147; white, 3, 14, 18, 22, 29, 31, 55, 120; white female, 2, 5, 7, 21–22, 24–25, 28, 47, 116, 125, 132, 134, 136, 149, 173n. 5

students of color *(see also* Black students; minority students), 2, 9, 42, 62, 64, 69, 73, 119, 121–24, 127, 130, 132, 136, 139, 144, 148, 161

T

Tannen, D., 152

Tatum, B. S., 3, 11, 146

teacher education programs, 5, 24, 120, 131, 135, 146–48, 172n.4, 174n. 1Ch.3

teacher preparation programs. *See* teacher education programs

teaching practices *(see also* pedagogy), 3, 7, 9, 14, 25, 35, 105, 122, 131–32, 134–35, 146, 174n. 1Ch.3

teachers: cooperating, 119, 126, 132, 147–48; white, 2–4, 6, 9, 14–16, 18, 21–22, 25, 31, 43, 45, 55, 67–68, 73, 90–91, 95, 99, 104, 117–27, 130–32, 143, 146–49, 152, 154, 161–63, 172n. 4, 174n. 1Ch.3, 175n. 1Ch.5

Terry, R. W., 14–15, 18, 175n. 1Ch.7
Thompson, B., 175n. 1Ch.7
transcription, 25, 152–56, 164; code, 157
Tripp, D., 41

V

Van Galen, J., 46, 124, 130
Vera, H., 16, 50, 57, 60, 108, 136, 163

W

Watkins, W., 10
Weiler, K., 12, 117
Weitzman, L. M., 18
Wellman, D., 16–17, 60, 65, 75, 95, 163
Welsh, J., 20
West, C., 16
white racial identity. *See* racial identity
White Racial Identity Attitude Scale, 17–18
white supremacy, 2, 15, 84, 102, 136
white talk, 31, 33, 37, 45–47, 52, 57, 60–61, 64, 69, 77–78, 87, 89, 110, 115, 152–53, 158–59, 162–65, 167–69, 174n. 1Ch.4; exemplars of, 158–69
whiteness, 1–7, 9, 12–18, 20–32, 35, 37–48, 59–60, 69, 73–74, 76–79, 87,

89, 94, 100, 102, 107, 110–11, 115–16, 120–21, 123, 125–26, 134, 136–37, 139–50, 152–56, 158–59, 162, 164–65, 167, 171n. 2, 172n. 3, 174n. 1Ch.4; representing, 40, 80–82, 85–87, 135, 173n. 4
whites: "bad" whites, 79, 95–99, 107, 154; and dualism, 60, 79, 95–96, 102, 105, 107, 120, 127, 136, 153; "good" whites, 95–99, 107, 154; as ideal, 79–80, 84, 88, 153; as individuals, 87, 95, 98, 99–102, 104–105, 108, 154, 165; as keepers of the American Dream, 79, 88, 153, 175n. 1Ch.5; as living a fairy tale, 79–84, 153; as members of racial group, 79, 87, 91, 95, 98–108, 154, 165; as normative, 79–80, 84–87, 103, 135, 153; as victims, 52, 109–11, 113–15, 122, 165
Wiggins, F., 16
work ethic, 2, 49–50, 52, 61–62, 66, 68, 83, 108, 122–23, 127, 132, 135

Y

Yang, J., 18

Z

zero-sum thinking, 57–58, 60, 89, 153
Zozakiewicz, C. A., 147